TEACHER'S GUIDE

Connected Mathematics 2™

Stretching and Shrinking

Understanding Similarity

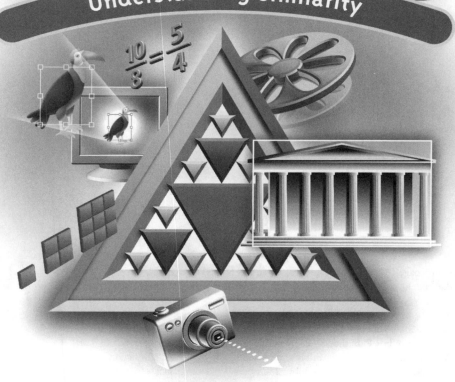

$$\frac{10}{8} = \frac{5}{4}$$

Glenda Lappan
James T. Fey
William M. Fitzgerald
Susan N. Friel
Elizabeth Difanis Phillips

PEARSON

Boston, Massachusetts · Glenview, Illinois · Shoreview, Minnesota · Upper Saddle River, New Jersey

Connected Mathematics™ was developed at Michigan State University with financial support from the Michigan State University Office of the Provost, Computing and Technology, and the College of Natural Science.

This material is based upon work supported by the National Science Foundation under Grant No. MDR 9150217 and Grant No. ESI 9986372. Opinions expressed are those of the authors and not necessarily those of the Foundation.

The Michigan State University authors and administration have agreed that all MSU royalties arising from this publication will be devoted to purposes supported by the Department of Mathematics and the MSU Mathematics Enrichment Fund.

13-digit ISBN 978-0-13-366193-4
10-digit ISBN 0-13-366193-8
1 2 3 4 5 6 7 8 9 10   11 10 09 08

Authors of Connected Mathematics

(from left to right) Glenda Lappan, Betty Phillips, Susan Friel, Bill Fitzgerald, Jim Fey

Glenda Lappan is a University Distinguished Professor in the Department of Mathematics at Michigan State University. Her research and development interests are in the connected areas of students' learning of mathematics and mathematics teachers' professional growth and change related to the development and enactment of K–12 curriculum materials.

James T. Fey is a Professor of Curriculum and Instruction and Mathematics at the University of Maryland. His consistent professional interest has been development and research focused on curriculum materials that engage middle and high school students in problem-based collaborative investigations of mathematical ideas and their applications.

William M. Fitzgerald (*Deceased*) was a Professor in the Department of Mathematics at Michigan State University. His early research was on the use of concrete materials in supporting student learning and led to the development of teaching materials for laboratory environments. Later he helped develop a teaching model to support student experimentation with mathematics.

Susan N. Friel is a Professor of Mathematics Education in the School of Education at the University of North Carolina at Chapel Hill. Her research interests focus on statistics education for middle-grade students and, more broadly, on teachers' professional development and growth in teaching mathematics K–8.

Elizabeth Difanis Phillips is a Senior Academic Specialist in the Mathematics Department of Michigan State University. She is interested in teaching and learning mathematics for both teachers and students. These interests have led to curriculum and professional development projects at the middle school and high school levels, as well as projects related to the teaching and learning of algebra across the grades.

Field Test Sites for CMP2

During the development of the revised edition of *Connected Mathematics* (CMP2), more than 100 classroom teachers have field-tested materials at 49 school sites in 12 states and the District of Columbia. This classroom testing occurred over three academic years (2001 through 2004), allowing careful study of the effectiveness of each of the 24 units that comprise the program. A special thanks to the students and teachers at these pilot schools.

Arkansas

Magnolia Public Schools
Kittena Bell*, Judith Trowell*; *Central Elementary School:* Maxine Broom, Betty Eddy, Tiffany Fallin, Bonnie Flurry, Carolyn Monk, Elizabeth Tye; *Magnolia Junior High School:* Monique Bryan, Ginger Cook, David Graham, Shelby Lamkin

Colorado

Boulder Public Schools
Nevin Platt Middle School: Judith Koenig

St. Vrain Valley School District, Longmont
Westview Middle School: Colleen Beyer, Kitty Canupp, Ellie Decker*, Peggy McCarthy, Tanya deNobrega, Cindy Payne, Ericka Pilon, Andrew Roberts

District of Columbia

Capitol Hill Day School: Ann Lawrence

Georgia

University of Georgia, Athens
Brad Findell

Madison Public Schools
Morgan County Middle School: Renee Burgdorf, Lynn Harris, Nancy Kurtz, Carolyn Stewart

Maine

Falmouth Public Schools
Falmouth Middle School: Donna Erikson, Joyce Hebert, Paula Hodgkins, Rick Hogan, David Legere, Cynthia Martin, Barbara Stiles, Shawn Towle*

Michigan

Portland Public Schools
Portland Middle School: Mark Braun, Holly DeRosia, Kathy Dole*, Angie Foote, Teri Keusch, Tammi Wardwell

Traverse City Area Public Schools
Bertha Vos Elementary: Kristin Sak; *Central Grade School:* Michelle Clark; Jody Meyers; *Eastern Elementary:* Karrie Tufts; *Interlochen Elementary:* Mary McGee-Cullen; *Long Lake Elementary:* Julie Faulkner*, Charlie Maxbauer, Katherine Sleder; *Norris Elementary:* Hope Slanaker; *Oak Park Elementary:* Jessica Steed; *Traverse Heights Elementary:* Jennifer Wolfert; *Westwoods Elementary:* Nancy Conn; *Old Mission Peninsula School:* Deb Larimer; *Traverse City East Junior High:* Ivanka Berkshire, Ruthanne Kladder, Jan Palkowski, Jane Peterson, Mary Beth Schmitt; *Traverse City West Junior High:* Dan Fouch*, Ray Fouch

Sturgis Public Schools
Sturgis Middle School: Ellen Eisele

Minnesota

Burnsville School District 191
Hidden Valley Elementary: Stephanie Cin, Jane McDevitt

Hopkins School District 270
Alice Smith Elementary: Sandra Cowing, Kathleen Gustafson, Martha Mason, Scott Stillman; *Eisenhower Elementary:* Chad Bellig, Patrick Berger, Nancy Glades, Kye Johnson, Shane Wasserman, Victoria Wilson; *Gatewood Elementary:* Sarah Ham, Julie Kloos, Janine Pung, Larry Wade; *Glen Lake Elementary:* Jacqueline Cramer, Kathy Hering, Cecelia Morris, Robb Trenda; *Katherine Curren Elementary:* Diane Bancroft, Sue DeWit, John Wilson; *L. H. Tanglen Elementary:* Kevin Athmann, Lisa Becker, Mary LaBelle, Kathy Rezac, Roberta Severson; *Meadowbrook Elementary:* Jan Gauger, Hildy Shank, Jessica Zimmerman; *North Junior High:* Laurel Hahn, Kristin Lee, Jodi Markuson, Bruce Mestemacher, Laurel Miller, Bonnie Rinker, Jeannine Salzer, Sarah Shafer, Cam Stottler; *West Junior High:* Alicia Beebe, Kristie Earl, Nobu Fujii, Pam Georgetti, Susan Gilbert, Regina Nelson Johnson, Debra Lindstrom, Michele Luke*, Jon Sorensen

Minneapolis School District 1
Ann Sullivan K–8 School: Bronwyn Collins; Anne Bartel* (Curriculum and Instruction Office)

Wayzata School District 284
Central Middle School: Sarajane Myers, Dan Nielsen, Tanya Ravnholdt

White Bear Lake School District 624
Central Middle School: Amy Jorgenson, Michelle Reich, Brenda Sammon

New York

New York City Public Schools
IS 89: Yelena Aynbinder, Chi-Man Ng, Nina Rapaport, Joel Spengler, Phyllis Tam*, Brent Wyso; *Wagner Middle School:* Jason Appel, Intissar Fernandez, Yee Gee Get, Richard Goldstein, Irving Marcus, Sue Norton, Bernadita Owens, Jennifer Rehn*, Kevin Yuhas

---

* indicates a Field Test Site Coordinator

Ohio

Talawanda School District, Oxford
Talawanda Middle School: Teresa Abrams, Larry Brock, Heather Brosey, Julie Churchman, Monna Even, Karen Fitch, Bob George, Amanda Klee, Pat Meade, Sandy Montgomery, Barbara Sherman, Lauren Steidl

Miami University
Jeffrey Wanko*

Springfield Public Schools
Rockway School: Jim Mamer

Pennsylvania

Pittsburgh Public Schools
Kenneth Labuskes, Marianne O'Connor, Mary Lynn Raith*; *Arthur J. Rooney Middle School:* David Hairston, Stamatina Mousetis, Alfredo Zangaro; *Frick International Studies Academy:* Suzanne Berry, Janet Falkowski, Constance Finseth, Romika Hodge, Frank Machi; *Reizenstein Middle School:* Jeff Baldwin, James Brautigam, Lorena Burnett, Glen Cobbett, Michael Jordan, Margaret Lazur, Tamar McPherson, Melissa Munnell, Holly Neely, Ingrid Reed, Dennis Reft

Texas

Austin Independent School District
Bedichek Middle School: Lisa Brown, Jennifer Glasscock, Vicki Massey

El Paso Independent School District
Cordova Middle School: Armando Aguirre, Anneliesa Durkes, Sylvia Guzman, Pat Holguin*, William Holguin, Nancy Nava, Laura Orozco, Michelle Peña, Roberta Rosen, Patsy Smith, Jeremy Wolf

Plano Independent School District
Patt Henry, James Wohlgehagen*; *Frankford Middle School:* Mandy Baker, Cheryl Butsch, Amy Dudley, Betsy Eshelman, Janet Greene, Cort Haynes, Kathy Letchworth, Kay Marshall, Kelly McCants, Amy Reck, Judy Scott, Syndy Snyder, Lisa Wang; *Wilson Middle School:* Darcie Bane, Amanda Bedenko, Whitney Evans, Tonelli Hatley, Sarah (Becky) Higgs, Kelly Johnston, Rebecca McElligott, Kay Neuse, Cheri Slocum, Kelli Straight

Washington

Evergreen School District
Shahala Middle School: Nicole Abrahamsen, Terry Coon*, Carey Doyle, Sheryl Drechsler, George Gemma, Gina Helland, Amy Hilario, Darla Lidyard, Sean McCarthy, Tilly Meyer, Willow Nuewelt, Todd Parsons, Brian Pederson, Stan Posey, Shawn Scott, Craig Sjoberg, Lynette Sundstrom, Charles Switzer, Luke Youngblood

Wisconsin

Beaver Dam Unified School District
Beaver Dam Middle School: Jim Braemer, Jeanne Frick, Jessica Greatens, Barbara Link, Dennis McCormick, Karen Michels, Nancy Nichols*, Nancy Palm, Shelly Stelsel, Susan Wiggins

---

* indicates a Field Test Site Coordinator

Reviews of CMP to Guide Development of CMP2

Before writing for CMP2 began or field tests were conducted, the first edition of *Connected Mathematics* was submitted to the mathematics faculties of school districts from many parts of the country and to 80 individual reviewers for extensive comments.

School District Survey Reviews of CMP

Arizona
Madison School District #38 (Phoenix)

Arkansas
Cabot School District, Little Rock School District, Magnolia School District

California
Los Angeles Unified School District

Colorado
St. Vrain Valley School District (Longmont)

Florida
Leon County Schools (Tallahassee)

Illinois
School District #21 (Wheeling)

Indiana
Joseph L. Block Junior High (East Chicago)

Kentucky
Fayette County Public Schools (Lexington)

Maine
Selection of Schools

Massachusetts
Selection of Schools

Michigan
Sparta Area Schools

Minnesota
Hopkins School District

Texas
Austin Independent School District, The El Paso Collaborative for Academic Excellence, Plano Independent School District

Wisconsin
Platteville Middle School

Individual Reviewers of CMP

Arkansas
Deborah Cramer; Robby Frizzell *(Taylor)*; Lowell Lynde *(University of Arkansas, Monticello)*; Leigh Manzer *(Norfork)*; Lynne Roberts *(Emerson High School, Emerson)*; Tony Timms *(Cabot Public Schools)*; Judith Trowell *(Arkansas Department of Higher Education)*

California
José Alcantar *(Gilroy)*; Eugenie Belcher *(Gilroy)*; Marian Pasternack *(Lowman M. S. T. Center, North Hollywood)*; Susana Pezoa *(San Jose)*; Todd Rabusin *(Hollister)*; Margaret Siegfried *(Ocala Middle School, San Jose)*; Polly Underwood *(Ocala Middle School, San Jose)*

Colorado
Janeane Golliher *(St. Vrain Valley School District, Longmont)*; Judith Koenig *(Nevin Platt Middle School, Boulder)*

Florida
Paige Loggins *(Swift Creek Middle School, Tallahassee)*

Illinois
Jan Robinson *(School District #21, Wheeling)*

Indiana
Frances Jackson *(Joseph L. Block Junior High, East Chicago)*

Kentucky
Natalee Feese *(Fayette County Public Schools, Lexington)*

Maine
Betsy Berry *(Maine Math & Science Alliance, Augusta)*

Maryland
Joseph Gagnon *(University of Maryland, College Park)*; Paula Maccini *(University of Maryland, College Park)*

Massachusetts
George Cobb *(Mt. Holyoke College, South Hadley)*; Cliff Kanold *(University of Massachusetts, Amherst)*

Michigan
Mary Bouck *(Farwell Area Schools)*; Carol Dorer *(Slauson Middle School, Ann Arbor)*; Carrie Heaney *(Forsythe Middle School, Ann Arbor)*; Ellen Hopkins *(Clague Middle School, Ann Arbor)*; Teri Keusch *(Portland Middle School, Portland)*; Valerie Mills *(Oakland Schools, Waterford)*; Mary Beth Schmitt *(Traverse City East Junior High, Traverse City)*; Jack Smith *(Michigan State University, East Lansing)*; Rebecca Spencer *(Sparta Middle School, Sparta)*; Ann Marie Nicoll Turner *(Tappan Middle School, Ann Arbor)*; Scott Turner *(Scarlett Middle School, Ann Arbor)*

Minnesota
Margarita Alvarez *(Olson Middle School, Minneapolis)*; Jane Amundson *(Nicollet Junior High, Burnsville)*; Anne Bartel *(Minneapolis Public Schools)*; Gwen Ranzau Campbell *(Sunrise Park Middle School, White Bear Lake)*; Stephanie Cin *(Hidden Valley Elementary, Burnsville)*; Joan Garfield *(University of Minnesota, Minneapolis)*; Gretchen Hall *(Richfield Middle School, Richfield)*; Jennifer Larson *(Olson Middle School, Minneapolis)*; Michele Luke *(West Junior High, Minnetonka)*; Jeni Meyer *(Richfield Junior High, Richfield)*; Judy Pfingsten *(Inver Grove Heights Middle School, Inver Grove Heights)*; Sarah Shafer *(North Junior High, Minnetonka)*; Genni Steele *(Central Middle School, White Bear Lake)*; Victoria Wilson *(Eisenhower Elementary, Hopkins)*; Paul Zorn *(St. Olaf College, Northfield)*

New York
Debra Altenau-Bartolino *(Greenwich Village Middle School, New York)*; Doug Clements *(University of Buffalo)*; Francis Curcio *(New York University, New York)*; Christine Dorosh *(Clinton School for Writers, Brooklyn)*; Jennifer Rehn *(East Side Middle School, New York)*; Phyllis Tam *(IS 89 Lab School, New York)*;

Marie Turini *(Louis Armstrong Middle School, New York)*; Lucy West *(Community School District 2, New York)*; Monica Witt *(Simon Baruch Intermediate School 104, New York)*

Pennsylvania
Robert Aglietti *(Pittsburgh)*; Sharon Mihalich *(Freeport)*; Jennifer Plumb *(South Hills Middle School, Pittsburgh)*; Mary Lynn Raith *(Pittsburgh Public Schools)*

Texas
Michelle Bittick *(Austin Independent School District)*; Margaret Cregg *(Plano Independent School District)*; Sheila Cunningham *(Klein Independent School District)*; Judy Hill *(Austin Independent School District)*; Patricia Holguin *(El Paso Independent School District)*; Bonnie McNemar *(Arlington)*; Kay Neuse *(Plano Independent School District)*; Joyce Polanco *(Austin Independent School District)*; Marge Ramirez *(University of Texas at El Paso)*; Pat Rossman *(Baker Campus, Austin)*; Cindy Schimek *(Houston)*; Cynthia Schneider *(Charles A. Dana Center, University of Texas at Austin)*; Uri Treisman *(Charles A. Dana Center, University of Texas at Austin)*; Jacqueline Weilmuenster *(Grapevine-Colleyville Independent School District)*; LuAnn Weynand *(San Antonio)*; Carmen Whitman *(Austin Independent School District)*; James Wohlgehagen *(Plano Independent School District)*

Washington
Ramesh Gangolli *(University of Washington, Seattle)*

Wisconsin
Susan Lamon *(Marquette University, Hales Corner)*; Steve Reinhart *(retired, Chippewa Falls Middle School, Eau Claire)*

Stretching and Shrinking
Understanding Similarity

> The Student Edition pages for the Unit Opener follow page 12.

Stretching and Shrinking
Understanding Similarity

Goals of the Unit

- Identify similar figures by comparing corresponding parts

- Use scale factors and ratios to describe relationships among the side lengths of similar figures

- Construct similar polygons

- Draw shapes on coordinate grids and then use coordinate rules to stretch and shrink those shapes

- Predict the ways that stretching or shrinking a figure affect lengths, angle measures, perimeters, and areas

- Use the properties of similarity to calculate distances and heights that can't be directly measured

Developing Students' Mathematical Habits

The overall goal of the *Connected Mathematics* curriculum is to help students develop sound mathematical practices. Through their work in this unit, students learn important questions to ask themselves about any situation that can be represented and modeled mathematically, such as:

- *What does the everyday use of the word "similar" mean? How does this differ from the mathematical meaning or use of the word?*

- *When two figures are similar, what is the same in each figure? What is different in each figure?*

- *How might we describe these differences?*

- *How do ratios relate to similarity?*

- *When two figures are similar, how can you describe the relationship between their areas? How can you describe the relationship between their perimeters?*

- *In what ways can you apply the ideas about similarity to use in the everyday world?*

Overview

Knowledge of similarity is important to the development of children's understanding of the geometry in their environment. In their immediate environment and in their studies of natural and social sciences, students frequently encounter phenomena that require familiarity with the ideas of enlargement, scale factors, area growth, indirect measurement, and other similarity-related concepts.

Similarity is an instance of proportionality. For example, if you increase the size of a diagram by 50%, then distances in the enlarged diagram are proportional to distances in the original diagram. Specifically, every distance in the enlargement is a constant multiple (1.5) of the corresponding distance in the original. It is generally understood that understanding proportional reasoning is an important stage in cognitive development.

Students in the middle grades often experience difficulty with ideas of scale. They confuse *adding* situations with *multiplying* situations. Situations requiring comparison by addition or subtraction come first in students' experience with mathematics and often dominate their thinking about any comparison situation, even those in which *scale* is the fundamental issue. For example, when considering the dimensions of a rectangle that began as 3 units by 5 units and was enlarged to a similar rectangle with a short side of 6 units, many students will say the long side is now 8 units rather than 10 units. They add 3 units to the 5 units rather than multiply the 5 units by 2, the scale factor. These students may struggle to build a useful conception that will help them distinguish between situations that call for addition and those that are multiplicative (calling for scaling up or down).

The problems in this unit are designed to help students begin to accumulate the knowledge and experiences necessary to make these kinds of distinctions and to reason about scaling in geometry situations. The next unit, *Comparing and Scaling*, continues to develop these ideas in numerical, rather than geometric, contexts.

Summary of Investigations

Investigation 1
Enlarging and Reducing Shapes

Similarity is introduced at an informal level. Students use their intuition about enlargements and reductions to answer questions. Students make drawings of similar figures using a pair of rubber bands. Then, they compare side lengths, angle measures, perimeters, and areas of the original and enlarged figures.

Investigation 2
Similar Figures

Students build a good working definition of *similar* in mathematical terms. They begin to see connections between geometry and algebra. Using the coordinate system, they draw several geometric figures. Some of the figures are similar to one another and others are not.

They explore algebraic rules that cause images to change size and to move about the coordinate plane. They also compare angle measures and lengths of corresponding sides informally as they investigate transformations. Students find that for two figures to be similar corresponding angles must be congruent and corresponding sides must grow or shrink by the same factor.

Investigation 3
Similar Polygons

Students deepen their understanding of what it means for two figures to be similar. In addition, they explore the relationship between the areas of similar figures. The idea that area does not grow at the same rate as side length when a figure is enlarged is difficult for students to grasp. Through experiments with rep-tiles (shapes where copies are put together to make larger, similar figures), students explore the relationship between the areas of two similar figures. They also discover how triangles are special. These experiences help them build mental images to support their evolving ideas about the relationship between scale factor and area.

Investigation 4

Similarity and Ratios

Students use equivalent ratios to test if figures are similar. They compare ratios of the sides within rectangles (length to width of one rectangle and length to width of the other). Students learn that for non-rectangular shapes such as triangles, you need information about angle measures as well. They learn that between two similar figures, you can find the length of missing sides using either ratios or scale factors.

Investigation 5

Using Similar Triangles and Rectangles

Students apply their knowledge about similarity of triangles to real-world problems. They use the shadow and mirror methods to find the height of a tall object. They compare their data to decide which method gives more consistent results. They also use similar triangles to find the distance across a physical feature, such as a river. In each problem, they find that triangles are similar if their corresponding angles are equal. In the ACE, they use their knowledge about similar rectangles to make similar rectangles and to find missing measurements.

Mathematics Background

The activities in the beginning of the unit elicit students' first notions about similarity as two figures with the same shape. Students may have difficulty with the concept of similarity because of the way the word is used in everyday language— family members are "similar" and houses are "similar." The unit begins by having students informally explore what it means for two geometric figures to be similar. They create similar figures using rubber bands. Early on, they begin to see that some attributes of similar figures are the same while others are not. For example, corresponding angle measures appear to be the same, but corresponding side lengths are different—yet these differences are predictable.

Students' experiences with photocopiers enlarging or shrinking pictures provide another familiar context to begin the exploration of similar figures.

Through the activities in *Stretching and Shrinking*, students will grow to understand that the everyday use of a word and its mathematical use may be different. For us to determine definitively whether two figures are similar, similarity must have a precise mathematical definition.

Similarity

Two figures are similar if:

- the measures of their corresponding angles are equal
- the lengths of their corresponding sides increase by the same factor, called the **scale factor**.

The two Figures A and B below are similar.

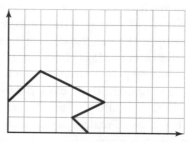

Figure A

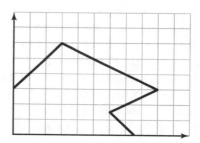

Figure B

The corresponding angle measures are equal. The side lengths from Figure A to Figure B grow by a factor of 1.5. Thus the scale factor from Figure A to Figure B is 1.5. (Figure A *stretches*, or is enlarged.) You can also say the scale factor from Figure B to Figure A is $\frac{1}{1.5}$, or $\frac{2}{3}$. (Figure B *shrinks*, or is reduced.)

Creating Similar Figures

The rubber-band stretcher introduced in Investigation 1 is a tool for physically producing a similarity transformation. It does not give precise results, but it is an effective way to introduce students to similarity transformations. More precision is gained in transformations using algebraic rules that specify how coordinates change. See Problem 1.2 in the Student Edition for instructions.

In this unit, students make figures on a coordinate system and use algebraic rules to transform them into similar figures. For example, if the coordinates of a figure are multiplied by 2, the algebraic transformation is from (x, y) to $(2x, 2y)$. In general, if the coordinates of a figure are (x, y), algebraic rules of the form $(nx + a, ny + b)$ will transform it into a similar figure with a scale factor of n. These algebraic rules are called *similarity transformations*, which are not introduced as vocabulary in this unit. In the preceding figures, Figure B has been transformed from Figure A by the rule $(1.5x, 1.5y)$.

Relationship of Area and Perimeter in Similar Figures

The *perimeters* of one rectangle A and rectangle B below are related by a scale factor of 2. The *area* increases by the square of the scale factor, or 4. This can be seen by dividing rectangle B into four rectangles (labeled A) congruent to rectangle A.

Similarity of Rectangles

Since all of the angles in rectangles are right angles, you need only check the ratios of the lengths of corresponding sides. For example, rectangles C and D are similar, but neither is similar to rectangle E.

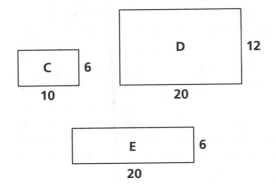

The scale factor from rectangle C to rectangle D is 2 because the length of each side of rectangle C multiplied by 2 gives the length of the corresponding side of rectangle D. The scale factor from rectangle D to rectangle C is $\frac{1}{2}$ because the length of each side of rectangle D multiplied by $\frac{1}{2}$ gives the length of the corresponding side of rectangle C. Rectangle E is not similar to rectangle C, because the lengths of corresponding sides do not increase by the same factor.

Similarity Transformations and Congruence

In general, algebraic rules of the form (nx, ny) are called similarity transformations, because they will transform a figure in the plane into a similar figure in the plane. If the figure described by the rule, (x, y), is compared to the figure described by the rule, (nx, ny), n is the scale factor from the original figure to the image. The scale factor from Figure A (x, y) to Figure B $(2x, 2y)$ is 2. The scale factor from Figure A (x, y) to Figure C $(3x, 3y)$ is 3. This is a special case where $n = 1$ in Figure A. If we compare two figures created by rules when $n \neq 1$ in both figures, then the scale factor is not n. An example is Figure B $(2x, 2y)$ and Figure C $(3x, 3y)$. They are similar to each other. But the scale factor from B to C is $\frac{3}{2}$.

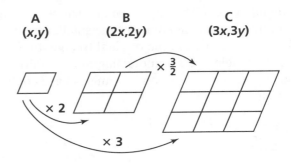

Note that similarity is transitive. If Figure A is similar to Figure B and Figure B is similar to Figure C, then Figure A is similar to Figure C.

In Problem 2.2, the students will see that adding to x and/or y moves the figure around on the grid, but does not affect its size. This means that a more general form of similarity transformations of this sort is $(nx + a, ny + b)$. Rules of this form, where the coefficient of both x and y is 1 [such as $(x + 3, y - 2)$], move the figure around, but the figure stays exactly the same shape and size (it is congruent to the original).

Congruent is a term from the sixth-grade unit *Shapes and Designs*. Note that the scale factor between two congruent figures is 1. Therefore, congruent figures are also similar.

There are other transformations in the plane that preserve congruence, such as flips and turns. These are studied in the eighth-grade unit *Kaleidoscopes, Hubcaps, and Mirrors*.

Comparing Area in Two Similar Figures Using Rep-Tiles

It is generally surprising to students that if you apply a scale factor of 2 to a figure, the area becomes 4 times as large. One approach is to have students calculate the area of a figure and that of its image and compare the results. In the first two investigations, area is explored informally. In Investigation 3, we use rep-tiles to demonstrate that when you apply a scale factor of 2, it requires four copies of the original figure. In this case, you are really measuring area using the original figure as the unit, rather than square inches or square centimeters. If congruent copies of a shape can be put together to make a larger, similar shape, the original shape is called a rep-tile. It takes four congruent triangles to create a larger similar triangle with a scale factor of 2 or nine congruent triangles to create a larger similar triangle with a scale factor of 3. The large triangle below is made from four congruent copies of the smaller triangle. The scale factor from the original triangle to the larger triangle is 2. From the diagram it is fairly easy to see that corresponding angles have equal measures.

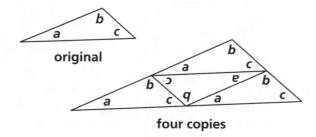

original

four copies

The following examples are also rep-tiles with a scale factor of 2 from the smaller shape to the larger shape.

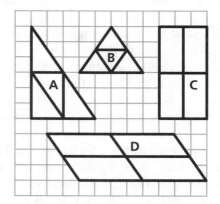

A misconception that can arise is the idea that tiling is related to similarity. Figures that tile may not make a larger, similar figure. In addition, any figure can be transformed into a larger or smaller image, regardless of whether the figure can tile the plane. Rep-tiles are special because they make area comparisons easy.

Equivalent Ratios

In similar figures, there are several equivalent ratios. Some are formed by comparing lengths *within* a figure. Others are formed by comparing lengths between two figures. For the rectangles below, the ratio of length to width is $\frac{10}{6}$ or $1.\overline{6}$ for rectangle P and $\frac{20}{12}$ or $1.\overline{6}$ for rectangle R.

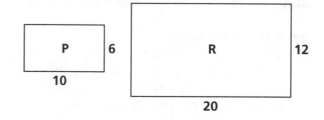

You can also look at the ratios of corresponding sides *across* two figures. In this situation it is width-to-width and length-to-length. The ratios are $\frac{12}{6}$ and $\frac{20}{10}$, respectively. These ratios are equivalent, and are also equivalent to 2, the scale factor. This second kind of ratio is not formally discussed in the unit, but students have used it informally when they divide corresponding side lengths between two similar figures to find the scale factor. This ratio also appears in an ACE.

The perimeter grows by a factor of 2 and the area grows by a scale factor of 2 × 2, or 4.

Similarity of Triangles

For polygons other than triangles, you must make sure that the lengths of corresponding sides increase by the same scale factor and that corresponding angle measures are equal when considering similarity.

In *Shapes and Designs*, students explored an important property of triangles—angles determine a triangle's shape. The property leads to the Angle-Angle-Angle Similarity Theorem for Triangles:

> If the measures of corresponding angles in two triangles are equal, then the two triangles are similar.

For triangles you only have to check the angles to determine whether two triangles are similar. However, this fact about triangles is only hinted at in the unit. At this stage of their development of understanding of similarity, it is best if students operate with the general definition that applies to all polygons:

> Corresponding angle measures are equal and corresponding side lengths grow by the same scale factor. The next section explains this theorem.

Angle-Angle-Angle Similarity for Triangles

The line that connects the midpoints of two opposite sides of a triangle is parallel to the third side and its length is equal to half the length of the opposite side. The parallel lines create equal corresponding angles.

Parallel lines also cut transversals into segments whose ratios are equal. In the following figure, segment DE is parallel to segment CB, so the ratios of the lengths of the segments AD to DC and the lengths of the segments AE to EB are equal.

That is, $\frac{AD}{DC} = \frac{AE}{EB}$.

These facts can be used to show that if the corresponding angles of one triangle are congruent to the

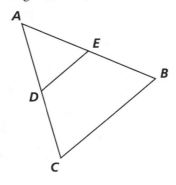

corresponding angles of another triangle then the two triangles are similar. This is known as the Angle-Angle-Angle Similarity Theorem. This is true only for triangles. Also, because you know that the angles of a triangle add to 180° you need only check two angles of a triangle in order to verify similarity.

This unit presents an alternative test for similarity. If the corresponding angle measures are equal, then instead of checking the ratio between corresponding sides (the scale factor), you could check the ratios of sides within each figure. Given the two figures below, if $\frac{FG}{GH} = \frac{KL}{LM}$ and $\frac{GH}{FH} = \frac{LM}{KM}$, then the figures are similar.

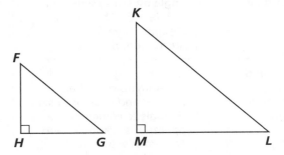

Solving Problems Using Similar Figures

Equivalent ratios can be used to solve interesting problems. For example, shadows can be thought of as sides of similar triangles because the sunlight hits the objects at the same angle. A building of unknown height and a meter stick, both of which are casting shadows, are shown below. To find the height of the building, you can use the scale factor between the lengths of the shadows. Since going from 0.25 to 10 involves a scale factor of 40, multiply the height of the meter stick by 40 to obtain the height of the building, 40 × 1 m = 40 m. You could also think of this as $\frac{x}{10} = \frac{1}{0.25}$. Finding the value of x that makes the ratios equivalent gives you the height of the building.

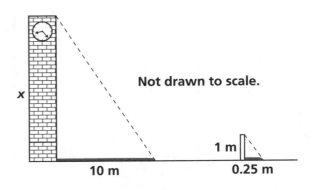

Not drawn to scale.

10 m   0.25 m

Big Idea	Prior Work	Future Work
Enlarging and shrinking plane figures	Finding angle measures, lengths, and areas of plane geometric figures (Shapes and Designs; Covering and Surrounding)	Scaling quantities, objects, and shapes up and down (Comparing and Scaling; Filling and Wrapping)
Identifying the corresponding parts of similar figures	Developing and applying concepts of vertex, angle, angle measure, side, and side length (Shapes and Designs; Covering and Surrounding)	Analyzing how two-dimensional shapes are affected by different isometries; generating isometric transformations (Kaleidoscopes, Hubcaps, and Mirrors)
Describing and producing transformations of plane figures	Constructing two-dimensional shapes (Shapes and Designs); using symbols to communicate operations (Variables and Patterns); exploring symmetries of a figure (Shapes and Designs)	Finding the equation of a line (Moving Straight Ahead); expressing linear relationships with symbols; determining whether linear expressions are equivalent (Say It With Symbols); writing directions for isometries in two dimensions (Kaleidoscopes, Hubcaps, and Mirrors)
Analyzing scale factors between figures; analyzing ratios within two figures; applying scale factors to solve two-dimensional geometric problems	Using factors and multiples (Prime Time); measuring two-dimensional figures (Covering and Surrounding); using ratios in fraction form (Bits and Pieces I; Bits and Pieces II); using maps (Variables and Patterns)	Scaling and comparing figures and quantities (Comparing and Scaling); using slope to solve problems involving linear relationships (Moving Straight Ahead)
Applying properties of similar figures	Exploring properties of two-dimensional shapes; finding areas, perimeters, and side lengths of shapes (Shapes and Designs; Covering and Surrounding)	Exploring ratios and proportional relationships (Comparing and Scaling); developing the concept of slope (Moving Straight Ahead)

Planning for the Unit

Pacing Suggestions and Materials

Investigations and Assessments	Pacing 45–50 min. classes	Materials for Students	Materials for Teachers
1 Enlarging and Reducing Shapes	$3\frac{1}{2}$ days	Rulers, number 16 3-inch rubber bands (2 per student), blank paper, masking tape, angle rulers; Labsheets 1.2A, 1.2B, 1.3, 1ACE Exercises 3, 4, 13	CMP Shapes Set (optional); Transparencies 1.1, 1.2
Mathematical Reflections	$\frac{1}{2}$ day		
2 Similar Figures	$4\frac{1}{2}$ days	Angle rulers, centimeter and half-centimeter grid paper; Labsheets 2.1A–C, 2.2A, 2.2B, 2.3, 2ACE Exercise 1	Transparent centimeter and half-centimeter grids (optional; copy grids onto transparency film); Transparencies 2.1A, 2.1B, 2.2, 2.3
Mathematical Reflections	$\frac{1}{2}$ day		
Assessment: Check Up 1	$\frac{1}{2}$ day		
3 Similar Polygons	$3\frac{1}{2}$ days	Blank paper, scissors (optional), ruler or other straightedge, quarter-inch grid paper; Labsheets 3.2, 3.3A, 3.3B, 3ACE Exercise 8, Shapes Set (optional)	Transparencies 3.2, 3.3A, 3.3B
Mathematical Reflections	$\frac{1}{2}$ day		
Assessment: Partner Quiz	1 day		
4 Similarity and Ratios	$3\frac{1}{2}$ days	Labsheets 4.2, 4.3	Transparencies 4.1A–C, 4.2, 4.3A–C
Mathematical Reflections	$\frac{1}{2}$ day		
Assessment: Check Up 2	$\frac{1}{2}$ day		
5 Using Similar Triangles and Rectangles	$3\frac{1}{2}$ days	Meter sticks, small mirrors, string and stakes, large marked area; Labsheet 5.3	String and stakes for laying out a "pond" (optional) Transparencies 5.1, 5.2, 5.3
Mathematical Reflections	$\frac{1}{2}$ day	Labsheet 5.3	Transparency LBLA
Looking Back and Looking Ahead	$\frac{1}{2}$ day		
Assessment: Unit Project	optional		
Assessment: Self Assessment	Take Home		
Assessment: Unit Test	1 day		

Total Time $24\frac{1}{2}$ days	**Materials for Use in All Investigations**	
For detailed pacing for Problems within each Investigation, see the Suggested Pacing at the beginning of each Investigation. For pacing with block scheduling, see next page.	Labsheets, calculators, blank transparencies and transparency markers (optional), student notebooks	Transparencies and transparency markers (optional)

Pacing for Block Scheduling (90-minute class periods)

Investigation	Suggested Pacing	Investigation	Suggested Pacing	Investigation	Suggested Pacing
Investigation 1	$2\frac{1}{2}$ **days**	**Investigation 3**	$2\frac{1}{2}$ **days**	**Investigation 5**	$2\frac{1}{2}$ **days**
Problem 1.1	$\frac{1}{2}$ day	Problem 3.1	1 day	Problem 5.1	$\frac{1}{2}$ day
Problem 1.2	1 day	Problem 3.2	$\frac{1}{2}$ day	Problem 5.2	$\frac{1}{2}$ day
Problem 1.3	$\frac{1}{2}$ day	Problem 3.3	$\frac{1}{2}$ day	Problem 5.3	1 day
Math Reflections	$\frac{1}{2}$ day	Math Reflections	$\frac{1}{2}$ day	Math Reflections	$\frac{1}{2}$ day
Investigation 2	$2\frac{1}{2}$ **days**	**Investigation 4**	**2 days**		
Problem 2.1	1 day	Problem 4.1	$\frac{1}{2}$ day		
Problem 2.2	$\frac{1}{2}$ day	Problem 4.2	$\frac{1}{2}$ day		
Problem 2.3	$\frac{1}{2}$ day	Problem 4.3	$\frac{1}{2}$ day		
Math Reflections	$\frac{1}{2}$ day	Math Reflections	$\frac{1}{2}$ day		

Vocabulary

Essential Terms Developed in This Unit	Additional Terms Referenced in This Unit	Terms Developed in Previous Units
complementary angles	fractal	congruent
corresponding angles	midpoint	parallel
corresponding sides	nested triangles	parallelogram
equivalent ratios	square	polygon
image	square root	probability
ratio		quadrilateral
rep-tile		ratio
scale factor		tessellation
similar		transformation
supplementary angles		

Go Online
PHSchool.com
For: Multiple Choice Skills Practice
Web Code: ank-5500

INTRODUCTION

Components

Use the chart below to quickly see which components are available for each Investigation.

Invest.	Labsheets	Additional Practice	Transparencies		Formal Assessment		Assessment Options	
			Problem	Summary	Check Up	Partner Quiz	Multiple-Choice	Question Bank
1	1.2A, 1.2B, 1.3, 1ACE Exercises 3, 4, 13	✔	1.1, 1.2				✔	✔
2	2.1A–C, 2.2A, 2.2B, 2.3, 2ACE Exercise 1	✔	2.1A, 2.1B, 2.2, 2.3		✔		✔	✔
3	3.2, 3.3A, 3.3B, 3ACE Exercise 8, Shapes Set (optional)	✔	3.2, 3.3A, 3.3B			✔	✔	✔
4	4.2, 4.3	✔	4.1A–C, 4.2, 4.3A–C		✔		✔	✔
5	5.3	✔	5.1, 5.2, 5.3				✔	✔
For the Unit	Quarter-inch grid paper	*ExamView* CD-ROM, Web site	LBLA		Unit Test, Notebook Check, Self Assessment		Multiple-Choice Items, Question Bank, *ExamView* CD-ROM	

Also Available for Use With This Unit

- Parent Guide: take-home letter for the unit
- Implementing CMP
- Spanish Assessment Resources
- Additional online and technology resources

Technology

The Use of Calculators

Connected Mathematics was developed with the belief that calculators should be available and that students should learn when their use is appropriate.

For this reason, we do not designate specific problems as "calculator problems." The calculations in *Stretching and Shrinking* involve only simple arithmetic, so nonscientific calculators are adequate.

Student Activity CD-ROM

Includes interactive activities to enhance the learning in the Problems within Investigations.

PHSchool.com

For Students Multiple-choice practice with instant feedback, updated data sources, data sets for Tinkerplots data software.

For Teachers Professional development, curriculum support, downloadable forms, and more.

See also www.math.msu.edu/cmp for more resources for both teachers and students.

ExamView® CD-ROM

Create multiple versions of practice sheets and tests for course objectives and standardized tests. Includes dynamic questions, online testing, student reports, and all test and practice items in Spanish. Also includes all items in the *Assessment Resources* and *Additional Practice*.

TeacherExpress™ CD-ROM

Includes a lesson planning tool, the Teacher's Guide pages, and all the teaching resources.

LessonLab Online Courses

LessonLab offers comprehensive, facilitated professional development designed to help teachers implement CMP2 and improve student achievement. To learn more, please visit PHSchool.com/cmp2.

Assessment Summary

Ongoing Informal Assessment

Embedded in the Unit
Problems Use students' work from the Problems to check student understanding.

ACE exercises Use ACE exercises for homework assignments to assess student understanding.

Mathematical Reflections Have students summarize their learning at the end of each Investigation.

Looking Back and Looking Ahead At the end of the unit, use the first two sections to allow students to show what they know about the unit.

Additional Resources
Teacher's Edition Use the Check for Understanding feature of some Summaries and the probing questions that appear in the *Launch, Explore,* or *Summarize* sections of all Investigations to check student understanding.

Self Assessment
Notebook Check Students use this tool to organize and check their notebooks before giving them to their teacher. Located in *Assessment Resources*.

Self Assessment At the end of the unit, students reflect on and provide examples of what they learned. Located in *Assessment Resources*.

Formal Assessment

Choose the assessment materials that are appropriate for your students.

Assessment	For Use After	Focus	Student Work
Check Up 1	Invest. 2	Skills	Individual
Check Up 2	Invest. 4	Skills	Individual
Partner Quiz	Invest. 3	Rich problems	Pair
Unit Test	The Unit	Skills, rich problems	Individual
Unit Project	The Unit	Rich problems	Individual or Group

Additional Resources
Multiple-Choice Items Use these items for homework, review, a quiz, or add them to the Unit Test.

Question Bank Choose from these questions for homework, review, or replacements for Quiz, Check Up, or Unit Test questions.

Additional Practice Choose practice exercises for each Investigation for homework, review, or formal assessments.

***ExamView* CD-ROM** Create practice sheets, review quizzes, and tests with this dynamic software. Give online tests and receive student progress reports. (Test items are also available in Spanish.)

Spanish Assessment Resources
Includes Partner Quiz, Check Up, Unit Test, Multiple-Choice Items, Question Bank, Notebook Check, and Self Assessment. Plus, the *ExamView* CD-ROM has all test items in Spanish.

Correlation to Standardized Tests

Investigation	NAEP	Terra Nova CAT6	Terra Nova CTBS	ITBS	SAT10	Local Test
1 Enlarging and Reducing Shapes	G2e, G2c	✔	✔			
2 Similar Figures	G2f, G4d		✔		✔	
3 Similar Polygons	G2e, G2f		✔		✔	
4 Similarity and Ratios	G2e, G2f	✔	✔			
5 Using Similar Triangles and Rectangles	G2e, G2f, G3c	✔	✔		✔	

NAEP National Assessment of Educational Progress

CAT6/Terra Nova California Achievement Test, 6th Ed.
CTBS/Terra Nova Comprehensive Test of Basic Skills

ITBS Iowa Test of Basic Skills, Form M
SAT10 Stanford Achievement Test, 10th Ed.

Stretching and Shrinking

Understanding Similarity

Glenda Lappan
James T. Fey
William M. Fitzgerald
Susan N. Friel
Elizabeth Difanis Phillips

PEARSON

Boston, Massachusetts · Glenview, Illinois · Shoreview, Minnesota · Upper Saddle River, New Jersey

Notes _____
_____
_____
_____

Stretching and Shrinking

Understanding Similarity

A teacher in disguise will appear for a few minutes at school each day for a week. The student who guesses the identity of the mystery teacher wins a prize. How might a photograph help in identifying the teacher?

A good map is similar to the place it represents. You can use a map to find actual distances of any place in the world. How can you estimate the distance from Cape Town, South Africa to Port Elizabeth, South Africa?

Here is a picture of Duke, a real dog. If you know the scale factor from Duke to the picture, how can you determine how long Duke is from his nose to the tip of his tail?

2   Stretching and Shrinking

Notes _____

_____

_____

_____

You probably use the word *similar* quite a bit in everyday conversation. For example, you might say that one song sounds similar to another song or that your friend's bike is similar to yours.

In many cases, you might use the word similar to describe objects and images that are the same shape but not the same size. A floor plan of a house is the same shape as the actual floor, but it is much smaller. The images on a movie screen are the same shape as the real people and objects they depict, but they are much larger.

You can order your school portrait in a variety of sizes, but your face will have the same shape in each photo.

In this unit, you will learn what it means for two shapes to be mathematically similar. The ideas you learn can help you answer questions like those on the previous page.

Notes _____

_____

_____

_____

Mathematical Highlights

Understanding Similarity

In *Stretching and Shrinking*, you will learn the mathematical meaning of similarity and explore the properties of similar figures.

You will learn how to

- Identify similar figures by comparing corresponding parts
- Use scale factors and ratios to describe relationships among the side lengths of similar figures
- Construct similar polygons
- Draw shapes on coordinate grids and then use coordinate rules to stretch and shrink those shapes
- Predict the ways that stretching or shrinking a figure affects lengths, angle measures, perimeters, and areas
- Use the properties of similarity to find distances and heights that you can't measure

As you work on the problems in this unit, make it a habit to ask yourself questions about situations that involve similar figures:

What is the same and what is different about two similar figures?

What determines whether two shapes are similar?

When figures are similar, how are the lengths, areas, and scale factor related?

How can I use information about similar figures to solve a problem?

Notes _____

_____

_____

_____

Introducing Your Students to Stretching and Shrinking

One way to introduce your students to this unit is ask them to think about two things that are similar to each other. Have students share their ideas and ask them to talk about what makes these things similar. Examples might include that one student's bicycle is similar to another's because they both have 10 speeds, or that one student's brother is similar to his sister because they both have brown hair.

Using the Unit Opener

You might ask students to think about circumstances in which they need a model of something that is smaller than the real thing (e.g., model airplanes, blueprints, and dollhouses). You might also ask them what situations require larger models (e.g., drawings of insects and plans for computer chips). Tell them that this unit is about the properties of these models.

In mathematics, we use the word *similar* to mean something very specific. This meaning will be the focus of this unit.

Discuss with your students the introductory problems located in the unit opener of the Student Edition. The problems will be answered within the unit, so students are not expected to be able to solve them here. The problems serve as an advanced organizer for what the students will encounter and learn to do during the unit. Take a few minutes to allow ideas from the students with the goal of generating enthusiasm for the kinds of situations in the unit.

You can use the unit goals to help the students to anticipate what is coming up in the unit and to build a set of expectations for the work of the students.

Using the Mathematical Highlights

The Mathematical Highlights page in the Student Edition provides information to students, parents, and other family members. It gives students a preview of the mathematics and some of the overarching questions that they should ask themselves while studying *Stretching and Shrinking*.

As they work through the unit, students can refer back to the Mathematical Highlights page to review what they have learned and to preview what is still to come. This page also tells students' families what mathematical ideas and activities will be covered as the class works through *Stretching and Shrinking*.

Using the Unit Project

An optional assessment item is the Shrinking or Enlarging Pictures project. Explain to students that they will enlarge or shrink a picture or cartoon of their choice using the technique of coordinate system rules to produce a similar image.

See the special section *Assigning the Unit Project* for more information. To help you assess the project, see the *Guide to the Unit Project* in the Assessment Resources section. Here you will find a rubric and samples of student projects. Each sample is followed by the teacher's comments about assessing the project.

There is an alternate project *All Similar Shapes* that can be assigned here.

Investigation 1 — Enlarging and Reducing Shapes

Mathematical and Problem-Solving Goals

- Informally introduce ideas about similarity
- Make similar figures
- Compare approximate measurements of corresponding parts in similar figures
- Determine which features of similar figures are different and which are the same
- Connect size changes to students' previous understanding of percent
- Use percents as a way to describe size change
- Make accurate comparisons of measurements of similar figures

Summary of Problems

Problem 1.1 Solving a Mystery

Students use the known size of a small object (magazine) in a photo of a mystery student giving away tickets to estimate the unknown actual size of a larger object (mystery student). Students are asked to express their informal ideas about the mathematical meaning of similarity.

Problem 1.2 Stretching a Figure

Students make a stretcher by tying two rubber bands together and use it to enlarge two different figures. They compare how general shape, line lengths, areas, perimeters, and angles are affected. This focuses students' attention on the preservation of shape.

Problem 1.3 Scaling Up and Down

The context of copier size factors introduces students to the use of scale factors other than 2.

Mathematics Background

For background on similar figures, see page 4.

	Suggested Pacing	Materials for Students	Materials for Teachers	ACE Assignments
All	$3\frac{1}{2}$ days	Angle rulers or protractors, centimeter and inch rulers		
1.1	1 day		Transparency 1.1, transparent inch ruler (optional)	1, 2, 8–12
1.2	1 day	Labsheet 1.2A and B (1 per student, based on handedness), 3 inch rubber bands (2 per student), masking tape, blank sheets of paper (at least 1 per student), Labsheet 1ACE Exercises 3, 4, and 13	Transparency 1.2, chart paper (optional), transparent centimeter ruler (optional), blank transparencies	3, 4, 13–18, 21–26
1.3	1 day	Labsheet 1.3 (1 per student)	Transparency of Labsheet 1.3 (optional), transparent grid paper (optional), transparent centimeter ruler (optional)	5–7, 19, 20
MR	$\frac{1}{2}$ day			

1.1 Solving a Mystery

Goal

- Informally introduce ideas about similarity

In this problem, a photo of a mystery teacher is shown and students use a known measure of a small object (magazine) to estimate an unknown measure of a larger object (mystery teacher).

Launch 1.1

In launching this problem, your goal is to understand what your students intuitively know about similar figures. In addition, you will want to assess their measurement skills.

Tell the story of the mystery teacher. Help students see what information they have and what they need to find.

Suggested Questions

- *What information do we have?* (the height of the real-life magazines, the height of the photo of the teacher and of the magazine)

- *What are we trying to find?* (the real-life height of the teacher)

- *How does the real-life teacher differ from the teacher in the photo?* (in the height and width; the real-life teacher is taller and wider.)

Be careful to leave the task of finding the teacher's height open enough so that you can learn what your students think about similar figures. Eliciting explicit strategies for finding the teacher's height in the launch could reduce your opportunity to assess your students' thinking.

Students can work in groups of 2 or 3.

Explore 1.1

Students can use rulers or edges of a piece of paper to make informal estimates of various measurements. Do not push for precise measurement at this time. Pay attention, though, to which students measure naturally and easily and which struggle with measurement. This will help you to plan your teaching in later problems in the unit where careful measurement is important.

Look for interesting strategies.

- Most students will likely measure the mystery teacher's height using the length of the magazine as a unit. They may say that the teacher is 7 magazines (or 70 in.) tall.

- Fewer students will notice that the real magazine is 20 times the size of the one in the picture, so the mystery teacher must be also. This gives approximately $3\frac{1}{2} \times 20 = 70$ in.

- Some students will measure the height in inches of the magazine and of the mystery teacher. They will then divide the height of the teacher by the height of the magazine to find how many magazines tall the teacher is. This is a more precise version of the first strategy.

Make sure students are clear about the comparisons that they are making. They may compare the real magazine to the magazine in the picture or the magazine in the picture to the teacher in the picture.

Summarize 1.1

Discuss students' perception of similar figures. They might say things like, "look alike," "same shape," "same features," "different size,". . .

Focus the summary on students' strategies. It is helpful for students to hear others' ideas while they are developing their own. You should expect some variation in the answers because all measurements are approximations. However, answers that are obviously unreasonable should be examined closely and efforts should be made to figure out why they are incorrect.

Suggested Questions

- *What would you expect the range of possible heights for the mystery teacher to be? If an answer is over 7 ft, is that reasonable? What about an answer of under 4 ft?*

Finally, ask students to summarize their procedures and apply them to other situations.

- *Can you think of some other times when you might want to use a photograph to estimate the size of something?*

- *In the movie theater, the image of the person is taller than the real person. How can you use the same techniques to estimate someone's height from their image on a movie screen?*

1.1

Solving a Mystery

Mathematical Goal

- Informally introduce ideas about similarity

Launch

Tell the story of the mystery teacher. Help students see what information they have and what they need to find. Discuss the relationship between the photo and the real scene.

Have students work in pairs or groups of 3.

Materials
- Transparency 1.1

Vocabulary
- similar

Explore

Pay attention to students' measuring strategies so that you can have more than one shared during the summary.

Make sure students are clear about the comparisons they are making. They may compare the real magazine to the magazine in the picture or the magazine in the picture to the teacher in the picture.

Materials
- rulers

Summarize

Discuss students' perception of the meaning of *similar*. Do not push for formal language; accept "look alike," "same shape," "same features," "different size,"...

Have students share their strategies with the class.

Discuss other situations where these ideas might be useful.

- *Can you think of some other times when you might want to use a photograph to estimate the size of something?*

- *In the movie theater, the image of the person is taller than the real person. How can you use the same techniques to estimate someone's height from their image on a movie screen?*

Materials
- student notebooks

ACE Assignment Guide
for Problem 1.1

Core 1, 2
Other *Connections* 8–12

Adapted For suggestions about adapting Exercise 1 and other ACE exercises, see the CMP *Special Needs Handbook*.
Connecting to Prior Units 8–12: *Covering and Surrounding*

Answers to Problem 1.1

A. about 72.5 in. or 6 ft $\frac{1}{2}$ in. tall;

One possible explanation: In the picture, the height of the *P. I. Monthly* is 0.5 in. We know that the height of the real magazine is 10 in. So the real magazine is $10 \div 0.5 = 20$ times larger than in the picture. The teacher should also be 20 times larger in real life than he/she is in the picture. The teacher's height in the picture is about $3\frac{5}{8}$ in. So the actual height is about $20 \times (3\frac{5}{8}) = 72.5$ in.

Note: Students are not expected to use the word *ratio* at this time. This term is introduced in Investigation 3.

The other likely explanation that students will give compares the magazine in the picture to the teacher in the picture. In this case, the teacher is $3\frac{5}{8} \div \frac{1}{2} = 7\frac{1}{4}$ times as tall as the magazine. Students may say that the teacher is $7\frac{1}{4}$ magazines tall. This should be true in real life as well. Since the height of the magazine is 10 in., the teacher is $10 \times 7\frac{1}{4} = 72.5$ in. tall.

B. Answers will vary. Some possible answers: The figures in the picture look the same as the original shapes except in size. The objects in the picture have the same shape as the actual objects.

1.2 Stretching a Figure

Goals

- Make similar figures
- Compare approximate measurements of corresponding parts in similar figures

In this problem, students use rubber bands to enlarge a figure. They compare the original figure to the enlargement to determine which features have changed and which have remained the same.

Transparent grids may be a helpful visual aid for some students to compare lengths of sides, perimeters, or areas of the figures. You may want to have them available throughout this unit.

You will need to demonstrate how to draw a figure using a rubber-band stretcher, either using chalk on the chalkboard or a marker on chart paper taped to the board. Test your setup before class so you know everything fits. Place the anchor point so that the enlarged drawing will not overlap the original. Choose a figure to enlarge that your students will find interesting, such as a popular cartoon character, a logo, a smiley face, or a ghost. Some teachers make a stretcher with larger rubber bands to make it easier for students to see what the teacher is doing at the board.

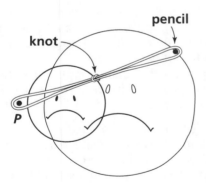

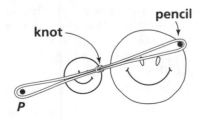

Launch 1.2

Members of the Mystery Club want to make a poster that shows their logo. To do this, they need to enlarge the logo found on the flyer that they have designed. Briefly discuss with students the desire to make a larger version of the original picture. Then tell them that you are going to demonstrate one method for doing so.

- *I have a super machine called a stretcher that will help me draw a copy of this figure. My machine has two parts. Watch me carefully while I make a stretcher before your very eyes!*

Tie the two rubber bands together by passing one band through the other and back through itself. Pull on the two ends, moving the knot to the center of the bands. You may need to pull on the knot so that each band forms half of the knot.

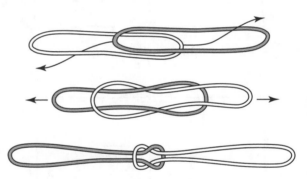

Hold your finished stretcher in the air and demonstrate its stretch. Then, use it to draw a copy of the figure as you describe the process.

- *Notice that I put one end of my stretcher on a point, called the anchor point, and hold it down securely without covering up any more of the band than necessary. I put the marker (chalk) through the other end and stretch the bands until the knot is just above part of my figure. I move my marker as I trace the figure with the knot. I try to keep the knot directly over the original figure as my marker draws the new figure. I do not look at the marker (chalk) as I draw. I only watch the knot. The more carefully the knot traces the original, the better my drawing will be.*

Finish the drawing and ask students to describe what occurred. They will probably say the two figures look alike but that the new one is larger. Until they have made their own drawings, you do not need to press for more specific observations or relationships.

Distribute two rubber bands, a blank sheet of paper, and Labsheet 1.2A (for right-handed students) or 1.2B (for left-handed students) to each student. Have students tape the two sheets to their desks using masking tape as shown below and in the Student Edition. Left-handed students will have the anchor point to their right and the blank sheet of paper to their left.

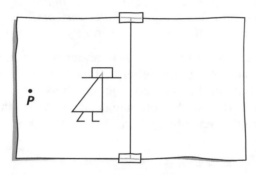

Right-handed Setup

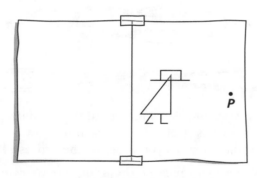

Left-handed Setup

Let the students make their stretchers. Some students will have a hard time tying the bands together and will need assistance. You may want to be sure everyone has made a stretcher before the class begins drawing.

Students should make their own sketches, then discuss their answers with a partner.

Explore 1.2

As students work, mention that their drawings will be more accurate if they hold the pencil vertically and keep the rubber bands as close to the point of the pencil as possible.

Remind students to trace the figure they are trying to copy with the knot, as they may be tempted to draw the object freehand. Accuracy is not the issue here, but students can get better drawings by being careful with the placement of the rubber bands on the pencil and the path of the knot on the figure.

A stretcher made from two rubber bands gives a figure enlarged by a factor of 2. This means the new length measures are twice as large as the original. Students may guess different factors for the growth of the lengths, which is fine at this stage, but it should be reasonably close to 2. In any case, this process is not very precise. Student error as well as variation in the length and stretchiness of the rubber bands will result in images that are not exactly twice as large.

Going Further
Students' work with the rubber-band stretchers often raises interesting questions.

Suggested Questions Encourage student exploration of interesting questions about the stretchers like:

- *What would happen if I made a three-band stretcher?* [Notice that with a three-band stretcher there are two knots. The size change is different based on whether you use the knot closer to the anchor point (3 times larger) or the knot closer to the pencil (1.5 times larger).]

- *Do I get exactly the same drawing if I switch the ends of my two-band stretcher?* [No. It is rarely the case that the two rubber bands are exactly alike in stretchiness and length. Furthermore, it is very difficult to get the bands to contribute equally to the knot. The net result is usually that the image is a bit more (less) than twice as large as the original in lengths. Switching the ends of the rubber band will then make the image a bit less (more) than twice as large.]

- *How could we use something like the rubber-band stretcher to make an image smaller than the original?* (This is a bit tricky, but possible to imagine. The standard stretcher method uses the knot to trace the smaller original and the end of the stretcher to trace the larger image. To shrink a figure, we need to switch the roles of the knot and the end. We would need to put a pencil at the knot and use the end of the stretcher to trace the original and have a friend or third hand to help.)

Summarize 1.2

Ask students to describe what they noticed about the figures they drew. Explain that the word *image* refers to a drawing made with a stretcher. Students should recognize that the two figures look alike and that the image is larger than the original.

Suggested Questions Encourage student exploration of interesting questions about the stretchers like:

- *What is the relationship between the side lengths of the original figure and the side lengths of the image?* (Side lengths of the image are double that of the original figure.)

Introduce the term *corresponding* at this point. This is the first place in the curriculum where the term is used. Students will need this vocabulary throughout this unit.

- *What is the relationship between the measures of corresponding angles?* (Their measures are the same.)

Blank transparencies are helpful to show how the angles compare. Copy one angle of a figure and then place it on top of the corresponding angle of the second figure. Or have both figures on transparencies and place one on top of the other on the overhead projector.

- *How does the area change?* (Students can informally compare the areas. They may use transparent grids or show informally how four of the smaller figures cover the larger figure. Or they may focus on the hat, which has a rectangular shape.)

Students may mention things other than that the side lengths have doubled. Do not be too concerned about the exactness of their observations at this stage, as long as their answers are reasonable for their drawings.

- *What happens if we change the anchor point?* (The image is still twice as large, but its location changes.)

Students are often amazed at the result of using a rubber band stretcher. It is helpful to have in mind that what makes the stretcher work is really similarity. In the first figure below you can see that when we knot two same size rubber bands together and the knot travels on a segment of the original figure, the drawing of a segment in the image will be twice the length of the segment in the original. The scale factor between the original and the image is 2.

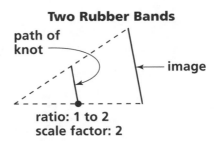

Two Rubber Bands

path of knot

image

ratio: 1 to 2
scale factor: 2

If we connected three rubber bands and use the first knot, we get an image that is 3 times as large.

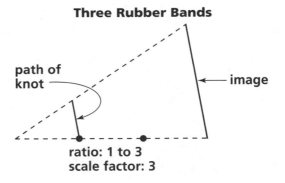

Three Rubber Bands

path of knot

image

ratio: 1 to 3
scale factor: 3

If we use the second knot, we get an image that is 1.5 times large.

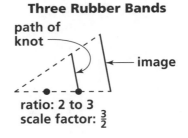

Three Rubber Bands

path of knot

image

ratio: 2 to 3
scale factor: $\frac{3}{2}$

1.2 Stretching a Figure

Mathematical Goals

- Make similar figures
- Compare approximate measurements of corresponding parts in similar figures

Launch

Briefly discuss with students the desire to make a larger version of the original picture, then tell them that you are going to demonstrate one method for doing so. Finish the drawing and ask students to describe what occurred.

Students should make their own sketches, then discuss their answers with a partner.

Materials
- Transparency 1.2
- Labsheets 1.2A and 1.2B (1 per student)
- #16 Rubber bands (2 per student)
- Blank paper
- Tape
- Angle rulers

Explore

Remind students to trace the figure they are trying to copy with the knot, as they may be tempted to draw the object freehand. Accuracy is not the issue here, but students can get better drawings by being careful with the placement of the rubber bands on the pencil and the path of the knot on the figure.

Encourage student exploration of interesting questions about the stretchers.

- *What would happen if I made a three-band stretcher? Do I get exactly the same drawing if I switch the ends of my two-band stretcher? How could we use something like the rubber band stretcher to make an image smaller than the original?*

Summarize

Ask students to describe what they noticed about the figures they drew. Explain that the word *image* will be used to refer to a drawing made with a stretcher. Students should recognize that the two figures look alike and that the image is larger than the original.

- *What is the relationship between the side lengths of the original figure and the side lengths of the image?*

Introduce the term *corresponding* at this point.

- *What about the relationship between the measures of corresponding angles?*

Materials
- Student notebooks
- Blank transparencies

Vocabulary
- image
- corresponding

continued on next page

Blank transparencies are helpful to show how the angles compare. Copy one angle of a figure and then place it on top of the corresponding angle of the second figure. Or have both figures on transparencies and place one on top of the other on the overhead projector.

- *How does the area change?*
- *What happens if we change the anchor point?*

ACE Assignment Guide for Problem 1.2

Core 14, 22
Other *Applications* 3, 4; *Connections* 13, 15–18, *Extensions* 21, 23–26; unassigned choices from previous problems
Labsheet 1ACE Exercises 3, 4, and 13 is available.

Adapted For suggestions about adapting ACE exercises, see the CMP *Special Needs Handbook*.
Connecting to Prior Units 13: *Covering and Surrounding;* 14–18: *Bits and Pieces III*

Answers to Problem 1.2

A. The general shapes of the two figures are the same.

The lengths of the corresponding line segments are different. The lengths in the image are twice as long as the corresponding lengths in the original.

The perimeters of the body and the hat in the image are twice as long as those in the original. Students may reason that since each line segment doubles, the perimeter, which is the sum of these doubled line segments, will also double. [Doubling each side individually then finding the perimeter is the same as finding the perimeter and then doubling it. This is intuitively the distributive property $2\ell + 2\ell + 2w + 2w = 2(\ell + \ell + w + w)$.]

The areas of the body and hat in the image are 4 times as large as those in the original. Students may see that approximately 4 of the original rectangles (hats) could fit into the enlarged rectangle (hat). If students say the areas are three or four times as large, this is fine at this stage. The important idea is that the area is more than twice as large.

The angles in the image are the same as the corresponding angles in the original.

Note that the answers above are true in the ideal case. In practice, the 2:1 ratio of the lengths (or the 4:1 ratio of the areas) will not always be observed. This is because of the imperfection of the bands and some differences in the application of the method. The result will be more accurate if the end of the rubber band on point *P* is fixed by holding a pin instead of holding by hand directly; if the image end of the band is held as close to the page as possible using the pencil; if the pencil chosen is as thin as possible since its thickness might cause the band in the image end to be shorter than it is supposed to be; if the bands are not stretched too much.

B. No matter which kind of figure you choose as the original, the observations in Question A will remain the same: The general shape will remain the same, the lengths and perimeters in the image will be twice as long as the lengths and perimeters in the original, while the areas will be four times as large and angles will remain the same.

1.3 Scaling Up and Down

Goals

- Use percents as a way to describe size change
- Make accurate comparisons of measurements of similar figures

This problem continues to focus on developing students' informal understanding of the concept of similarity. It uses the context of copier size factors to introduce scale factors other than 2. Connecting back to the sixth-grade rational number units, the use of scale factors of 75% and 150% is explored.

Launch 1.3

Set up the photocopier context by talking with students about the rubber-band stretchers and other methods for enlarging figures.

Suggested Questions

- *If you wanted to make a very good enlargement of a figure, would you use a rubber-band stretcher?* (No)

- *What other ways do you know of to make a larger copy of something?* (Students might mention a poster-making machine, an overhead projector and a photocopy machine. You will likely have many students who know that a photocopier can make enlargements and reductions, but have never used one to do this. Be prepared to tell students that we enter a percent into the photocopier to tell it what size to make the copy.)

Use the transparency of Labsheet 1.3 to do a quick review of basic percent concepts. Cover up the captions under each figure. Tell students that the middle figure is the original.

> *Estimate the percent Daphne entered into the photocopier in order to get the smaller image on the left. Write your estimate in your notebook.* (Student estimates can vary widely. Most will recognize that the smaller image is more than half of the original and so will guess something between 50% and 100%. This is as much precision as you ought to expect at this stage. Repeat the estimation with the enlarged

figure. Make sure that students realize that the result of entering 100% into the photocopier would be an image identical to the original.)

Students can work in small groups of 2 to 3.

Explore 1.3

Pay attention to how well your students are measuring. This is the first problem in this unit where more precision really makes sense, yet the comparisons are still relatively simple. Use this time to have students practice this important skill.

Suggested Questions This is also an opportunity to review operations with percents.

- *What is the measurement of the base of the triangle in the smaller figure?* [If the original figure's base is 1.5 in., the smaller figure's base ought to be 75% of this ($1\frac{1}{8}$ in.). Most students will get this first by measuring. Encourage some of this computation as well for review and practice.]

Look for ways that they use to compare features such as length and area.

- Some students will see immediately that the percents given are the right comparison.

- Some students will feel more comfortable comparing with fractions (the lengths on the smaller figure are about $\frac{3}{4}$ of the original).

Summarize 1.3

Discuss the questions. Ask students to explain their reasoning. This will give you insights into their understanding of percents. Be sure to discuss angle measures, side measures, and area.

Students may use adding strategies rather than multiplying by a common factor. For example, they may divide the side lengths of the original figure by four equal segments and then subtract one of the segments to get the side length of the figure that has been reduced to 75%.

To get the side length of the figure that is increased to 150% students may divide the side lengths of the original figure into two equal segments and then add one of the segments to the original.

Suggested Question To review percents and to encourage the students to see the multiplying effects of increasing/decreasing by percents, ask:

- *If I want to enlarge a figure by 25%, will the image be larger or smaller than the original? What number do I enter in the photocopier?* (To increase a figure by 25%, you multiply the figure by a factor of 1.25. Ask the class to explain why this is true.)

Draw a square on a transparent grid on the overhead to show what happens to an increase of 25%. To make the enlargement, first enlarge two adjacent sides of the original square and then complete the square.

Compare the two squares. (If the original side length is 1, then the new side length is 1.25. So the lengths grew by a factor of 1.25. That is, each side length is multiplied by 1.25.)

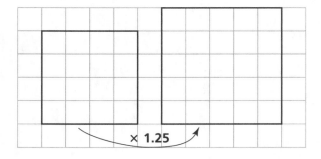

Repeat this demonstration on a unit square with a decrease of 25%. In this case the scale factor is 0.75.

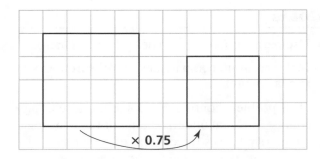

Suggested Question You could also ask the class to compare the smaller figure to the larger figure.

- *How is the photocopy similar to the rubber-band method of creating similar figures?* (Students will likely say that they are alike in that they each produce similar figures, but rubber bands can only enlarge figures.)

Some students may also trace over the figures in order to compare them.

You can also demonstrate how an overhead projector creates similar figures.

- Cut out three rectangles, two of which are similar. The third rectangle should not be similar to either of these rectangles. Be sure the third non-similar rectangle is larger than the smaller rectangle in the similar pair.

- Put the smallest rectangle on the overhead and then tape the other larger similar rectangle on the screen. Move the overhead until the image of the small rectangle on the overhead exactly fits the similar rectangle that is taped to the screen.

- Repeat the process with the third rectangle. Tape this rectangle to the screen and try to move the projector to the smaller rectangle to fit the rectangle taped to the screen. What happens is that you will be able to make either the lengths or widths match, but not both.

You can use this summary to launch the next investigation that introduces another method for creating similar figures using a coordinate grid.

1.3 Scaling Up and Down

Mathematical Goals

- Use percents as a way to describe size change
- Make accurate comparisons of measurements of similar figures

Launch

Set up the photocopier context by talking with students about the rubber band stretchers and other methods for enlarging figures.

- *If you wanted to make a very good enlargement of a figure, would you use a rubber-band stretcher?*
- *What other ways do you know of to make a larger copy of something?*

Tell students that we enter a percent into the photocopier to tell it what size to make the copy. Do a quick review of basic percent concepts using a transparency of Labsheet 1.3. Tell students that the middle figure is the original.

- *Estimate the percent Daphne entered into the photocopier in order to get the smaller image on the left. Write your estimate in your notebook.*

Do not expect perfect estimates. This problem is intended to increase students' ability to work with percents in this way.

Students can work in small groups of 2 to 3.

Materials

- Transparency of Labsheet 1.3 (optional)
- Labsheet 1.3 (optional)
- Rulers
- Angle rulers

Explore

Pay attention to students' measuring skills and provide assistance where necessary.

Look for ways that they use to compare features such as length and area. Some students will see immediately that the percents given are the right comparison. Others will feel more comfortable comparing with fractions.

Summarize

Discuss the questions. Ask students to explain their reasoning. Try to gain insight into their understanding of percents.

Review percents and help students to see the multiplying effects of increasing or decreasing by percents.

- *If I want to enlarge a figure by 25%, will the image be larger or smaller than the original? What number do I enter in the photocopier?*

Draw a square on a transparent grid on the overhead to show an increase of 25%. To make the enlargement, first enlarge two adjacent sides of the original square and then complete the square. Compare the two squares. Repeat this demonstration with a decrease of 25%.

Materials

- Student notebooks

ACE Assignment Guide for Problem 1.3

Differentiated Instruction
Solutions for All Learners

Core 6, 7

Other *Applications* 5; *Connections* 19, 20; unassigned choices from previous problems

Adapted For suggestions about adapting ACE exercises, see the CMP *Special Needs Handbook*.
Connecting to Prior Units 19: *Covering and Surrounding*; 20: *Bits and Pieces III*

Answers to Problem 1.3

A. The side lengths of the small design are 0.75 (or 75% or $\frac{3}{4}$) times as long as the side lengths of the original design. The side lengths of the large design are 1.5 times as large as the side lengths of the original design. Finally, side lengths in the largest figure are 2 times the side lengths of the smallest figure. Some students may use additive strategies. See the discussion in the summary.

B. The angle measures remain the same.

C. The perimeters of the small design are 0.75 times as long as the perimeters of the original design. The perimeters of the large design are 1.5 times as large as the perimeters of the original design.

D. Some possible answers: The area of the smallest design is a little more than half the area of the original design. The area of the largest design is a little more than double the area of the original design. The area of the largest design is about 4 times the area of the smallest design. (You can show this by having students see how many of the smallest rectangles fit in the largest "hat.")

E. The length and perimeter comparison factors are the same as the copier size factors; they are just the same numbers written in decimal form: $0.75 = 75\%$, $1.5 = 150\%$. For the rectangular part of the design, students may reason that since the sides are changed by a factor, the area (which is the product of the sides—length and width) is changed by a product of the factor and itself. (Note: The area comparison factors are the squares of the copier size factors: $0.5625 = 0.75 \times 0.75$ and $2.25 = 1.5 \times 1.5$.) In the next investigation, the copier size factor is named the *scale factor*.

Investigation 1

Enlarging and Reducing Shapes

In this investigation, you will explore how some properties of a shape change when the shape is enlarged or reduced.

1.1 Solving a Mystery

The Mystery Club at P.I. Middle School meets monthly. Members watch videos, discuss novels, play "whodunit" games, and talk about real-life mysteries. One day, a member announces that the school is having a contest. A teacher in disguise will appear a few minutes at school each day for a week. Any student can pay $1 for a guess at the identity of the mystery teacher. The student with the first correct guess wins a prize.

The club decides to enter the contest together. Each member brings a camera to school in hopes of getting a picture of the mystery teacher.

How might a photograph help in identifying the mystery teacher?

Notes _____

_____

_____

_____

Problem **1.1** Introduction to Similarity

One of Daphne's photos looks like the picture below. Daphne has a copy of the *P.I. Monthly* magazine shown in the picture. The *P.I. Monthly* magazine is 10 inches high. She thinks she can use the magazine and the picture to estimate the teacher's height.

A. What do you think Daphne has in mind? Use this information and the picture to estimate the teacher's height. Explain your reasoning.

The adviser of the Mystery Club says that the picture is similar to the actual scene.

B. What do you suppose the adviser means by *similar*? Is it different from saying that two students in your class are similar?

ACE **Homework starts on page 12.**

6   Stretching and Shrinking

Notes _____

_____

_____

_____

Michelle, Daphne, and Mukesh are the officers of the Mystery Club. Mukesh designs this flier to attract new members.

Daphne wants to make a large poster to publicize the next meeting. She wants to redraw the club's logo, "Super Sleuth," in a larger size. Michelle shows her a clever way to enlarge the figure by using rubber bands.

Notes
_____
_____
_____
_____

Instructions for Stretching a Figure

1. Make a "two-band stretcher" by tying the ends of two identical rubber bands together. The rubber bands should be the same width and length. Bands about 3 inches long work well.

2. Take the sheet with the figure you want to enlarge and tape it to your desk. Next to it, tape a blank sheet of paper. If you are right-handed, put the blank sheet on the right. If you are left-handed, put it on the left (see the diagram below).

3. With your finger, hold down one end of the rubber-band stretcher on point *P*. Point *P* is called the anchor point. It must stay in the same spot.

4. Put a pencil in the other end of the stretcher. Stretch the rubber bands with your pencil until the knot is on the outline of your picture.

5. Guide the knot around the original picture while your pencil traces out a new picture. (Don't allow any slack in the rubber bands.) The new drawing is called the **image** of the original.

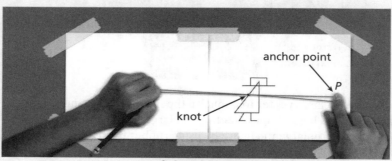

Left-handed setup

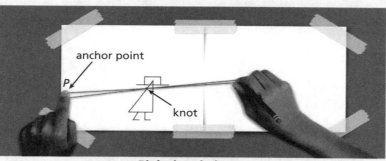

Right-handed setup

Notes _____

_____

_____

_____

Problem 1.2 Comparing Similar Figures

Use the rubber-band method to enlarge the figure on the Mystery Club flier. Draw as carefully as you can, so you will be able to compare the size and shape of the image to the size and shape of the original figure.

A. Tell how the original figure and the image are alike and how they are different. Compare these features:

- the general shapes of the two figures
- the lengths of the line segments in the hats and bodies
- the areas and perimeters of the hats and bodies
- the angles in the hats and bodies

Explain each comparison you make. For example, rather than simply saying that two lengths are different, tell which lengths you are comparing and explain how they differ.

B. Use your rubber-band stretcher to enlarge another simple figure, such as a circle or a square. Compare the general shapes, lengths, areas, perimeters, and angles of the original figure and the image.

ACE Homework starts on page 12.

Did You Know?

Measurement is used in police work all the time. For example, some stores with cameras place a spot on the wall 6 feet from the floor. When a person standing near the wall is filmed, it is easier to estimate the person's height. Investigators take measurements of tire marks at the scene of auto accidents to help them estimate the speed of the vehicles involved. Photographs and molds of footprints help the police determine the shoe size, type of shoe, and the weight of the person who made the prints.

Go Online
PHSchool.com
For: Information about police work.
Web Code: ane-9031

Notes _____

_____

_____

_____

Scaling Up and Down

In studying similar figures, we need to compare their sides and angles. In order to compare the right parts, we use the terms **corresponding sides** and **corresponding angles.** Each side in one figure has a corresponding side in the other figure. Also, each angle has a corresponding angle. The corresponding angles and sides of the triangles are given.

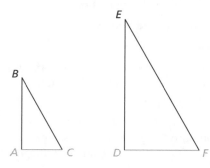

Corresponding sides
AC and *DF*

AB and *DE*

BC and *EF*

Corresponding angles
A and *D*

B and *E*

C and *F*

Daphne thinks the rubber-band method is clever, but she believes the school copier can make more accurate copies in a greater variety of sizes. She makes a copy with the size factor set at 75%. Then, she makes a copy with a setting of 150%. The results are shown on the next page.

10   Stretching and Shrinking

STUDENT PAGE

Notes _____

_____

_____

_____

(10) 28

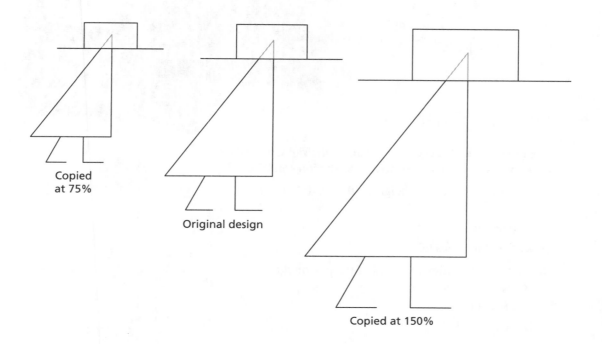

Copied
at 75%

Original design

Copied at 150%

Problem 1.3 **Corresponding Sides and Angles**

A. For each copy, tell how the side lengths compare to the corresponding side lengths in the original design.

B. For each copy, tell how the angle measures compare to the corresponding angle measures in the original design.

C. Describe how the perimeter of the triangle in each copy compares to the perimeter of the triangle in the original design.

D. Describe how the area of the triangle in each copy compares to the area of the triangle in the original design.

E. How do the relationships in the size comparisons you made in Questions A–D relate to the copier size factors used?

ACE Homework starts on page 12.

Investigation 1 Enlarging and Reducing Shapes **11**

Notes _____

_____

_____

_____

Applications

For Exercises 1 and 2, use the drawing at the right, which shows a person standing next to a construction scaffold.

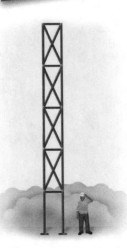

1. Find the approximate height of the scaffold if the person is

   a. 6 feet tall

   b. 5 feet 6 inches tall

2. Find the approximate height of the person if the scaffold is

   a. 28 feet tall

   b. 36 feet tall

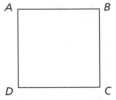

3. Copy square *ABCD* and anchor point *P* onto a sheet of paper. Use the rubber-band method to enlarge the figure. Then answer parts (a)–(d) below.

P

A   B

D   C

   a. How do the side lengths of the original figure compare to the side lengths of the image?

   b. How does the perimeter of the original figure compare to the perimeter of the image?

   c. How do the angle measures of the original figure compare to the angle measures of the image?

   d. How does the area of the original figure compare to the area of the image? How many copies of the original figure would it take to cover the image?

STUDENT PAGE

Notes _____

_____

_____

_____

4. Copy parallelogram *ABCD* and anchor point *P* onto a sheet of paper. Use the rubber-band method to enlarge the figure. Then, answer parts (a)–(d) from Exercise 3 for your diagram.

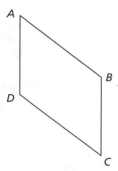

•
P

5. The diagram below is the original floor plan for a dollhouse. The diagram on the right is the image of the floor plan after you reduce it with a copier.

Go Online
PHSchool.com

For: Multiple-Choice Skills
        Practice
Web Code: ana-2154

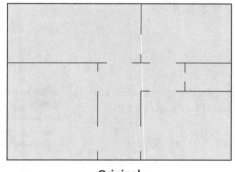

Original

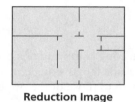

Reduction Image

a. Estimate the copier size factor used. Give your answer as a percent.

b. How do the segment lengths in the original plan compare to the corresponding segment lengths in the image?

c. Compare the area of the entire original floor plan to the area of the entire image. Then, do the same with one room in both plans. Is the relationship between the areas of the rooms the same as the relationship between the areas of the whole plans?

d. The scale on the original plan is 1 inch = 1 foot. This means that 1 inch on the floor plan represents 1 foot on the actual dollhouse. What is the scale on the smaller copy?

Investigation 1 Enlarging and Reducing Shapes **13**

Notes _____

_____

_____

_____

6. **Multiple Choice** Suppose you reduce the design below with a copy machine. Which of the following can be the image?

A.

B.

C.

D.

7. Suppose you copy a drawing of a polygon with the given size factor. How will the side lengths, angle measures, and perimeter of the image compare to those of the original?

a. 200% **b.** 150% **c.** 50% **d.** 75%

Homework Help Online
PHSchool.com
For: Help with Exercise 7
Web Code: ane-2107

Connections

For Exercises 8–12, find the perimeter (or circumference) and the area of each figure.

8.

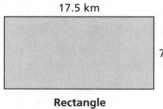

17.5 km

7.5 km

Rectangle

9.

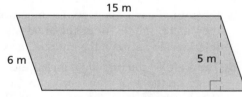

15 m

6 m

5 m

Parallelogram

14 Stretching and Shrinking

Notes _____

_____

_____

_____

10.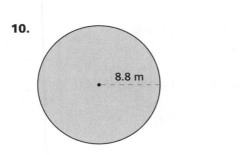

8.8 m

11.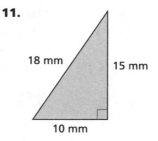

18 mm   15 mm

10 mm

12.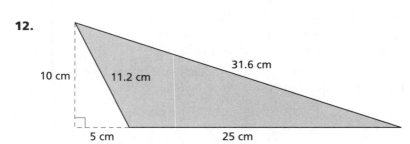

31.6 cm

10 cm   11.2 cm

5 cm   25 cm

13. Copy the circle and anchor point *P* onto a sheet of paper. Make an enlargement of the circle using your two-band stretcher.

•
P

C

    a. How do the diameters of the circles compare?

    b. How do the areas of the circles compare?

    c. How do the circumferences of the circles compare?

14. Find the given percent of each number. Show your work.

    a. 25% of 120   **b.** 80% of 120

    c. 120% of 80   **d.** 70% of 150

    e. 150% of 200   **f.** 200% of 150

15. Multiple Choice What is the 5% sales tax on a $14.00 compact disc?

    A. $0.07   **B.** $0.70   **C.** $7.00   **D.** $70.00

16. Multiple Choice What is the 15% service tip on a $25.50 dinner in a restaurant?

    F. $1.70   **G.** $3.83   **H.** $5.10   **J.** $38.25

Notes _____

_____

_____

_____

17. Multiple Choice What is the 28% tax on a $600,000 cash prize?

    A. $16,800   **B.** $21,429   **C.** $168,000   **D.** $214,290

18. Multiple Choice What is the 7.65% Social Security/Medicare tax on a paycheck of $430?

    F. $3.29   **G.** $5.62   **H.** $32.90   **J.** $60.13

19. A circle has a radius of 4 centimeters.

    a. What are the circumference and the area of the circle?

    b. Suppose you copy the circle using a size factor of 150%. What will be the radius, diameter, circumference, and area of the image?

    c. Suppose you copy the original circle using a size factor of 50%. What will be the radius, diameter, circumference, and area of the image?

20. While shopping for sneakers, Juan finds two pairs he likes. One pair costs $55 and the other costs $165. He makes the following statements about the prices.

"The expensive sneakers cost $110 more than the cheaper sneakers."

"The expensive sneakers cost three times as much as the cheaper sneakers."

    a. Are both of his statements accurate?

    b. How are the comparison methods Juan uses similar to the methods you use to compare the sizes and shapes of similar figures?

    c. Which method is more appropriate for comparing the size and shape of an enlarged or reduced figure to the original? Explain.

Notes _____

_____

_____

_____

Extensions

21. A movie projector that is 6 feet away from a large screen shows a rectangular picture that is 3 feet wide and 2 feet high.

 a. Suppose the projector is moved to a point 12 feet from the screen. What size will the picture be (width, height, and area)?

 b. Suppose the projector is moved to a point 9 feet from the screen. What size will the picture be (width, height, and area)?

22. Circle B is an enlargement of a smaller circle A, made with a two-band stretcher. Circle A is not shown.

Circle B

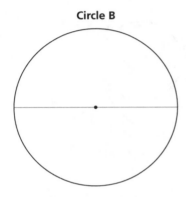

 a. How does the diameter of circle B compare to the diameter of circle A?

 b. How does the area of circle B compare to the area of circle A?

 c. How does the circumference of circle B compare to the circumference of circle A?

Investigation 1 Enlarging and Reducing Shapes   **17**

Notes _____

_____

_____

_____

23. Make a three-band stretcher by tying three rubber bands together. Use this stretcher to enlarge the "Super Sleuth" drawing from Problem 1.2.

   a. How does the shape of the image compare to the shape of the original figure?

   b. How do the lengths of the segments in the two figures compare?

   c. How do the areas of the two figures compare?

24. Two copies of a small circle are shown side by side inside a large circle. The diameter of the large circle is 2 inches.

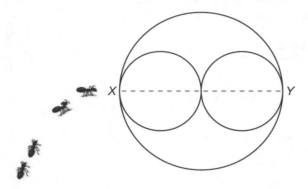

   a. What is the combined area of the two small circles?

   b. What is the area of the region inside the large circle that is *not* covered by the two small circles?

   c. Suppose an ant walks from X to Y. It travels only along the perimeter of the circles. Describe possible paths that the ant can travel. Which path is the shortest? Explain.

Notes _____

_____

_____

_____

25. Suppose you enlarge some triangles, squares, and circles with a two-band stretcher. You use an anchor point inside the original figure, as shown in the sketches below.

   a. In each case, how does the shape and position of the image compare to the shape and position of the original?

   b. What relationships do you expect to find between the side lengths, angle measures, perimeters, and areas of the figures?

   c. Test your ideas with larger copies of the given shapes. Make sure the shortest distance from the anchor point to any side of a shape is at least one band length.

26. Suppose you make a stretcher with two different sizes of rubber band. The band attached to the anchor point is twice as long as the band attached to the pencil.

   a. If you use the stretcher to enlarge polygons, what relationships do you expect to find between the side lengths, angle measures, perimeters, and areas of the figures?

   b. Test your ideas with copies of some basic geometric shapes.

Investigation 1 Enlarging and Reducing Shapes   **19**

Notes _____

_____

_____

_____

Mathematical Reflections 1

In this investigation, you solved problems that involved enlarging (stretching) and reducing (shrinking) figures. You used rubber-band stretchers and copy machines. These questions will help you summarize what you learned.

Think about your answers to these questions. Discuss your ideas with other students and your teacher. Then write a summary of your findings in your notebook.

1. When you enlarge or reduce a figure, what features stay the same?

2. When you enlarge or reduce a figure, what features change?

3. Rubber-band stretchers, copy machines, overhead projectors, and movie projectors all make images that are similar to the original shapes. What does it mean for two shapes to be similar? That is, how can you complete the sentence below?

    "Two geometric shapes are similar if . . ."

Notes _____

_____

_____

_____

Investigation 1

ACE Assignment Choices

Differentiated Instruction
Solutions for All Learners

Problem 1.1
Core 1, 2
Other *Connections* 8–12

Problem 1.2
Core 14, 22
Other *Applications* 3, 4; *Connections* 13, 15–18; *Extensions* 21–26; unassigned choices from previous problems

Problem 1.3
Core 6, 7
Other *Applications* 5; *Connections* 19, 20; unassigned choices from previous problems

Adapted For suggestions about adapting Exercise 1 and other ACE exercises, see the CMP *Special Needs Handbook*.
Connecting to Prior Units 8–13, 19: *Covering and Surrounding*; 14–18, 20: *Bits and Pieces III*

Applications

1. **a.** 30 ft
   b. 27 ft 6 in.

2. **a.** approx. 5 ft 7 in.
   b. approx. 7 ft $2\frac{1}{2}$ in.

3. **and 4.** (NOTE: Labsheet 1ACE has left-handed and right-handed versions of these questions)
   a. The new lengths are 2 (scale factor) times the original lengths.
   b. The perimeter of the new figure is 2 (scale factor) times the original perimeter.
   c. Angles remain the same.
   d. Area of the new figure is 4 times the original area. It takes 4 copies of the original figure to cover its stretched image.

5. **a.** 50%; Students can use a side of a piece of paper to compare the side lengths of the floor plan.
   b. The line segments in the reduced plan are half as long as the corresponding line segments in the original plan (or the line segments in the original plan are twice the lengths of the corresponding sides in the reduced plan).
   c. Area of the whole house in the original plan is about 4 times the area of the reduced plan. The relationship between a room in the original plan and in the reduced plan is the same as the relationship between the whole plans.
   d. 1 inch represents 2 ft

6. Answer is (C) since its height to width ratio is the same as in the original figure.

7. Angle measures do not change in each case. Side lengths and the perimeter are:
   a. 2 times as long
   b. 1.5 times as long
   c. $\frac{1}{2}$ times as long
   d. $\frac{3}{4}$ times as long

Connections

8. perimeter = 50 km;
   area = 131.25 km^2

9. perimeter = 42 m;
   area = 75 m^2

10. perimeter ≈ 55.29 m;
    area ≈ 243.28 m^2

11. perimeter = 43 mm
    area = 75 mm^2

12. perimeter = 67.8 cm
    area = 125 cm^2

13. (NOTE: Labsheet 1ACE has left-handed and right-handed versions of this exercise.)

   a. Diameter of the image circle is 2 times as long as the diameter of the original circle.

   b. Area of the image circle is 4 times as big as the area of the original circle.

   c. Circumference of the image circle is 2 times as long as the circumference of the original circle.

14. a. 30   b. 96   c. 96
    d. 105   e. 300   f. 300

15. B   16. G   17. C   18. H

19. a. Circumference is about 25.13 cm. Area is about 50.27 cm^2.

   b. radius = 6 cm
      diameter = 12 cm
      circumference ≈ 37.7 cm
      area ≈ 113.1 cm^2

   c. radius = 2 cm
      diameter = 4 cm
      circumference ≈ 12.57 cm
      area ≈ 12.57 cm^2

20. a. Both statements are accurate.

   b. One can use similar statements in comparing sizes of shapes. For example, for question 19b, one could say: "Diameter of the image circle is 2 in. longer than the diameter of the original circle." or "Diameter of the image circle is 1.5 times as long as the diameter of the original circle."

   c. The second method is more appropriate because each size will be enlarged or reduced by the same factor. However, the exact amount of increase or decrease of the lengths will be different.

Extensions

21. a. The width and height would be 2 times as large as the first picture.
      width = 6 ft
      height = 4 ft
      area = 24 square ft

   b. The width and height would be 1.5 times as large as the first picture.
      width = 4.5 ft
      height = 3 ft
      area = 13.5 square ft

22. a. Diameter of B is 2 times as long as the diameter of A.

   b. Area of B is 4 times as large as the area of A.

   c. Circumference of B is 2 times as long as the circumference of A.

23. Note that there are two possible interpretations of this problem. Most students will use the knot closest to the anchor point to trace the original figure. This is the interpretation assumed in the answers that follow. Some students may use the knot closer to the pencil. This will give different results. See the discussion in the "Going Further" section of Problem 1.2 in this Teacher's Guide.

   a. The shapes are similar to each other.

   b. The lengths in the image figure are 3 times as long as the lengths in the original figure.

   c. The areas in the image figure are 9 times as big as the areas in the original figure.

24. a. About 1.57 square in.

   b. About 1.57 square in.

   c. Path (1): along the outer circle. Path (2): along the outsides of the two smaller circles. Both paths are the same length (3.14 in. long each.) You can see this by the similarity of the large circle to the smaller one. The scale factor from the smaller to the larger circle is 2. So, the circumference of the large circle is twice as long as the circumference of the small one. Hence, walking along half of the circumference of the large circle is the same distance as walking along the full circumference of the small one, the same length as path (2).

25. a. The size of the image would still be the same as in the case when the anchor point is outside. However, in this case the image figure would enclose the original figure.

   b. Sizes of sides and perimeters would be 2 times as long as the original figure. Angle measures would not change. Area would be 4 times as big as the area of the original figure.

   c. Answers will vary.

26. a. The lengths are 1.5 times as long as the original figure. Angle measures do not change. The perimeter is 1.5 times as large as the original figure. Area would be $1.5 \times 1.5 = 2.25$ times as large as the original figure.

b. Answers will vary.

Possible Answers to Mathematical Reflections

1. The shape will remain the same except in size. The angle measures of corresponding angles will also remain the same.

2. Each length in the image will stretch or shrink by the same factor; hence the areas seem to change in some predictable pattern.

3. Two geometric shapes are similar if one can be obtained from the other by applying a stretch or a shrink, keeping the general shape of the figure unchanged, in which all the lengths are changed by the factor or multiplied by the same number (i.e., the same scaling factor), and all the corresponding angles are kept the same.

Note that if the scale factor or ratio is 1, then the two figures are still similar and in this case we say they are congruent, which tells us that a translation will also yield a similar figure. Students may not use ratio at this time. They may use "multiplied by the same factor."

Students will continue to develop deeper understandings as they move through the unit. At this stage we are looking for intuitive, informal answers that shape stays the same, but size may change.

Investigation 2 Similar Figures

Mathematical and Problem-Solving Goals

- Use algebraic rules to produce similar figures on a coordinate grid
- Focus student attention on both lengths and angles as criteria for similarity
- Contrast similar figures with non-similar figures
- Understand the role multiplication plays in similarity relationships
- Understand the effect on the image if a number is added to the *x*- and *y*-coordinates
- Develop more formal ideas of the meaning of similarity, including the vocabulary of scale factor
- Understand the relationships of angles, side lengths, perimeters and areas of similar polygons

Summary of Problems

Problem 2.1 Drawing Wumps

Students graph members of the Wump family, plus other figures that claim to be in the Wump family. Members of the Wump family are similar to one another. The impostors are not similar, but one is distorted vertically and one is distorted horizontally. Students compare the shapes, side lengths, and angles of the figures they draw.

Problem 2.2 Hats Off to the Wumps

Students investigate the effect that altering a rule for transforming a figure has on the shape and location of the figure on a coordinate grid.

Problem 2.3 Mouthing Off and Nosing Around

Students continue to work with the Wump family as they investigate side lengths, angles, perimeters, and areas of similar rectangles and triangles. The vocabulary of scale factor is introduced.

Mathematics Background

For background on similar rectangles and congruence, see page 5.

	Suggested Pacing	Materials for Students	Materials for Teachers	ACE Assignments
All	$4\frac{1}{2}$ days	Centimeter and inch rulers, angle rulers or protractors		
2.1	2 days	Labsheet 2.1A (1 per student), Labsheet 2.1B (at least 1 per student, 2 if each student draws all Wumps), Labsheet 2.1C (optional, for special needs students), Labsheet 2ACE Exercise 1	Transparent 4 × 4 board (optional, see Launch), Transparencies of Labsheets 2.1A and 2.1B (optional)	1, 2, 14–15, 29
2.2	1 day	Labsheets 2.2A and 2.2B (1 of each per student), Labsheet 2.1C (optional, for special needs students)	Transparency 2.2 (optional), Transparency of Labsheet 2.2B (optional)	3, 4, 16–18, 30, 31
2.3	1 day	Labsheet 2.3 (1 per student)	Transparency 2.3 (optional)	5–13, 19–28, 32, 33
MR	$\frac{1}{2}$ day			

2.1 Drawing Wumps

Goals

- Use algebraic rules to produce similar figures on a coordinate grid
- Focus student attention on both lengths and angles as criteria for similarity
- Contrast similar figures with non-similar figures

The use of numbers to locate points in a plane is a very useful and important idea in mathematics. In this investigation, students will learn how to make similar and non-similar shapes using a coordinate system. They will graph Mug Wump, some of Mug's family, and some other figures that claim to be in Mug Wump's family. Zug and Bug are both similar to Mug (and so they are similar to each other) and belong to his family. Glug and Lug are not similar because they are distorted either vertically or horizontally and they are not Wumps.

Meeting Special Needs

We have included Labsheet 2.1C with larger spacing on the grids for students who may struggle with either seeing or working with the smaller grids on the regular labsheets.

Launch 2.1

If your students need to review graphing, you might introduce them to tic-tac-toe on a 4 × 4 board (explained below). The winner is the person who gets four in a row first (horizontally, vertically, or diagonally). The players take turns telling you two numbers which designate the location of the *intersection* point for their X or their O. This is different from the traditional game where the X's and O's are placed in the middle of each square. With little instruction, nearly every student will learn how to graph points in a hurry. This is a variation of the Four In a Row game that was introduced in the *Shapes and Designs* unit.

Use a transparent 4 × 4 board or draw five horizontal and five vertical lines, equally spaced.

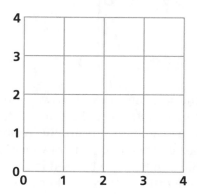

Suggested Questions Check to see that students start with an estimate.

- *How many of you know how to play tic-tac-toe?*

- *How many do you need in a row to win?* (three)

- *Today we will play a different game of tic-tac-toe. You will need four in a row to win.*

- *We'll play the left side of the class against the right side of the class. The left side can go first and tell me two numbers.*

Have the first player tell you two numbers. If the numbers are between 0 and 4, they will be on the board. Otherwise, they will be off the board. For example, if a student says 5, 1, start at zero and count until you get to four and say, "Oops, they fell off the board!" Then let the other team have a turn. The students quickly learn to use the correct numbers and they quickly recognize that the order of the two numbers is important.

In future games, you can change the number scheme by moving the origin to a different place in the grid and by using negatives, fractions, etc.

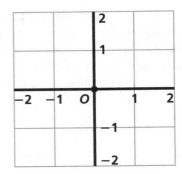

After the students know their way around a coordinate grid, introduce the story of the video game whose star characters are the Wump family.

Students may need help in drawing Mug Wump because the points are to be used in sets that are connected in order. You could do part of Mug as a whole class to make sure they know how to locate and connect the four sets of points.

In addition, the students will need help in interpreting the symbolic rules for the points.

Suggested Questions

- *The points for Zug are found from the points for Mug. The rule is (2x, 2y). What do you think this rule tells us to do to a Mug point to get a Zug point?* (Multiply each coordinate by 2 or double the numbers for the coordinates.)

- *What do the other rules tell you to do for Lug, Bug, and Glug?* (For Lug we multiply Mug's x-coordinate by 3 and keep Mug's y-coordinate the same. For Bug we multiply each coordinate by 3. For Glug we keep x the same and multiply the y-coordinate by 3.)

- *Go through your table and compute the new value of the x and y for each point. Remember that you are always starting with Mug's x- and y-coordinates. Then locate the points and connect them in sets as you did for Mug.*

When you feel your students are ready, launch the challenge of drawing all of the figures according to the rules given and comparing the final figures to see which ones look like they belong to the Wump family and which ones do not.

Have students divide up the work in their groups of 3 or 4. Be sure that each student draws

Mug and at least two other characters. They can share their work as a group so that collectively the group has all five figures.

Explore 2.1

Help students plot and connect the points.

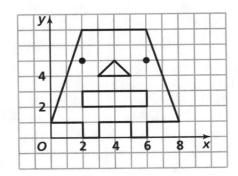

Part 2 is the mouth.
Part 3 is the nose.
Part 4 is the eyes.
Students may need help starting over to get the mouth, nose, and eyes.

Summarize 2.1

It is very helpful to have copies of the figures on transparencies for the overhead. Two sets are provided as transparencies. In one set, the figures are on a dot grid and in the other set, the figures are on a blank transparency. You can cut the figures out and then move them around on the overhead to show the comparisons that the students are describing.

Suggested Questions

- *How would you describe to a friend the growth of the figures that you drew?* (They all increased in size. Some grew taller and wider, while one just grew taller and one just grew wider.)

- *Which figures seem to belong to the Wump family and which do not?* (Mug, Zug, and Bug have the same shape, but Lug and Glug are distorted.)

- *Are Lug and Glug related? Did they grow into the same shape?* (No; Lug is wide and short while Glug is narrow and tall.)

- *In earlier units in CMP, we learned that both angles and the lengths of edges help determine the shape of the figure. How do the corresponding angles of the five figures compare?*

Put the figures on the overhead and compare corresponding angles. The nice thing about having these on transparencies is that you can superimpose the angles that you want to compare. This reinforces that when you measure angles, you measure the amount of turn between the edges and not the lengths of the edges. In Mug, Zug, and Bug, the corresponding angles are equal. In Mug and Lug (or Glug), the corresponding angles (except the right angles) are not equal.

- *Now let's look at some corresponding lengths for the five figures. Are the lengths related? Are some of them related and others not?*

- *How do the lengths in similar Wumps compare?* (Compare some of the lengths to show that in Mug, Bug, and Zug, the corresponding lengths grow the same way. They are multiplied by the same number. Students will begin to notice that if the coefficient of both the x- and y-coordinates of the rule are the same, the figure is similar to the original. If the coefficients are different, the figure will change more in one direction than the other and will be distorted. One special case that you should help students notice is the case where we multiply the x and y by 1 to get a new figure. In this case the figures are similar. Even more, they are congruent. You get a figure of exactly the same size and shape. This case will occur in Problem 2.2.

Another interesting experiment to do as a part of this summary is to use the overhead projector to compare Mug and Bug. Try to project Mug onto a picture of Bug by taping Bug to the overhead screen or a clear wall. Then place Mug on the overhead and project Mug onto the figure of Bug. Move the projector closer or farther away to see if you can get the two to fit. The image of Mug should fit exactly onto Bug. Do the same for Mug and Glug. The image of Mug will not fit exactly onto Glug. (Note: Try this on your own before doing it with the class.)

2.1 Drawing Wumps

Mathematical Goals

- Use algebraic rules to produce similar figures on a coordinate grid
- Focus student attention on both lengths and angles as criteria for similarity
- Contrast similar figures with non-similar figures

Launch

Review graphing on the coordinate plane with a round of Four in a Row.

Introduce the story of the video game whose star characters are the Wump family. Help students draw Mug Wump, noting that the points are to be used in sets that are connected in order. Do part of Mug with the whole class to make sure they know how to locate and connect the four sets of points. Help students to interpret the symbolic rules for the points.

Have students divide up the work in their groups of 3 or 4. Be sure that each student draws Mug and at least two other characters.

Materials

- Transparency 2.1A and 2.1B
- Labsheets 2.1A and 2.1B
- Labsheet 2.1C (optional; for special needs students)
- Labsheet 2ACE Exercise 1

Explore

Help students plot and connect the points (in particular, remind them which number in the pair corresponds to which axis). Students may need help starting over to get the mouth, nose, and eyes.

Summarize

Have copies of the figures on transparencies for the overhead so you can move them around to illustrate the comparisons students are discussing.

- *How would you describe the growth of the figures that you drew?*
- *Which figures seem to belong to the Wump family and which do not?*
- *Are Lug and Glug related? Did they grow into the same shape?*
- *How do the corresponding angles of the five figures compare?*
- *Are the lengths of the five figures related? Are some of the lengths related and others not?*

Materials

- Student notebooks

ACE Assignment Guide for Problem 2.1

Core 1
Other *Applications* 2, *Connections* 14–15, *Extensions* 29

Adapted For suggestions about adapting ACE exercises, see the CMP *Special Needs Handbook*.
Connecting to Prior Units 14–15: *Bits and Pieces II*

Answers to Problem 2.1

A. Mug is a small figure with a triangular nose, a rectangular mouth, square legs, points for eyes, and a body shaped like a trapezoid.

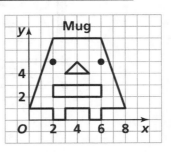

B. 1.

	Mug Wump	Zug	Lug	Bug	Glug
Rule	(x, y)	(2x, 2y)	(3x, y)	(3x, 3y)	(x, 3y)
Point			Part 1		
A	(0, 1)	(0, 2)	(0, 1)	(0, 3)	(0, 3)
B	(2, 1)	(4, 2)	(6, 1)	(6, 3)	(2, 3)
C	(2, 0)	(4, 0)	(6, 0)	(6, 0)	(2, 0)
D	(3, 0)	(6, 0)	(9, 0)	(9, 0)	(3, 0)
E	(3, 1)	(6, 2)	(9, 1)	(9, 3)	(3, 3)
F	(5, 1)	(10, 2)	(15, 1)	(15, 3)	(5, 3)
G	(5, 0)	(10, 0)	(15, 0)	(15, 0)	(5, 0)
H	(6, 0)	(12, 0)	(18, 0)	(18, 0)	(6, 0)
I	(6, 1)	(12, 2)	(18, 1)	(18, 3)	(6, 3)
J	(8, 1)	(16, 2)	(24, 1)	(24, 3)	(8, 3)
K	(6, 7)	(12, 14)	(18, 7)	(18, 21)	(6, 21)
L	(2, 7)	(4, 14)	(6, 7)	(6, 21)	(2, 21)
M	(0, 1)	(0, 2)	(0, 1)	(0, 3)	(0, 3)
Part 2 (start over)					
N	(2, 2)	(4, 4)	(6, 2)	(6, 6)	(2, 6)
O	(6, 2)	(12, 4)	(18, 2)	(18, 6)	(6, 6)
P	(6, 3)	(12, 6)	(18, 3)	(18, 9)	(6, 9)
Q	(2, 3)	(4, 6)	(6, 3)	(6, 9)	(2, 9)
R	(2, 2)	(4, 4)	(6, 2)	(6, 6)	(2, 6)
Part 3 (start over)					
S	(3, 4)	(6, 8)	(9, 4)	(9, 12)	(3, 12)
T	(4, 5)	(8, 10)	(12, 5)	(12, 15)	(4, 15)
U	(5, 4)	(10, 8)	(15, 4)	(15, 12)	(5, 12)
V	(3, 4)	(6, 8)	(9, 4)	(9, 12)	(3, 12)
Part 4 (start over)					
W	(2, 5)	(4, 10)	(6, 5)	(6, 15)	(2, 15)
X	(6, 5)	(12, 10)	(18, 5)	(18, 15)	(6, 15)

B. 2.

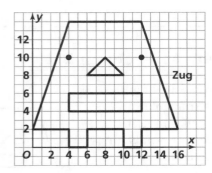

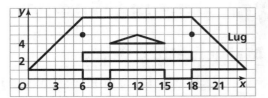

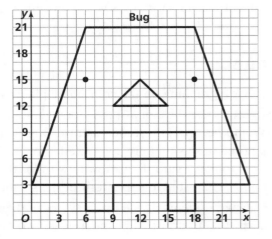

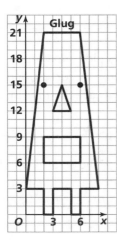

C. 1. Zug and Bug are big versions of Mug, so they are the other Wumps. Lug is too wide and Glug is too tall. They are imposters.

2. All have a triangular nose, a rectangular mouth, and the same kind of body figure.

3. From Mug to Zug and Bug, the angles and the general shape stayed the same. From Mug to Zug, the lengths doubled and from Mug to Bug they tripled. From Mug to Lug and Glug, corresponding lengths did not grow the same. Lug is the same height as Mug but three times as wide. Glug is the same width as Mug but three times as tall. Many of their angles differ from Mug's.

2.2 Hats Off to the Wumps

Goals

- Understand the role multiplication plays in similarity relationships
- Understand the effect on the image if a number is added to the x- and y-coordinates

The figure is a hat for Mug. The hat is made from a rectangle and a triangle and has 6 vertices. This makes the figure simple enough that the students can concentrate on what is happening as we manipulate the rule by adding to each coordinate and/or multiplying each coordinate by a number.

Launch 2.2

Tell the students that this problem is related to drawing the Wump family and impostors. In this case they are looking at hats for the Wump family.

Hand out Labsheets 2.2A and B. Have students look at the table and the grids that are provided. They should have little trouble drawing the figures. However, it is important that the students start the problem knowing that the main point of the problem is to look back over their drawings and make sense of what adding or multiplying in the rule does to the image. After they have the set of hats to look at, challenge students to find a way to predict what will happen to the image only by analyzing the rule and not drawing the figure.

Let students work in pairs.

Explore 2.2

Suggested Questions As students catch on, ask further questions as you go around the room.

- *What rule would give the largest possible image on the grids provided?*
- *Make up a rule that would place the image in another quadrant.*

Challenge the students to make up rules to fit your constraints.

Even though the students have not studied negative numbers formally and may not have much experience with all four quadrants of a coordinate system, many students can figure out how to move the figure around.

Additionally, you might ask students to write a rule that would put the hat in the right place on the grid to fit on each Wump's head and to transform the hat to the right size and location for the impostors [some of these questions are asked in Applications, Connections, Extensions (ACE) 32 of this investigation].

Some students may have difficulties comparing the hats across the grids. To help them, you might have students draw two or more hats on the same grid. If students use a different color for each hat, it will be easier to differentiate the images.

Summarize 2.2

This is an opportunity to superimpose the images and the original on transparencies to examine what happens to the angles.

Suggested Questions Ask students what happened with each of the rules.

- *Are the images similar to the original? Why or why not?* [For $(x + 2, y + 3), (x - 1, y + 4)$, and $(0.5x, 0.5y)$, the images are all similar to the original. For $(x + 2, 3y)$ and $(2x, 3y)$, the images do not keep the same shape.]

You can use the following questions as part of the summary. Ask for explanations and/or demonstrations. Be sure to focus on the last question before and give some examples of new rules for students to predict what would happen.

- *What rule would make a hat with line segments $\frac{1}{3}$ the length of Hat 1's line segments?* $(\frac{1}{3}x + 2, \frac{1}{3}y + 3)$
- *What happens to a figure on a coordinate grid when you add to or subtract from its coordinates?* (It relocates the figure on the grid.)
- *What rule would make a hat the same size as Hat 1 but moved up 2 units on the grid?* $(x + 2, y + 5)$

- *What rule would make a hat with line segments twice as long as Hat 1's line segments and moved 8 units to the right?* $(2x + 10, 2y + 3)$

- *Describe a rule that moves Hat 1 and does not produce a similar figure.* [One possible answer: $(x + 4, 3y + 3)$.]

- *What are the effects of multiplying each coordinate by a number?* (If the numbers are the same, then the figures are similar. If the numbers are different, then the figures are not similar.)

Note: This last response is not an exact answer, but it is what students will be able to say from their experiences so far. In the unit *Accentuate the Negative*, students will return to this question and see that it is the coefficient without regard to its sign that makes the difference. If you multiply the x by -2 and the y by 2, you still get a similar figure.

- *What effect does the rule $(5x - 5, 5y + 5)$ have on the original hat?* (The figure would be similar. Its sides will be 5 times as large and the image will be moved to the left five units and up five units.)

- *What about the rule $(\frac{1}{4}x, 4y - \frac{5}{6})$?* (This rule would not give a similar figure. The figure is shrunk horizontally and stretched vertically. It is also moved down $\frac{5}{6}$ of a unit.)

- *Make up a rule that will shrink the figure, keep it similar and move it to the right and up.* [Many possibilities. Here is one: $(\frac{2}{3}x + 2, \frac{2}{3}y + 1)$.]

2.2 Hats Off to the Wumps

Mathematical Goals

- Understand the role multiplication plays in similarity relationships
- Understand the effect on the image if a number is added to the x- and y-coordinates

Launch

Tell the students that this problem is related to drawing the Wump family and impostors. In this case we are looking at hats for the Wump family. Hand out Labsheets 2.2A and B. It is important that the students know that the main point of the problem is to look back over their drawings and make sense of what adding or multiplying in the rule does to the image.

Have students individually draw the hats, then discuss the questions in the text with a partner. After they have the set of hats to look at, challenge students to find a way to predict what will happen to the image only by analyzing the rule and not drawing the figure.

Materials
- Transparency 2.2
- Labsheets 2.2A and 2.2B
- Labsheet 2.1C (optional; for special needs students)

Explore

As students catch on, ask further questions as you go around the room.
- *What rule would give the largest possible image on the grids provided?*
- *Make up a rule that would place the image in another quadrant.*

Have students draw more hats on the same grid using different colors.

Summarize

This is an opportunity to superimpose the images and the original on transparencies to examine what happens to the angles. Ask students:
- *Are the images similar to the original? Why or why not?*

Ask for explanations and/or demonstrations. Be sure to focus on these questions:
- *What happens to a figure on a coordinate grid when you add to or subtract from its coordinates?*
- *What are the effects of multiplying each coordinate by a number?*

Give some examples of new rules for students to predict what would happen.

Materials
- Student notebooks

ACE Assignment Guide for Problem 2.2

Differentiated Instruction
Solutions for All Learners

Core 3, 4, 16–17
Other *Connections* 18; *Extensions* 30, 31; unassigned choices from previous problems

Adapted For suggestions about adapting Exercise 3 and other ACE exercises, see the CMP *Special Needs Handbook*.
Connecting to Prior Units 16–18: *Bits and Pieces III*

Answers to Problem 2.2

A. Answers will vary. Hat 1 will move 2 units to the right and 3 units up without changing its size or shape. Hat 2 will move 1 unit left and 4 units up also without changing its size or shape. Hat 3 will be located 2 units to the right, and it will be 3 times as high (stretched vertically). Hat 4 will shrink vertically and horizontally by the same factor: 0.5. Hat 5 will be stretched both vertically and horizontally, but more in the vertical direction.

B. (Figure 1)

Rule: (x, y)

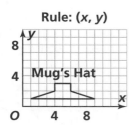

Rule: $(x + 2, y + 3)$

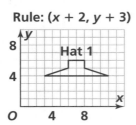

Rule: $(x - 1, y + 4)$

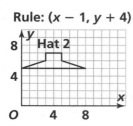

Rule: $(x + 2, 3y)$

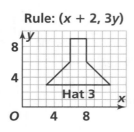

Rule: $(0.5x, 0.5y)$

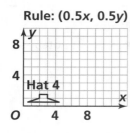

Rule: $(2x, 3y)$

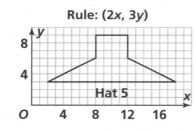

C. 1. The angles and side measures of Hats 1 and 2 are exactly the same as Mug's Hat. The width of Hat 3 is the same as the width of Mug's Hat, but its height is 3 times as long and the bottom angles have larger measures. Both the width and height of Hat 4 are half as long as Mug's Hat, while its corresponding angles are the same. The width of Hat 5 is 2 times as long as the width of Mug's Hat, while its height is 3 times as long and it has larger angle measures at the bottom.

2. Hat 1, Hat 2, and Hat 4 are similar to Mug's Hat, since they have the same shapes, corresponding angles, and their sides have been multiplied by the same factor (for Hats 1 and 2 the factor is 1 and for Hat 4 it is 0.5). Hat 4 is similar because it is the same shape only smaller. Its side lengths changed by the same factor, and all its angles have the same measure as Mug's Hat.

D. 1. $(\frac{x}{3}, \frac{y}{3})$

2. $(1.5x, 1.5y)$

3. $(x + 1, y + 5)$

E. Some possible answers: $(3x - 2, y - 2)$; $(4x, 3y)$. In fact, if you choose any two positive numbers a and b, which are not equal to each other, then (ax, by) is not similar to Mug's. Any rule $(ax + r, by + s)$, where r and s are any two numbers (positive or negative does not matter), gives an image that is not similar to Mug's, where a and b are still not equal to each other.

Figure 1

Point	Mug's Hat (x, y)	Hat 1 $(x + 2, y + 3)$	Hat 2 $(x - 1, y + 4)$	Hat 3 $(x + 2, 3y)$	Hat 4 $(0.5x, 0.5y)$	Hat 5 $(2x, 3y)$
A	(1, 1)	(3, 4)	(0, 5)	(3, 3)	(0.5, 0.5)	(2, 3)
B	(9, 1)	(11, 4)	(8, 5)	(11, 3)	(4.5, 0.5)	(18, 3)
C	(6, 2)	(8, 5)	(5, 6)	(8, 6)	(3, 1)	(12, 6)
D	(6, 3)	(8, 6)	(5, 7)	(8, 9)	(3, 1.5)	(12, 9)
E	(4, 3)	(6, 6)	(3, 7)	(6, 9)	(2, 1.5)	(8, 9)
F	(4, 2)	(6, 5)	(3, 6)	(6, 6)	(2, 1)	(8, 6)
G	(1, 1)	(3, 4)	(0, 5)	(3, 3)	(0.5, 0.5)	(2, 3)

Goals

- Develop more formal ideas of the meaning of similarity, including the vocabulary of scale factor

- Understand the relationships of angles, side lengths, perimeters and areas of similar polygons

Students continue working with the Wump family and investigate side lengths, angles, perimeters, and area of similar rectangles and triangles.

We will begin to form a more precise definition of the meaning of *similar* in mathematics. In this investigation students will use the idea of *same shape* to discover that similar figures have *corresponding angles* that have the same measure and that *corresponding sides* grow by a common factor. We will call this factor the *scale factor* because it tells us the scale of enlargement or reduction (stretching or shrinking) between the figures. The scale factor only applies to similar figures. In non-similar figures there may be some relationship between the edges, but the scale for all pairs of corresponding edges may not be the same. The scale factor from Mug to Zug is 2, and from Mug to Bug the scale factor is 3. This means that all linear measures of parts of the figures, such as length of sides or perimeter, are multiples of the corresponding parts in the original object. One of the difficult and surprising things to students is that even though the lengths increase or decrease by the same factor, the areas are enlarged by the square of this factor. So Zug's nose is $2^2 = 4$ times the area of Mug's nose, and Bug's nose is $3^2 = 9$ times the area of Mug's nose.

Even though we do not study volume in this unit, for completeness you might want to remember that the pattern continues; volume grows by the cube of the scale factor between the edges. In the seventh-grade unit *Filling and Wrapping* we complete the picture of what happens when we grow similar three-dimensional figures by looking at volume and surface area.

Launch 2.3

Discuss the Getting Ready with students. Get them to talk about the relationship between the scale factors when going from the large shape to the smaller shape and vice versa. On a transparent grid, draw the hats of the Wump family and the impostors (or put up the transparency of the hats over a transparent grid paper).

Suggested Questions

- *How does Zug's hat compare with Mug's hat?* (Its side lengths are double that of Mug's hat.)

- *How many Mug hats can you put in Zug's hat?* (4)

- *How do the perimeters compare between Mug and Zug?* (Zug's perimeter is double Mug's.)

- *Do these patterns apply for Mug to Bug? For Mug to Glug? For Mug to Lug?* (Only for Mug to Bug where the side lengths and perimeter of Bug are triple that of Mug's.)

- *The hats of the set of figures are all made from a triangle and rectangle, but they are not all similar. How can you tell if two rectangles (or triangles) are similar? What information should you collect?* (Students should say something about the measures of corresponding angles—that they are equal, congruent or the same size. They should also say something about the lengths of corresponding sides. They may suggest gathering information on perimeter and area of the hats. They may not mention scale factor.)

This is a good time to talk about scale factor.

- *Use two similar hats and ask the students to compare the lengths. The number that one side length is multiplied by to get the corresponding side length is the* scale factor.

You may have done this earlier in the unit, but this problem is the first time the term appears in the student edition. It will be important vocabulary for the remainder of the unit.

Tell the class that the challenge is to use the criteria of corresponding angles and side lengths to determine which rectangles (mouths) and which triangles (noses) are similar.

- Corresponding angles have the same measure.

- Corresponding side lengths from one figure to the other are multiplied by the same scale factor.

Because *corresponding* sides and angles constitute an essential idea, you may want to be explicit with students about the need for labeling figures. The vertices of the Wump mouths and noses are not labeled. You could label these vertices to clear up any difficulties referring to specific sides later.

Students can work in pairs and then share their work with a larger group.

Explore 2.3

As the students work in pairs, look for students who are having trouble sorting out corresponding sides when finding side lengths.

Urge the students to organize their work. They can record their measurements on the figures. If they use a chart, they will need some way to distinguish the sides (such as "vertical" and "horizontal" or "base" and "height").

To compare areas, some students may find the area of each rectangle and triangle by using formulas for areas. Others may count the squares that cover each figure.

If some students finish early, encourage them to draw two more rectangles—one that is similar to the Wump family's mouth and one that is not similar. Repeat for triangles. Be sure to use these figures in the summary.

Summarize 2.3

Go over the answers. Ask for explanations. For rectangles J and L, students may talk about the width growing by 2 and the length growing by 2. The perimeters also grow by a factor of 2. This gives you an opportunity to help students describe the growth in a different way. We say that the widths, lengths, and perimeters grow by a scale factor of 2. Note that rectangle L is Mug's mouth and triangle O is Mug's nose.

Suggested Questions Ask questions such as:

- *I want to grow a new Wump from Wump 1 (Mug). The scale factor is 9. What are the dimensions and perimeter of the new Wump's mouth?* ($36 \times 9; p = 90$)

- *If the scale factor is 75, what are the measurements of the new mouth?* (300 by 75)

- *Why are the dimensions 300 by 75? What rule would produce this figure?* (The scale factor tells what to multiply the old sides by to get the new sides. Since Mug's mouth is 4 by 1, the new mouth is 4×75 by 1×75 or 300 by 75. The rule is ($75x$, $75y$).)

Note that these questions connect back to *Variables and Patterns*. Students are looking for a general rule to express Wump family mouths.

- *Why does the perimeter grow the same way as the lengths of the sides of a rectangle?* [Students should be able to explain that the perimeter is really a length, so it behaves like the width and length. Some might say that the perimeter = $2(\ell + w)$ and if the scale factor is 2, then the new perimeter = $2(2\ell + 2w)$ and this is just double the original perimeter. A few students might recognize that $2(2\ell + 2w) = 2 \times 2(\ell + w)$ or that in the expression $2(2\ell + 2w)$, the factor, $(2\ell + 2w)$, is the perimeter of the original rectangle.]

- *Let's go the reverse direction. How can you find the scale factor from the original to the image if all you have are the dimensions of the two similar figures?* (We need to divide the length of a side of the image by the length of the corresponding side of the original figure.)

Once you feel students have some ideas about similarity and scale factor, probe students' understanding of similarity by asking some of the above questions in reverse:

- *If the perimeter of the mouth of a new Wump family member is 150, what is the length, width, and area of its mouth? What scale factor was used to grow this new Wump from Mug 1?* [If the perimeter is 150, then I must find a number that when the original perimeter (10) is multiplied by this number, the product is 150. That is, $10 \times \blacksquare = 150$. So students divide 150 by 10 to get 15, which is the scale factor. Therefore, the length = 60, width = 15, and area = 900.]

- *If the area of the mouth of a new Wump family member is 576, what are the length and width of its mouth?* (Students might reason as follows: the new area, 576, is found by multiplying the original area, 4, by a number. That is, $576 = 4 \times \blacksquare$. You divide 576 by 4 to get 144. This is the square of the scale factor. You must find what number squared (or times itself) is 144. The answer is 12, which is the scale factor. Therefore, the width $= 12$, the length $= 48$, and the perimeter $= 120$.]

If your class is ready, you could ask:

- *What scale factor is needed to produce a new mouth (rectangle) whose perimeter is 5?* (This requires students to shrink the original rectangle by a scale factor of $\frac{1}{2}$.)

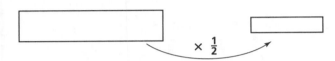

Repeat some of the questions above for triangles. It is best if you use the original nose (triangle O) as the reference.

As part of the summary or as an extension you could extend the idea of similar rectangles to similar quadrilaterals.

- *On grid paper, draw a quadrilateral (or a parallelogram) that is not a rectangle.*
- *Make a similar quadrilateral using a scale factor of 2.* (To do this, students need to keep corresponding angles congruent. Limiting it to non-rectangular parallelograms would be a bit easier.)
- *Compare the corresponding lengths of the two figures.*
- *Compare the measures of the corresponding angles.*
- *How can you decide if two figures are similar?* (When their angles are the same measure and their sides grow by the same scale factor.)

2.3 Mouthing Off and Nosing Around

Mathematical Goals

- Develop more formal ideas of the meaning of similarity, including the vocabulary of scale factor
- Understand the relationships of angles, side lengths, perimeters, and areas of similar polygons

Launch

Review Problem 2.2 and ask students for ways to tell whether two figures are similar. Introduce the term *scale factor* to express the comparison between the side lengths of similar figures.

Tell the class that the challenge is to use the criteria of corresponding angles and side lengths to determine which rectangles (mouths) and which triangles (noses) are similar.

Students can work in pairs and then share their work with a larger group.

Materials
- Transparency 2.3
- Labsheet 2.3
- Angle rulers
- Centimeter grid paper

Explore

Look for students who are having trouble sorting out corresponding sides. Urge students to organize their work.

Note whether your students use counting or formulas to find areas.

Have some students draw two more rectangles—one that is similar to the Wump family's mouth and one that is not similar. Repeat for triangles. Use these figures in the summary.

Summarize

Go over the answers. Ask for explanations. Ask questions such as:

- *I want to grow a new Wump from Wump 1 (Mug). Rectangle L is Mug's mouth. The scale factor is 9. What are the dimensions and perimeter of the new Wump's mouth?*
- *If the scale factor is 75, what are the measurements of the new mouth?*
- *Why are the dimensions 300 by 75? What rule would produce this figure?*
- *Why does the perimeter grow the same way as the lengths of the sides of a rectangle?*

Once you feel students have some ideas about similarity and scale factor, probe students' understanding of similarity by asking some of the above questions in reverse:

- *If the perimeter of the mouth of a new Wump family member is 150, what are the length, width, and area of its mouth? What scale factor was used to grow this new Wump from Mug 1?*
- *How can you decide if two figures are similar?*

Materials
- Student notebooks

ACE Assignment Guide for Problem 2.3

Differentiated Instruction
Solutions for All Learners

Core 5–6, 9–13
Other *Applications* 7, 8; *Connections* 19–28; *Extensions* 32, 33; unassigned choices from previous problems

Adapted For suggestions about adapting ACE exercises, see the CMP *Special Needs Handbook*.
Connecting to Prior Units 19: *Covering and Surrounding*; 20–25: *Bits and Pieces II*

Answers to Problem 2.3

A. Both Marta and Zack are correct because determining the scale factor depends on whether you are going from the larger rectangle to the smaller one or from the smaller rectangle to the larger one. The scale factor from L to J is 2 and the scale factor from J to L is 0.5.

B. Rectangles (mouths) J, L, and N are similar to each other. For the scale factor, students may go from small to large or large to small.

Scale factors from small to large: L to J is 2, L to N is 3, and J to N is $\frac{3}{2}$.

Scale factors from large to small: J to L is $\frac{1}{2}$, N to L is $\frac{1}{3}$, and N to J is $\frac{2}{3}$.

C. Triangles (noses) O, R, and S are similar to each other.

Scale factors from small to large: O to R is 2; O to S is 3; and R to S is $\frac{3}{2}$.

Scale factors from large to small: R to O is $\frac{1}{2}$ (reciprocal of 2); S to O is $\frac{1}{3}$ (reciprocal of 3); S to R is $\frac{2}{3}$ (reciprocal of $\frac{3}{2}$).

D. 1. Yes, because the perimeter of the larger rectangle is the scale factor times the perimeter of the small rectangle. This is because you have increased all sides by the same scale factor. Therefore, the perimeter, which is the sum of all the sides, will also be increased by the same scale factor.

2. The area of the larger rectangle is the 'square of the scale factor' times the area of the small rectangle. For example, students may see that the scale factor from rectangle L to N is 3, and that nine rectangle L's fit into rectangle N. Therefore, the scale factor for the area is 3×3, which is the same as the 'square of the scale factor' of the sides: 3^2.

E. 1. Answers will vary. The sides of the rectangle must be enlarged by the same factor to get similar rectangles.

2. Answers will vary. The sides of the new triangle will not grow by the same factor. The angle measures will not be the same, and it will not look like an enlarged or shrunken version of the original triangle.

3. Answers will vary. The sides of the new rectangle will not be multiplied by the same scale factor. Although the angles will have the same measures, the new rectangle will not look like an enlarged or shrunken version of the original rectangle.

F. You can divide the length in the second figure by the corresponding length in the first figure. You can also find a number that the length of the first (original) figure is multiplied by to get the length of the corresponding length in the second figure (image).

Similar Figures

Zack and Marta want to design a computer game that involves several animated characters. Marta asks her uncle Carlos, a programmer for a video game company, about computer animation.

Carlos explains that the computer screen can be thought of as a grid made up of thousands of tiny points, called pixels. To animate a figure, you need to enter the coordinates of key points on the figure. The computer uses these key points to draw the figure in different positions.

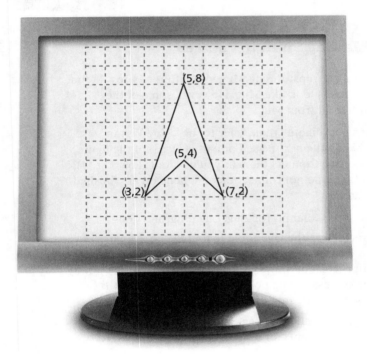

Sometimes the figures in a computer game need to change size. A computer can make a figure larger or smaller if you give it a rule for finding key points on the new figure, using key points from the original figure.

Investigation 2 Similar Figures   **21**

Notes _____

_____

_____

_____

2.1 Drawing Wumps

Zack and Marta's computer game involves a family called the Wumps. The members of the Wump family are various sizes, but they all have the same shape. That is, they are similar. Mug Wump is the game's main character. By enlarging or reducing Mug, a player can transform him into other Wump family members.

Zack and Marta experiment with enlarging and reducing figures on a coordinate grid. First, Zack draws Mug Wump on graph paper. Then, he labels the key points from *A* to *X* and lists the coordinates for each point. Marta writes the rules that will transform Mug into different sizes.

Problem 2.1 Making Similar Figures

Marta tries several rules for transforming Mug into different sizes. At first glance, all the new characters look like Mug. However, some of the characters are quite different from Mug.

A. To draw Mug on a coordinate graph, refer to the "Mug Wump" column in the table on the next page. For parts (1)–(3) of the figure, plot the points in order. Connect them as you go along. For part (4), plot the two points, but do not connect them. When you are finished, describe Mug's shape.

B. In the table, look at the columns for Zug, Lug, Bug, and Glug.

   1. For each character, use the given rule to find the coordinates of the points. For example, the rule for Zug is $(2x, 2y)$. This means that you multiply each of Mug's coordinates by 2. Point *A* on Mug is $(0, 1)$, so the corresponding point on Zug is $(0, 2)$. Point *B* on Mug is $(2, 1)$, so the corresponding point *B* on Zug is $(4, 2)$.

   2. Draw Zug, Lug, Bug, and Glug on separate coordinate graphs. Plot and connect the points for each figure, just as you did to draw Mug.

C. 1. Compare the characters to Mug. Which are the impostors?

   2. What things are the same about Mug and the others?

   3. What things are different about the five characters?

ACE Homework starts on page 28.

For: Mug Wumps, Reptiles, and Sierpinski Triangles Activity
Visit: PHSchool.com
Web Code: and-2201

Notes _____

_____

_____

_____

Coordinates of Game Characters

Rule	Mug Wump (x, y)	Zug (2x, 2y)	Lug (3x, y)	Bug (3x, 3y)	Glug (x, 3y)
Point	**Part 1**				
A	(0, 1)	(0, 2)			
B	(2, 1)	(4, 2)			
C	(2, 0)				
D	(3, 0)				
E	(3, 1)				
F	(5, 1)				
G	(5, 0)				
H	(6, 0)				
I	(6, 1)				
J	(8, 1)				
K	(6, 7)				
L	(2, 7)				
M	(0, 1)				
	Part 2 (Start Over)				
N	(2, 2)				
O	(6, 2)				
P	(6, 3)				
Q	(2, 3)				
R	(2, 2)				
	Part 3 (Start Over)				
S	(3, 4)				
T	(4, 5)				
U	(5, 4)				
V	(3, 4)				
	Part 4 (Start Over)				
W	(2, 5) (make a dot)				
X	(6, 5) (make a dot)				

Notes _____

_____

_____

_____

2.2 Hats Off to the Wumps

Zack experiments with multiplying Mug's coordinates by different whole numbers to make other characters. Marta asks her uncle how multiplying the coordinates by a decimal or adding numbers to or subtracting numbers from each coordinate will affect Mug's shape. He gives her a sketch for a new shape (a hat for Mug) and some rules to try.

Mug's Hat

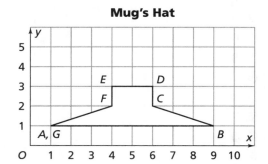

Problem 2.2 Changing a Figure's Size and Location

A. Look at the rules for Hats 1–5 in the table. Before you find any coordinates, predict how each rule will change Mug's hat.

B. Copy and complete the table. Give the coordinates of Mug's hat and the five other hats. Plot each new hat on a separate coordinate grid and connect each point as you go.

Rules for Mug's Hat

Point	Mug's Hat (x, y)	Hat 1 (x + 2, y + 3)	Hat 2 (x − 1, y + 4)	Hat 3 (x + 2, 3y)	Hat 4 (0.5x, 0.5y)	Hat 5 (2x, 3y)
A	(1, 1)					
B	(9, 1)					
C						
D						
E						
F						
G						

24 Stretching and Shrinking

Notes _____

_____

_____

_____

C. 1. Compare the angles and side lengths of the hats.

   2. Which hats are similar to Mug's hat? Explain why.

D. Write rules that will make hats similar to Mug's in each of the following ways.

   1. The side lengths are one third as long as Mug's.

   2. The side lengths are 1.5 times as long as Mug's.

   3. The hat is the same size as Mug's, but has moved right 1 unit and up 5 units.

E. Write a rule that makes a hat that is *not* similar to Mug's.

 Homework starts on page 28.

2.3 Mouthing Off and Nosing Around

How did you decide which of the computer game characters were members of the Wump family and which were imposters?

In general, how can you decide whether or not two shapes are similar?

Your experiments with rubber-band stretchers, copiers, and coordinate plots suggest that for two figures to be **similar,** there must be the following correspondence between the figures.

- The side lengths of one figure are multiplied by the same number to get the corresponding side lengths in the second figure.

- The corresponding angles are the same size.

The number that the side lengths of one figure can be multiplied by to give the corresponding side lengths of the other figure is called the **scale factor.**

How can I decide whether or not two shapes are similar?

Investigation 2 Similar Figures   **25**

Notes _____

_____

_____

_____

The rectangles below are similar. The scale factor from the smaller rectangle to the larger rectangle is 3.

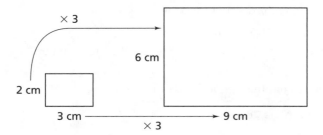

- What is the scale factor from the larger rectangle to the smaller rectangle?

The diagram shows a collection of mouths (rectangles) and noses (triangles) from the Wump family and from some impostors.

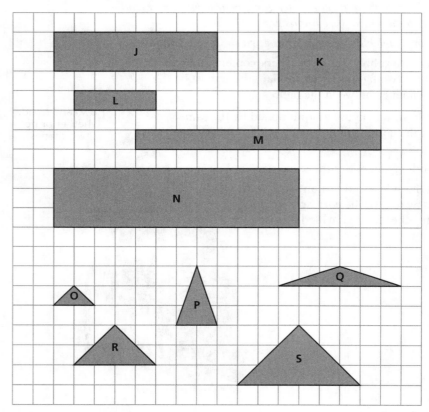

Notes _____

_____

_____

_____

A. After studying the noses and mouths in the diagram, Marta and Zack agree that rectangles J and L are similar. However, Marta says the scale factor is 2, while Zack says it is 0.5. Is either of them correct? How would you describe the scale factor so there is no confusion?

B. Decide which pairs of rectangles are similar and find the scale factor.

C. Decide which pairs of triangles are similar and find the scale factor.

D. 1. Can you use the scale factors you found in Question B to predict the relationship between the perimeters for each pair of similar rectangles? Explain.

  2. Can you use the scale factors in Question B to predict the relationship between the areas for each pair of similar rectangles? Explain.

E. For parts (1)–(3), draw the figures on graph paper.

  1. Draw a rectangle that is similar to rectangle J, but is larger than any rectangle shown in the diagram. What is the scale factor from rectangle J to your rectangle?

  2. Draw a triangle that is *not* similar to any triangle shown in the diagram.

  3. Draw a rectangle that is *not* similar to any rectangle shown in the diagram.

F. Explain how to find the scale factor from a figure to a similar figure.

ACE Homework starts on page 28.

Did You Know?

You can make figures and then rotate, slide, flip, stretch, and copy them using a computer graphics program. There are two basic kinds of graphics programs. Paint programs make images out of pixels (which is a short way of saying "picture elements"). Draw programs make images out of lines that are drawn from mathematical equations.

The images you make in a graphics program are displayed on the computer screen. A beam of electrons activates a chemical in the screen, called phosphor, to make the images appear on your screen. If you have a laptop computer with a liquid crystal screen, an electric current makes the images appear on the screen.

Go Online
PHSchool.com
For: Information about computer images
Web Code: ane-9031

Notes _____

_____

_____

_____

Applications

1. This table gives key coordinates for drawing the mouth and nose of Mug Wump. It also gives rules for finding the corresponding points for four other characters—some members of the Wump family and some impostors.

Coordinates of Characters

	Mug Wump	Glum	Sum	Tum	Crum
Rule	**(x, y)**	**(1.5x, 1.5y)**	**(3x, 2y)**	**(4x, 4y)**	**(2x, y)**
Point	Mouth				
M	(2, 2)				
N	(6, 2)				
O	(6, 3)				
P	(2, 3)				
Q	(2, 2) (connect *Q* to *M*)				
	Nose (Start Over)				
R	(3, 4)				
S	(4, 5)				
T	(5, 4)				
U	(3, 4) (connect *U* to *R*)				

a. Before you find coordinates or plot points, predict which characters are the impostors.

b. Copy and complete the table. Then plot the figures on grid paper. Label each figure.

c. Which of the new characters (Glum, Sum, Tum, and Crum) are members of the Wump family, and which are impostors?

d. Choose one of the new Wumps. How do the mouth and nose measurements (side lengths, perimeter, area, angle measures) compare with those of Mug Wump?

e. Choose one of the impostors. How do the mouth and nose measurements compare with those of Mug Wump? What are the dimensions?

Notes _____

_____

_____

_____

f. Do your findings in parts (b)–(e) support your prediction from part (a)? Explain.

2. a. Design a Mug-like character of your own on grid paper. Give him/her eyes, a nose, and a mouth.

 b. Give coordinates so that someone else could draw your character.

 c. Write a rule for finding coordinates of a member of your character's family. Check your rule by plotting the figure.

 d. Write a rule for finding the coordinates of an impostor. Check your rule by plotting the figure.

3. a. On grid paper, draw triangle ABC with vertex coordinates $A(0, 2)$, $B(6, 2)$ and $C(4, 4)$.

For: Multiple-Choice Skills Practice
Web Code: ana-2254

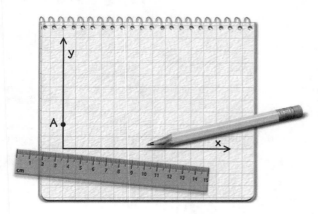

 b. Apply the rule $(1.5x, 1.5y)$ to the vertices of triangle ABC to get triangle PQR. Compare the corresponding measurements (side lengths, perimeter, area, angle measures) of the two triangles.

 c. Apply the rule $(2x, 0.5y)$ to the vertices of triangle ABC to get triangle FGH. Compare the corresponding measurements (side lengths, perimeter, area, angle measures) of the two triangles.

 d. Which triangle, PQR or FGH, seems similar to triangle ABC? Why?

4. a. On grid paper, draw parallelogram $ABCD$ with vertex coordinates $A(0, 2)$, $B(6, 2)$, $C(8, 6)$, and $D(2, 6)$.

 b. Write a rule to find the vertex coordinates of a parallelogram $PQRS$ that is larger than, but similar to, $ABCD$. Test your rule to see if it works.

 c. Write a rule to find the vertex coordinates of a parallelogram $TUVW$ that is smaller than, but similar to, $ABCD$. Test your rule.

Investigation 2 Similar Figures   **29**

Notes

For Exercises 5–6, study the size and shape of the polygons shown on the grid below.

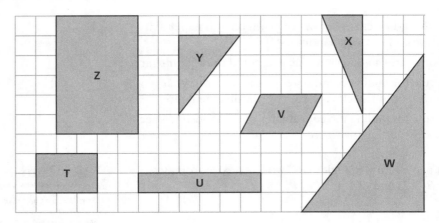

5. **Multiple Choice** Choose the pair of similar figures.

   A. Z and U   **B.** U and T   **C.** X and Y   **D.** Y and W

6. Find another pair of similar figures. How do you know they are similar?

Homework Help Online
PHSchool.com
For: Help with Exercise 6
Web Code: ane-2206

7. Copy the figures below accurately onto your own grid paper.

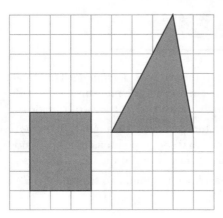

   a. Draw a rectangle that is similar, but not identical, to the given rectangle.

   b. Draw a triangle that is similar, but not identical, to the given triangle.

   c. How do you know the figures you drew are similar to the original figures?

30   Stretching and Shrinking

Notes _____

_____

_____

_____

8. Use the diagram of two similar polygons.

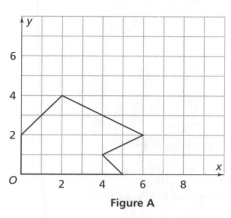

Figure A

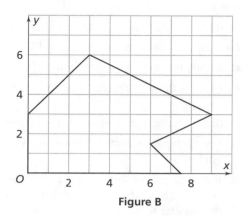

Figure B

a. Write a rule for finding the coordinates of a point on Figure B from the corresponding point on Figure A.

b. Write a rule for finding the coordinates of a point on Figure A from the corresponding point on Figure B.

c. i. What is the scale factor from Figure A to Figure B?

   ii. Use the scale factor to describe how the perimeter and area of Figure B are related to the perimeter and area of Figure A.

d. i. What is the scale factor from Figure B to Figure A?

   ii. Use the scale factor to describe how the perimeter and area of Figure A are related to the perimeter and area of Figure B.

9. a. Suppose you make Figure C by applying the rule $(2x, 2y)$ to the points on Figure A in Exercise 8. Find the coordinates of the vertices of Figure C.

b. i. What is the scale factor from Figure A to Figure C?

   ii. Use the scale factor to describe how the perimeter and area of Figure C are related to the perimeter and area of Figure A.

c. i. What is the scale factor from Figure C to Figure A?

   ii. Use the scale factor to describe how the perimeter and area of Figure A are related to the perimeter and area of Figure C.

   iii. Write a coordinate rule in the form (mx, my) that can be used to find the coordinates of any point in Figure A from the corresponding points of Figure C.

Investigation 2 Similar Figures   **31**

Notes _____
_____
_____
_____

10. What is the scale factor from an original figure to its image if the image is made using the given method?

    a. a two-rubber-band stretcher

    b. a copy machine with size factor 150%

    c. a copy machine with size factor 250%

    d. the coordinate rule $(0.75x, 0.75y)$

11. a. Study the polygons below. Which pairs seem to be similar figures?

    b. For each pair of similar figures, list the corresponding sides and angles.

    c. For each pair of similar figures, estimate the scale factor that relates side lengths in the larger figure to the corresponding side lengths in the smaller figure.

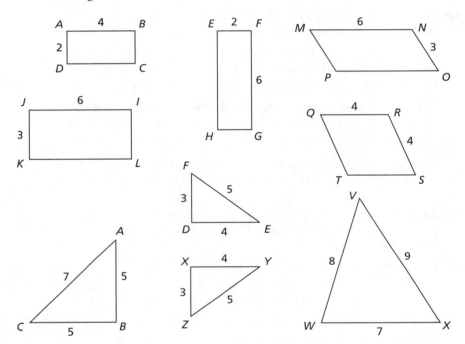

12. On grid paper, draw a rectangle with an area of 14 square centimeters. Label it *ABCD*.

    a. Write and use a coordinate rule that will make a rectangle similar to rectangle *ABCD* that is three times as long and three times as wide. Label it *EFGH*.

Notes _____

_____

_____

_____

b. How does the perimeter of rectangle *EFGH* compare to the perimeter of rectangle *ABCD*?

c. How does the area of rectangle *EFGH* compare to the area of rectangle *ABCD*?

d. How do your answers to parts (b) and (c) relate to the scale factor from rectangle *ABCD* to rectangle *EFGH*?

13. Suppose a student draws the figures below. The student says the two shapes are similar because there is a common scale factor for all of the sides. The sides of the larger figure are twice as long as those of the smaller figure. What do you say to the student to explain why they are *not* similar?

1 cm   2 cm

Connections

For Exercises 14–15, the rule $\left(x, \frac{3}{4}y\right)$ is applied to a polygon.

14. Is the image similar to the original polygon? Explain.

15. The given point is on the original polygon. Find the image of the point.

    a. $(6, 8)$ **b.** $(9, 8)$ **c.** $\left(\frac{3}{2}, \frac{4}{3}\right)$

Multiple Choice For Exercises 16–17, what is the scale factor as a percent that will result if the rule is applied to a point (x, y) on a coordinate grid?

16. $(1.5x, 1.5y)$

    A. 150%   **B.** 15%   **C.** 1.5%   **D.** None of these

17. $(0.7x, 0.7y)$

    F. 700%   **G.** 7%   **H.** 0.7%   **J.** None of these

Notes _____

_____

_____

_____

18. The rule $\left(x + \frac{2}{3}, y - \frac{3}{4}\right)$ is applied to a polygon. Find the coordinates of the point on the image that corresponds to each of these points on the original polygon.

   a. $(5, 3)$ **b.** $\left(\frac{1}{6}, \frac{11}{12}\right)$ **c.** $\left(\frac{9}{12}, \frac{4}{5}\right)$

19. A good map is similar to the place it represents. Below is a map of South Africa.

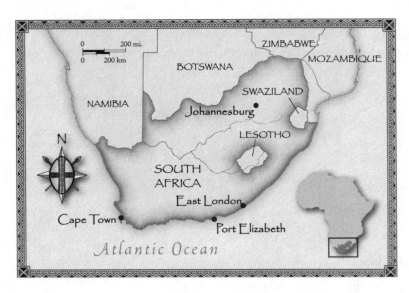

   a. Use the scale to estimate the distance from Cape Town to Port Elizabeth.

   b. Use the scale to estimate the distance from Johannesburg to East London.

   c. What is the relationship between the scale for the map and a "scale factor"?

Find each quotient.

20. $\frac{1}{2} \div \frac{1}{4}$ **21.** $\frac{1}{4} \div \frac{1}{2}$ **22.** $\frac{3}{7} \div \frac{4}{7}$

23. $\frac{4}{7} \div \frac{3}{7}$ **24.** $\frac{3}{2} \div \frac{3}{5}$ **25.** $1\frac{1}{2} \div \frac{3}{8}$

26. At a bake sale, 0.72 of a pan of corn bread has not been sold. A serving is 0.04 of a pan.

   a. How many servings are left?

   b. Use a hundredths grid to show your reasoning.

Notes _____

_____

_____

_____

27. Each pizza takes 0.3 of a large block of cheese. Charlie has 0.8 of a block of cheese left.

   a. How many pizzas can he make?

   b. Use a diagram to show your reasoning.

28. Use the grid for parts (a)–(c).

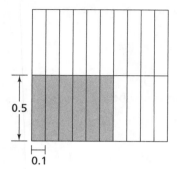

0.5

0.1

   a. What part of the grid is shaded?

   b. If the grid shows the part of a pan of spinach appetizers left, how many servings are left if a serving is 0.04?

   c. Use the grid picture to confirm your answer.

Extensions

29. Select a drawing of a comic strip character from a newspaper or magazine. Draw a grid over the figure or tape a transparent grid on top of the figure. Identify key points on the figure and then enlarge the figure by using each of these rules. Which figures are similar? Explain.

   a. $(2x, 2y)$ **b.** $(x, 2y)$ **c.** $(2x, y)$

30. Suppose you use the rule $(3x + 1, 3y - 4)$ to transform Mug Wump into a new figure.

   a. How will the angle measures in the new figure compare to corresponding angle measures in Mug?

   b. How will the side lengths of the new figure compare to corresponding side lengths of Mug?

   c. How will the area and perimeter of this new figure compare to the area and perimeter of Mug?

Investigation 2 Similar Figures   **35**

Notes _____

_____

_____

_____

31. The vertices of three similar triangles are given.

- triangle ABC: $A(1, 2), B(4, 3), C(2, 5)$
- triangle DEF: $D(3, 6), E(12, 9), F(6, 15)$
- triangle GHI: $G(5, 9), H(14, 12), I(8, 18)$

a. Find a rule that changes the vertices of triangle ABC to the vertices of triangle DEF.

b. Find a rule that changes the vertices of triangle DEF to the vertices of triangle GHI.

c. Find a rule that changes the vertices of triangle ABC to the vertices of triangle GHI.

32. If you drew Mug and his hat on the same grid, his hat would be at his feet instead of on his head.

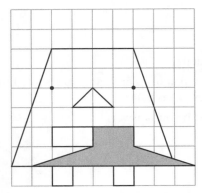

a. Write a rule that puts Mug's hat centered on his head.

b. Write a rule that changes Mug's hat to fit Zug and puts the hat on Zug's head.

c. Write a rule that changes Mug's hat to fit Lug and puts the hat on Lug's head.

33. Films are sometimes modified to fit a TV screen. Find out what that means. What exactly is modified? If Mug is in a movie that has been modified, is he still a Wump when you see him on the TV screen?

Notes _____

_____

_____

_____

Mathematical Reflections 2

In this investigation, you drew a character named Mug Wump on a coordinate grid. Then you used rules to transform Mug into other characters. Some of the characters you made were similar to Mug Wump and some were not. These questions will help you summarize what you learned.

Think about your answers to these questions. Discuss your ideas with other students and your teacher. Then write a summary of your findings in your notebook.

1. How did you decide which characters were similar to Mug Wump and which were *not* similar?

2. What types of rules produced figures similar to Mug Wump? Explain.

3. What types of rules produced figures that were *not* similar to Mug Wump? Explain.

4. When a figure is transformed to make a similar figure, some features change and some stay the same. What does the scale factor tell you about how the figure changes?

Notes _____

_____

_____

_____

Investigation 2

ACE
Assignment Choices

Differentiated Instruction
Solutions for All Learners

Problem 2.1

Core 1
Other *Applications* 2, *Connections* 14–15,
Extensions 29

Problem 2.2

Core 3, 4, 16–17
Other *Connections* 18; *Extensions* 30, 31;
unassigned choices from previous problems

Problem 2.3

Core 5–6, 9–13
Other *Applications* 7, 8; *Connections* 19–28;
Extensions 32, 33; unassigned choices from
previous problems

Adapted For suggestions about adapting
Exercise 3 and other ACE exercises, see the
CMP *Special Needs Handbook.*
Connecting to Prior Units 14–15, 20–25: *Bits and
Pieces II*; 16–18: *Bits and Pieces III*; 19: *Covering
and Surrounding*

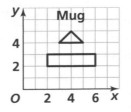

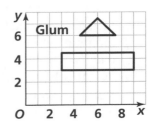

Note: The order of Sum and Tum is switched
below.

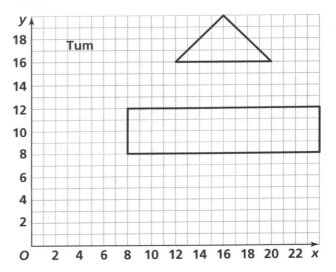

Applications

1. **a.** Sum and Crum are impostors.

   b.

	Mug Wump	Glum	Sum	Tum	Crum
Rule	(x, y)	(1.5x, 1.5y)	(3x, 2y)	(4x, 4y)	(2x, y)
Point	Mouth				
M	(2, 2)	(3, 3)	(6, 4)	(8, 8)	(4, 2)
N	(6, 2)	(9, 3)	(18, 4)	(24, 8)	(12, 2)
O	(6, 3)	(9, 4.5)	(18, 6)	(24, 12)	(12, 3)
P	(2, 3)	(3, 4.5)	(6, 6)	(8, 12)	(4, 3)
Q	(2, 2)	(3, 3)	(6, 4)	(8, 8)	(4, 2)
	Nose				
R	(3, 4)	(4.5, 6)	(9, 8)	(12, 16)	(6, 4)
S	(4, 5)	(6, 7.5)	(12, 10)	(16, 20)	(8, 5)
T	(5, 4)	(7.5, 6)	(15, 8)	(20, 16)	(10, 4)
U	(3, 4)	(4.5, 6)	(9, 8)	(12, 16)	(6, 4)

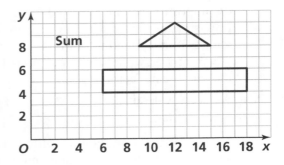

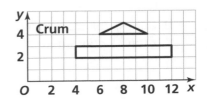

ACE ANSWERS 2

c. Glum and Tum are members. Sum and Crum are impostors.

d. For Glum: Mouth lengths, nose lengths, and perimeters are 1.5 times as long as the corresponding lengths of Mug. The angles are the same. The areas are 2.25 times as large [since 1.5 × 1.5 = 2.25 which is scale factor × scale factor = (scale factor)^2.] The mouth height is 1.5 units and the width is 6 units. The nose width is 3 units and the height is 1.5 units.

For Tum: Mouth lengths, nose lengths, and perimeters are 4 times as long as the corresponding lengths and perimeter of Mug. The angles are the same. The areas are 16 times as large. The dimensions of the mouth are 16 units by 4 units and the nose has a width of 8 units and a height of 4 units.

e. For Sum: The height of the mouth and the height of the nose are 2 times as long while the width of the mouth and width of the nose are 3 times as long as the corresponding lengths of Mug. The mouth is 12 units wide and 2 units high and the nose is 6 units wide and 2 units high.

For Crum: The heights of the mouth and the nose are the same as the corresponding heights of Mug. The width of the mouth and the nose is 2 times as long as the corresponding widths of Mug.

f. Yes, the findings support the prediction that the impostors will be Sum and Crum. Impostors are those who have different scale factors applied to both the x- and y-coordinates, while family members have the same scale factor applied.

2. a. Answers will vary.

b. Answers will vary.

c. The rule is that one should multiply both x- and y-coordinates by the same number k: (kx, ky).

d. Choose different numbers multiplying the x- and y-coordinates: (kx, ry), where k is not equal to r.

3. a–c.

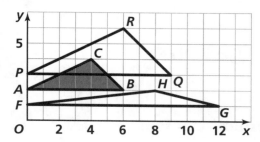

b. The side lengths and perimeter of triangle PQR are 1.5 times the side lengths and perimeter of triangle ABC. The angle measures of triangle ABC and PQR are the same and the area of triangle PQR is 2.25 times (the scale factor squared) the area of triangle ABC.

c. In comparing triangle ABC to triangle FGH, the side lengths of triangle FGH grew by different size scale factors. Therefore, the perimeter of triangle FGH did not grow by the same scale factor as the side lengths, and the angle measures are not the same. Finally, the area of triangle FGH is the same as the area of triangle ABC. (**Note:** Doubling the base and halving the height makes the areas equal.)

d. Triangle PQR is similar to triangle ABC since the corresponding lengths are enlarged by the same factor.

4. a.

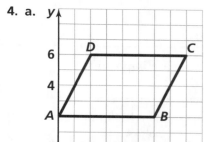

b. Choose any number k greater than 1. The rule is (kx, ky).

c. Choose any positive number s smaller than 1. The rule is (sx, sy).

5. D

6. Z and T are similar. The comparison of small sides with each other and the larger sides with each other gives the scale factor, 2 or $\frac{1}{2}$.

7. a. Answers will vary.

   b. Answers will vary.

   c. A possible answer is "The comparison of small sides with each other and the larger sides with each other gives the same scale factor."

8. a. $(1.5x, 1.5y)$

   b. $(\frac{1}{1.5}x, \frac{1}{1.5}y)$ or $(\frac{2}{3}x, \frac{2}{3}y)$

   c. i. 1.5

     ii. The perimeter of B is 1.5 times as large as the perimeter of A and the area of B is 2.25 times as large as the area of A. The perimeter relationship is given by the same factor as the constant number multiplying the x- and y-coordinates, i.e., the scale factor. The area relationship is given by the square of this number.

   d. i. $\frac{1}{1.5}$ or $\frac{2}{3}$

     ii. The perimeter of A is $\frac{2}{3}$ times as small as the perimeter of B while the area of A is $\frac{4}{9}$ times as small as the area of B. The perimeter is given by the same factor as the constant number multiplying the x- and y-coordinates. The area relationship is given by the square of this number.

9. a. coordinates of corner points of C: $(0, 0)$, $(0, 4)$, $(4, 8)$, $(12, 4)$, $(8, 2)$ and $(10, 0)$

   b. i. The scale factor is 2.

     ii. The perimeter of C is 2 times as large. The area of C is "square of 2" or 4 times as large. The factor for the perimeter is the same as the constant number multiplying the x- and y-coordinates in the rules. For the area relationship, the square of this number is taken.

   c. i. $\frac{1}{2}$

     ii. The perimeter of A is $\frac{1}{2}$ times as small as the perimeter of B. The area of A is $\frac{1}{4}$ times as small as the area of B. The factor for the perimeter is the same as the reciprocal of the constant number

multiplying the x- and y-coordinates in the rule. For the area relationship, the square of this number is taken.

     iii. $(\frac{1}{2}x, \frac{1}{2}y)$

10. a. 2   **b.** 1.5   **c.** 2.5   **d.** 0.75

11. a. Rectangles $ABCD$ and $IJKL$ seem to be similar. Triangles DFE and XZY seem to be similar. You need to know angle measures to be sure they are similar.

   b. For the first pair above, the corresponding angles are:

     A and J (or L) B and I (or K)

     C and L (or J) D and K (or I)

     The corresponding sides are:

     AB and JI (or LK) BC and IL (or KJ)

     CD and LK (or JI) DA and KJ (or IL)

     For the second pair, the corresponding angles are:

     F and Z E and Y D and X

     The corresponding sides are:

     FE and ZY ED and YX DF and XZ

   c. The scale factor from the larger to the smaller figure for the rectangles is $\frac{2}{3}$. The scale factor for the triangles is 1. Note that triangles DEF and XYZ have corresponding sides of equal length. These are congruent triangles.

12. a. $(3x, 3y)$

   b. The perimeter of rectangle $EFGH$ varies because the perimeter of rectangle $ABCD$ varies. It is three times as long as the perimeter of the rectangle $ABCD$.

   c. Area of rectangle $EFGH$ is nine times as large as the area of the rectangle $ABCD$.

   d. The answer to part (b) is the same as the scale factor and the answer to part (c) is the square of the scale factor.

13. Answers will vary. Student answers should mention the fact that the angles in the two figures are different from each other. In the figure on the left, the angles are all the same measure and obtuse. In the figure on the right, there are some obtuse angles and some acute angles.

ACE ANSWERS 2

Connections

14. No; because $1 \neq \frac{3}{4}$. The image will look shorter as it will shrink vertically.

15. a. $(6, 6)$ **b.** $(9, 6)$ **c.** $(\frac{3}{2}, 1)$

16. A   **17.** J

18. a. $(\frac{17}{3}, \frac{9}{4})$ **b.** $(\frac{5}{6}, \frac{1}{6})$ **c.** $(\frac{17}{12}, \frac{1}{20})$

19. a. About 662 km or 410 miles

     b. About 760 km or 470 miles

     c. The scale on the map gives the lengths of two corresponding sides—one from the map and one from the real world. The ratio of those lengths gives the scale factor between the map and a fictitious map, which is similar to the first, but the size is the same as the distances in the real world.

20. 2   **21.** $\frac{1}{2}$ **22.** $\frac{3}{4}$

23. $\frac{4}{3}$ or $1\frac{1}{3}$ **24.** $\frac{5}{2}$ or $2\frac{1}{2}$ **25.** 4

26. a. $0.72 \div 0.04 = 18$ servings.

     b. One possible answer: $4 \times 4\frac{1}{2} = 18$ servings

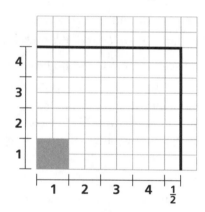

27. a. $0.8 \div 0.3 = 2$ pizzas and 0.66 of another or remainder 0.2 of the block of cheese.

     b.

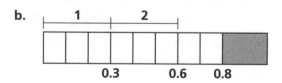

28. a. $0.5 \times 0.6 = 0.3$ of the grid

     b. $0.3 \div 0.04 = 7.5$ servings

     c.

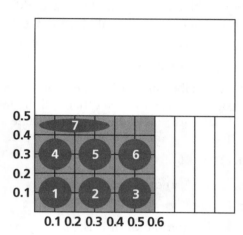

Extensions

29. Answers will vary. In part (a), one gets a similar figure, which is two times as big. In part (b) and part (c), the image will not be similar. It will be two times as high in part (b) while keeping the same width and two times as wide in part (c) while keeping the same height.

30. a. Angle measures remain the same.

     b. Side lengths will be three times as long.

     c. Area will be nine times as large. Perimeter will be three times as large.

31. a. $(3x, 3y)$

     b. $(x + 2, y + 3)$

     c. $(3x + 2, 3y + 3)$

32. a. $(x - 1, y + 6)$

     b. $(2x - 2, 2y + 12)$

     c. $(3x - 3, y + 6)$

33. The rectangle of a movie screen is not similar to the rectangle of a TV screen, in general. The width of the movie screen is usually much longer than its height, while the width and height of a TV screen are close to each other, i.e. more like a square. The reduction may be performed in three different ways:
(1) It is performed so that the width of the theatre picture fits exactly onto the width of the TV screen, and the same scale is used to reduce the height. In this case Mug will still be a Wump but there will be a blank area at the bottom or the top of the TV screen.

(2) The reduction is performed so that the height of the movie screen fits exactly onto the height of the TV screen, and the same scale is used to reduce the width. In this case Mug will still be a Wump but a part of the picture will be cut from the left and/or right side since it will be outside of the TV screen range.

(3) Different scales are used to reduce the width and the height so that the whole picture will fit onto the TV screen. However, in this case, the images will be distorted a little bit and Mug will not be a Wump anymore. Because of this, the reduction method is not usually applied in practice.

Possible Answers to Mathematical Reflections

1. Answers will vary, but essentially, similar figures have the same shape. Students might talk about angles being the same or side lengths all doubling or tripling. They might mention that Glug and Lug were distorted, and therefore, not similar to Mug, because each changed in only one direction.

2. Rules of the form $(2x, 2y)$ and $(3x, 3y)$ produced figures that were similar to Mug. In these rules, x and y are multiplied by the same number, stretching or shrinking the new figure by the same factor in both vertical and horizontal directions.

3. Rules such as $(3x, y)$ and $(x, 3y)$ did not produce similar figures. These rules stretch the figure in only one direction, which makes it fatter or thinner than the original. Rules of the form $(nx + a, ny + b)$ also produce figures similar to the original, but the image is moved a units horizontally and b units vertically. For example, $(2x + 7, 2y - 4)$ makes a figure similar to but twice as large as the original and moved to the right 7 units and down 4 units.

4. If the scale factor is larger than 1, then the new figure will be bigger than the original figure. The new lengths and perimeters will be the scale factor times as large, while the new areas will be the *square of the scale factor* times as large. If the scale factor is less than 1, then the new figure will be smaller than the original figure. The same relationships mentioned above will hold between lengths in the two figures and the areas of the two figures.

Investigation 3 Similar Polygons

Mathematical and Problem-Solving Goals

- Construct similar quadrilaterals from smaller, congruent figures

- Connect the ratio of the areas of two similar figures to the scale factor

- Construct similar triangles from smaller, congruent figures

- Generalize the relationship between scale factor and area

- Generalize the relationship between scale factor and area to scale factors less than 1

- Subdivide a figure into smaller, similar figures

- Use scale factors to make similar shapes

- Find missing measures in similar figures using scale factor

Summary of Problems

Problem 3.1 Rep-Tile Quadrilaterals

Students use four congruent quadrilaterals to make a larger, similar quadrilateral. They find that the scale factor from the smaller to the larger quadrilateral is 2 and that the side lengths and perimeter grow by a factor of 2 while the area grows by a factor of $2^2 = 4$. They then add additional small quadrilaterals to their figures to make another larger similar quadrilateral with 3 as the scale factor from the smallest to the largest quadrilateral.

Problem 3.2 Rep-Tile Triangles

Students repeat the procedure in Problem 3.1 with triangles. They also reverse the process by subdividing a triangle into four congruent triangles, each similar to the original.

Problem 3.3 Scale Factors and Similar Shapes

Students use a given scale factor to make a figure similar to a specific triangle or rectangle. In Question C of the problem, students find missing side lengths in two similar figures. The strategy that they use at this point is to first find the scale factor and then use it to multiply the given side length to obtain the missing corresponding side length. In the next investigation they will find missing lengths by using ratios.

Mathematics Background

For background on comparing area in two similar figures using rep-tiles, see page 6.

	Suggested Pacing	Materials for Students	Materials for Teachers	ACE Assignments
All	$3\frac{1}{2}$ days	Centimeter and inch rulers; angle rulers or protractors, scissors (optional)		
3.1	1 day	Blank sheets of paper (at least 1 per student), blank transparency film (optional; 1 per group or pair), transparency markers (optional; 1 per group or pair)	Shapes Set (optional)	1–3, 22–25, 33, 34
3.2	1 day	Labsheet 3.2 (1 per student), blank sheets of paper (at least 1 per student), blank transparency film (optional; 1 per group or pair), transparency markers (optional; 1 per group or pair)	Transparency 3.2 (optional), Shapes Set (optional)	4–6, 26–31, 35–37
3.3	1 day	Labsheet 3.3A (1 per student), Labsheet 3.3B (optional; 1 per student) Labsheet 3 ACE Exercise 8	Transparencies 3.3A and 3.3B (optional)	7–21, 32, 38–42
MR	$\frac{1}{2}$ day			

3.1 Rep-Tile Quadrilaterals

Goals

- Construct similar quadrilaterals from smaller, congruent figures

- Connect the ratio of the areas of two similar figures to the scale factor.

This problem focuses on rep-tiling. Students are challenged to find ways to put multiple copies of figures together to make a larger similar figure. This is followed by a question in Problem 3.2 that goes the other way: sub-dividing a triangle into smaller triangles, each similar to the original. In each of these contexts, students study how the areas of two similar figures are related to the scale factor. To save time, you can let students use the Shapes Sets to trace figures. If they fold a piece of paper in fourths, trace a figure, and then cut it they will have four congruent copies of that figure. They could also use several congruent quadrilaterals from the Shapes Set.

This problem is designed to help students focus on scale factor and the relationship between the areas of similar figures. It is generally surprising to students that if we apply a scale factor of 2 to a figure, the area becomes four times as large. At this stage, we have chosen not to have students be concerned with area calculations. Instead, we use rep-tiles to demonstrate that when we wish to apply a scale factor of 2, it requires four copies of the original figure. In this case, we are really measuring area using the original figure as the unit, rather than square inches or square centimeters.

Launch 3.1

Launch the activity by demonstrating what is meant by a repeating tile or "rep-tile."

- *Today we are going to investigate several kinds of shapes to see which shapes are rep-tiles. I am going to show two patterns on the overhead. The first one is a rep-tile and the second one is not a rep-tile. Look at the figures carefully and tell me what you think a rep-tile is.* (A regular hexagon will tessellate because it fits together with no overlaps or underlaps and has a pattern that can be

continued forever. However, there is no larger regular hexagon in the pattern formed by the small hexagons. The regular hexagon tessellates, but is not a rep-tile. However, if you put four squares together you can make a larger square that is similar to the small squares. Students will find other figures for which this is the case.)

Show squares and hexagons from the Shapes Set or cut out from transparent paper. Students will say that each tessellates.

Suggested Questions

- *What is different about the resulting figures that might make one a rep-tile and the other not?* (Ask questions until you get the students to see that the larger figure made from the squares is similar to the original figure, while the large figure made from hexagons is not a hexagon, and so cannot be similar to the original. This self-similar feature is what makes a figure a rep-tile.)

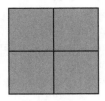

- *In this problem, you are going to work with quadrilaterals. For each quadrilateral, your challenge is to determine whether it is possible to put together several identical small quadrilaterals to form a larger version of the same quadrilateral. When it is possible, you will sketch how the shapes fit together and then answer some questions about the measurements of the figures.*

Students can work in small groups on this problem.

Some students have greater spatial skills than others and may find rep-tiles more quickly. For those who are struggling, make some suggestions about how they can systematically explore the possibilities. Point out that it is reasonable to assume edges that are the same length must be placed together. However, there are usually two ways to place two matching edges together, as one of the shapes can be flipped.

Encourage students to make a sketch of their rep-tiles for the summary. You may also want to have students record their work in a table like this one:

Shape	Larger Shape	Number of Tiles	Scale Factor

Some teachers have students make a small poster for each rep-tile the class finds. They display these posters and then have a handy reference for future discussions about the relationship between area and scale factor.

As students add more rectangles to the rep-tile in Question A, encourage them to look for patterns.

- *How many rectangles will it take to make the next similar figure formed from the rep-tile? We will call these similar figures rep-tile figures. How many rectangles to make the 10th rep-tile figure, etc.?*

Going Further

The four parallelograms below form a larger parallelogram, but it is not similar to the original. You might ask students to decide for themselves whether this is true and explain why.

Because it is unlikely that students will have found a trapezoid that is a rep-tile, you could tell them that one does exist (see Problem 3.1 Question A answers) and challenge them to find it or you can provide them with a copy of the trapezoid so they can investigate how the rep-tile figure is formed.

Summarize 3.1

Go over the answers. Be sure that students give reasons for why each rep-tile figure is similar to the original rectangle or parallelogram. They will probably use scale factor in some way to compare lengths.

Suggested Questions If they don't use scale factors, ask:

- *How does the side of the original rectangle (parallelogram) compare to the rep-tile figure's side?* (Focus students on the growth in terms of multiplying by a common factor.)

- *How do the angles of the original rectangle (parallelogram) compare to the angles of the rep-tile figure?* (Make sure students see that the angles are the same.)

- *Remember the common factor is called the scale factor and it is used to scale up or down to make similar figures.*

Call on different groups to come to the overhead to demonstrate their rep-tile figures and patterns that they observed. Students should give reasons for how the scale factor is related to lengths, perimeter, and area.

Once the students have observed that the scale factor from one of the small rectangles to the larger rep-tile figure is 2, discuss the perimeter and area. To help some students see the area relationship, tell them the following:

- *Assume that the original rectangle had an area of 1 square unit. Since it takes four of them to form the rep-tile figure, the area grows by a factor of 4 or 2 × 2 or 2^2.*

The following discussion refers to rectangles. You can include parallelograms from the start or repeat the discussion after you have discussed rectangles in Question B parts (1)–(3).

Take four copies of the smaller rectangle and make the first rep-tile figure.

Suggested Questions Ask:

- *How many more smaller rectangles do I need to make the next larger rep-tile figure?* (5) *How many are there all together?* (9)

- *How many more do I need to add to this rep-tile figure to make the next larger rep-tile figure?* (7) *How many are there all together?* (16)

- *Predict what will happen to the next rep-tile figure (the 10th rep-tile figure).*

The number pattern associated with this sequence of rep-tiles is

$$1 \ (1\text{st})$$
$$1 + 3 = 4 \ (2\text{nd})$$
$$1 + 3 + 5 = 9 \ (3\text{rd})$$
$$1 + 3 + 5 + 7 = 16 \ (4\text{th})$$
$$1 + 3 + 5 + 7 + 9 = 25 \ (5\text{th})$$

and so on until

$$1 + 3 + 5 + 7 + 9 + \ldots + 19 = 100 \ (10\text{th}).$$

Students may say that the pattern is adding consecutive odd integers and the sum is the square of the number of odd integers in the sum. For example, the sum of the first 5 odd integers is 5^2 or 25. The sum of the first 10 odd integers is 10^2 or 100. Some students may verbalize this to say that the sum of the first n odd integers is n^2.

The following diagram is a geometric interpretation of the above sequence using squares:

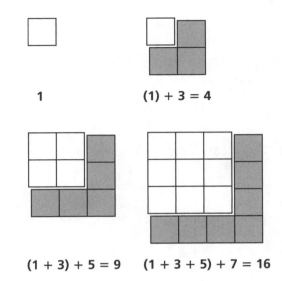

1   (1) + 3 = 4

(1 + 3) + 5 = 9   (1 + 3 + 5) + 7 = 16

Repeat the above questions for parallelograms or trapezoids.

3.1 Rep-Tile Quadrilaterals

Mathematical Goals

- Construct similar quadrilaterals from smaller, congruent figures
- Connect the ratio of the areas of two similar figures to the scale factor

Launch

Demonstrate what is meant by a *rep-tile*.

- *Today we are going to investigate several kinds of shapes to see which shapes are rep-tiles. I am going to show two patterns on the overhead. The first one is a rep-tile and the second one is not a rep-tile. Look at the figures carefully and tell me what you think a rep-tile is.*

Show squares and hexagons.

- *What is different about the resulting figures that might make one a rep-tile and the other not?*

Ask questions to get students to see that the larger figure made from the squares is similar to the original figure, while the large figure made from hexagons is not a hexagon.

- *You are going to work with quadrilaterals. For each quadrilateral, your challenge is to determine whether it is possible to put together several identical small quadrilaterals to form a larger version of the same quadrilateral. When possible, you will sketch how the shapes fit together and then answer some questions about their measurements.*

Have students work in small groups of 3 or 4.

Materials
- Blank paper
- Scissors
- Rulers or other straightedges
- Shapes Set (optional)

Vocabulary
- rep-tile

Explore

Suggest to struggling students that they systematically explore possibilities. Point out that it is reasonable to assume edges of the same length are placed together and there are two ways to do this.

Encourage students to make a sketch of their rep-tiles for the summary. You may also have students record their work in a table. Have a group of students make a small poster for each rep-tile the class finds. Display these posters as a handy reference for future discussions.

Ask questions about patterns and predicting.

- *How many rectangles will it take to make the next similar figure formed from the rep-tile? We will call these similar figures rep-tile figures. How many rectangles to make the 10th rep-tile figure, etc.?*

Materials
- Shapes Set (optional)

Summarize

Have students justify each similar figure. Ask questions that prompt thinking about the scale factor. Focus students' attention also on angles.

Help students see the area relationship. Make a rep-tile figure with four quadrilaterals.

Materials
- Student notebooks

continued on next page

- *How many more smaller rectangles (or parallelograms, etc.) do I need to make the next larger rep-tile figure? How many all together?*

- *How many more do I need to add to this rep-tile figure to make the next larger rep-tile figure? How many are there all together?*

- *Predict what will happen to the next rep-tile figure (the 10th rep-tile figure).*

ACE Assignment Guide for Problem 3.1

Differentiated Instruction
Solutions for All Learners

Core 1, 2
Other *Applications* 3; *Connections* 22–25; *Extensions* 33, 34; unassigned choices from previous exercises

Adapted For suggestions about adapting Exercise 1 and other ACE exercises, see the CMP *Special Needs Handbook.*
Connecting to Prior Units 22–24: *Shapes and Designs*; 25: *Bits and Pieces II*

Answers to Problem 3.1

A. All of these shapes can fit together to make a larger shape that is similar to the original. Some possible sketches:

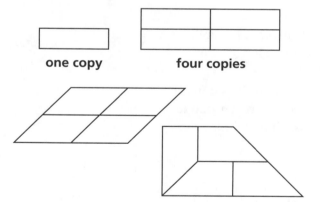

one copy   four copies

B. 1. The scale factor is 2 because the lengths of the sides of the large rectangle are twice the lengths of the original rectangle.

2. The perimeter of the large figure is two times the perimeter of the small figure (scale factor is 2).

3. Because the area of the large figure is the number of copies of the original rectangle, the area of the large figure is four times the

area of the small figure (i.e., the square of the scale factor).

C. 1 and **2.** Possible answers:

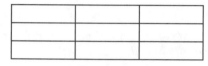

nine copies
scale factor = 3

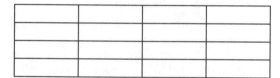

sixteen copies
scale factor = 4

3. Answers may vary. Students will most likely find a rectangle with a scale factor of either 3 or 4. If the answer is 4, the length of the sides of the new rep-tile figure will be four times the length of the sides of the original. You can find the scale factor by seeing that 4 = 3 + 1 (the length of the original side) gives you the length of the new rectangle's side. Another way to think about it is the length of the sides of the new rep-tile figure in Question C is 2 times the length of the sides in Question A, which was 2 times the length of the original. Therefore, the scale factor would be (2 × 2) or 4.

4. Answers will vary depending on shape and rep-tile figure used. The side length in the large rectangle is the scale factor times the length of the corresponding side in the small rectangle. The perimeter of the large rectangle is the scale factor times the perimeter of the small rectangle. The area of the large rectangle is "the square of the scale factor" times the area of the small rectangle.

3.2 Rep-Tile Triangles

Goals

- Construct similar triangles
- Generalize the relationship between scale factor and area
- Generalize the relationship between scale factor and area to scale factors less than 1
- Subdivide a figure into smaller, similar figures

In this problem, students repeat the rep-tiling procedure from Problem 3.1 with triangles. Students also reverse the process. They take a triangle and subdivide it into four congruent triangles that are similar to the original triangle.

Launch 3.2

Tell the class that they will now investigate triangles to see which ones rep-tile. They will need several copies of congruent triangles. Have them make them as was described in Problem 3.1.

Some students will find these triangles more difficult to sketch than the rectangles. You may want to have these students cut out paper copies of the triangles to glue on a larger sheet of paper rather than sketch them.

Students can work in pairs or small groups. Each student should have a record of the work.

Explore 3.2

As you move around, make sure that the students have arranged the triangles in such a way that the new triangle is similar to the smaller triangles. Make sure that students have a way to compare the lengths of the smaller triangles to the larger.

You might ask students if they have checked angle measures and how they might do this. Some may use a transparency to copy and compare. They should notice that corresponding angles are congruent because they used congruent triangles to form the rep-tile figure. They need to make sure that they are comparing corresponding angles.

Summarize 3.2

The summary for this problem is much like that for Problem 3.1. Ask different groups to come to the overhead and demonstrate their work. Be sure they give explanations. Encourage the class to verify the explanations or to ask questions.

Ask questions that focus on scale factor and its relationship to the areas of the similar figures. You want students to be able to articulate that the area of the rep-tile figure is the square of the scale factor times the original area and to have mental images of the rep-tile and rep-tile figures to help this make sense.

If time allows, discuss the case of triangles: We can add on another row of congruent triangles to the bottom of the triangle and form a larger and larger similar triangle. The pattern of how many we need to add each time is interesting. Note that we add 3 and then 5, and then 7 and so on. Each time we add the next larger odd number of triangles to form the bottom row.

Suggested Question

- *We seem to get square numbers for the total number of triangles each time. Why do these odd numbers add together to give the square numbers?*

The following pictures will help show the pattern.

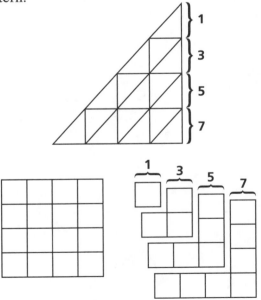

The rep-tiling patterns suggest a method for subdividing a triangle into smaller congruent similar triangles. Students might suggest making smaller figures that have a scale factor of 2 from the small to the large, subdividing each side length of the larger triangle. Connect the midpoints. A similar method using a scale factor of 3 can be used by subdividing each side length into thirds and connecting the corresponding points.

Be sure that the students understand the relationship between scale factor and perimeter and between scale factor and area.

Suggested Questions Ask:

- *If the area of one triangle is 15 square units and the scale factor between this triangle and a similar triangle is 2.5, what is the area of a similar triangle?* (93.75 square units)

- *If the area of one triangle is 15 square units and the scale factor between this triangle and a similar triangle is 0.5, what is the area of a similar triangle?* (3.75 square units)

Sketch a triangle on the overhead. Ask:

- *Can you subdivide this triangle into smaller congruent triangles? What is the scale factor? How do the perimeters and areas compare?*

- *Can you use this triangle to show how copies of it can be used to make a larger similar triangle? What is the scale factor? How do the perimeters and areas compare?*

There are other patterns the students may observe such as the midpoint line of a triangle is parallel to the opposite side and is half the length of the opposite side. You can also ask questions about corresponding angles and what this information says about the midpoint line and the opposite side.

Mathematics Background
For background on parallel lines, see page 7.

3.2 Rep-Tile Triangles

Mathematical Goals

- Construct similar triangles
- Generalize the relationship between scale factor and area
- Generalize the relationship between scale factor and area for scale factors less than 1
- Subdivide a figure into smaller, similar figures

Launch

Tell the class that they will now investigate triangles. Hand out the materials to make them.

Some students will find these triangles more difficult to sketch than the rectangles. You may want to have these students cut out paper copies of the triangles to glue on a larger sheet of paper rather than sketch them.

Students can work in pairs or small groups. Each student should have a record of the work.

Materials
- Transparency 3.2
- Blank paper
- Scissors
- Rulers or other straightedges
- Shapes Set (optional)

Explore

Make sure that the students' new triangles are similar to the smaller triangles and they have a way to compare the lengths of the smaller triangles to the larger. Encourage students to check angle measures.

Materials
- Blank transparencies
- Labsheet 3.2 (optional)

Summarize

Ask different groups to come to the overhead and demonstrate their work.

Ask questions that focus on scale factor and its relationship to the areas of the similar figures. You want students to be able to articulate that the area of the rep-tile figure is the square of the scale factor times the original area.

Demonstrate that we can continue to generate larger similar triangles by adding longer and longer rows of small triangles.

- *We seem to get square numbers for the totals each time. Why do these odd numbers add together to give the square numbers?*

The rep-tiling patterns suggest a method for subdividing a triangle into smaller congruent similar triangles. Ask students for their strategies.

Be sure that the students understand the relationship between scale factor and perimeter and between scale factor and area. Ask:

- *Suppose the area of one triangle is 15 square units and the scale factor between this triangle and a similar triangle is 2.5. What is the area of the similar triangle?*

- *Suppose the area of one triangle is 15 square units and the scale factor between this triangle and a similar triangle is 0.5. What is the area of the similar triangle?*

Materials
- Student notebooks

continued on next page

Sketch a triangle on the overhead. Ask:

- *Can you subdivide this triangle into smaller congruent triangles?*
  What is the scale factor? How do the perimeters and areas compare?

ACE Assignment Guide for Problem 3.2

Core 4–6
Other *Connections* 26–31, *Extensions* 35–37;
unassigned choices from previous problems

Adapted For suggestions about adapting ACE
exercises, see the CMP *Special Needs Handbook*.
Connecting to Prior Units 26–28: *Bits and Pieces
III*; 29–31: *Shapes and Designs*

Answers to Problem 3.2

A. All of the triangles (right, isosceles, and
scalene) fit together to make a larger triangle
that is similar to the original. One possible
sketch:

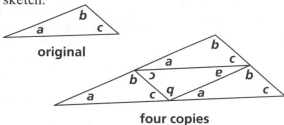

B. 1. Answers will vary. One answer according to
Question A is: The scale factor is 2 because
the side lengths of the new triangle are all
two times the side lengths of the original
triangle.

2. The perimeter of the large triangle is 2
times the perimeter of the small triangle
(scale factor is 2).

3. The area of the large triangle is 4 (i.e. the
square of the scale factor) times the area of
the small triangle, and because four of the
original triangles fit into the larger triangle.

C. 1–2. One possible answer: (Figure 1)

3. Scale factor is 4, since the side lengths
are four times that of the original.

4. The sides and perimeter of the large
triangle is the scale factor (i.e. 4) times the
sides and perimeter of the small triangle,
respectively. The area of the large triangle
is 16 (i.e., the square of the scale factor)
times the area of the small triangle.

D. Students may have a variety of strategies. One
possibility is for each triangle, find the
midpoints of each of its sides and join them
by drawing straight lines connecting each of
the midpoints to form smaller similar
triangles. The process looks like this:

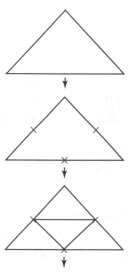

The other two triangles will be subdivided like this:

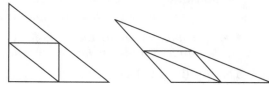

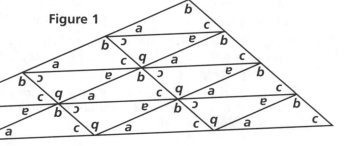

Figure 1

3.3 Scale Factors and Similar Shapes

Goals

- Use scale factors to make similar shapes

- Find missing measures in similar figures using scale factor

In this problem, students use a given scale factor to make a figure similar to a specific triangle or rectangle, and to find missing side lengths in two similar figures. The strategy at this point is first to find the scale factor and then to use it to multiply the given side length to obtain the missing corresponding side length. In the next investigation, they will find missing lengths using ratios.

Launch 3.3

Display rectangle A and triangle B on the overhead. Tell the class that their challenge is to make similar figures given the scale factor, area, or perimeter of the new figure.

The class can work in pairs. Be sure that the students have quarter-inch grid paper.

Explore 3.3

Suggested Question If students are having a hard time getting started, you might ask:

- *If the scale factor is 2.5, what will the new side length look like? How will it compare to the side length of the original figure?* (It will be 2.5 times as long.)

Check if students are using the correct scale factor in the parts that give information about area. For example, if the area is nine times the original area, students must note that the area grows by the square of the scale factor. In this case, the scale factor is 3.

If students are having trouble with corresponding parts, ask which side has the shortest length in each rectangle. Then ask for the longest.

Look for students who solve the problem in interesting ways. Be sure to call on these students during the summary.

Summarize 3.3

As the students present their solutions, be sure they explain their reasoning and methods. To find the missing lengths in Question C, students might find the scale factor using two of the known corresponding lengths. They will then use the scale factor to multiply the given length to get the unknown length. Be sure that they are going in the right direction. That is, they need to find the scale factor from the figure with the given length to the figure with the unknown length.

As a summary activity you could hand out copies of Labsheet 3.3B for students to extend their understanding of similarity to other polygons.

Suggested Question

- *In each set, decide which polygons are similar. Explain.* (Rectangles A and C are similar, as are parallelograms B and C, decagons A and B and stars A and C. For the rectangles, we need to check only the side lengths. For the others, we need to check the angle measurements as well.)

By the end of this investigation, students should have a firm understanding of the two criteria for identifying similar figures and the role of the scale factor and its relationship to length, perimeter, and area.

Check for Understanding

Sketch the following rectangle on the board.

- *If the rectangle is enlarged by a scale factor of 3, what is the perimeter of the new rectangle? What is the area of the new rectangle?* (perimeter: 63 units and area: 202.5 units²)

3.3 Scale Factors and Similar Shapes

Mathematical Goals

- Use scale factors to make similar shapes
- Find missing measures in similar figures using scale factor

Launch

Display rectangle A and triangle B on the overhead. Challenge the class to make similar figures given the scale factor, area, or perimeter of the new figure.

Be sure that the students have quarter-inch grid paper.

The class can work in pairs.

Materials

- Transparencies 3.3A and 3.3B
- Quarter-inch grid paper
- Labsheet 3.3A (optional)

Explore

If students are having a hard time getting started, you might ask:

- *If the scale factor is 2.5, what will the new side length look like? How will it compare to the side length of the original figure?*

Check to see if students are using the correct scale factor in the parts that give information about area.

Look for interesting ways that students solve the problem. Be sure to call on these students during the summary.

Summarize

Be sure students explain their reasoning and methods. To find the missing lengths in Question C, students might find the scale factor using two of the known corresponding lengths. They will then use the scale factor to multiply the given length to get the unknown length. Hand out copies of Labsheet 3.3B for students to extend their understanding of similarity to other polygons.

- *In each set, decide which polygons are similar. Explain.*

By the end of this investigation, students should have a firm understanding of the two criteria for identifying similar figures and the role of the scale factor and its relationship to length, perimeter, and area.

Materials

- Student notebooks
- Labsheet 3.3B (optional)

ACE Assignment Guide
for Problem 3.3

Core 7–18
Other *Applications* 19–21; *Connections* 32; *Extensions* 38–42; unassigned choices from previous problems
Labsheet 3ACE Exercise 8 is available.

Adapted For suggestions about adapting ACE exercises, see the CMP *Special Needs Handbook*

Answers to Problem 3.3

A. 1.

10 by 20

2.

2 by 4

3.

12 by 24

B. 1.

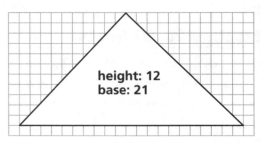

height: 12
base: 21

2.

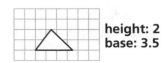

height: 2
base: 3.5

C. 1. Side *AD* is 4 cm. This side corresponds to side *EH*. One possible method is 6.75 ÷ 3 = 2.25. This gives the scale factor: 2.25. Then 9 ÷ 2.25 = 4. Alternatively, 9 ÷ 6.75 = $\frac{4}{3}$, and $\frac{4}{3}$ times 3 gives side *AD*, which is 4 cm.

2. a. Side *AB* corresponds to side *DE*. The scale factor from *AB* to *DE* is 1.25.

   b. Side *DF* is 3.75 cm. Side *FE* is 6.25 cm (5 × 1.25 = 6.25), as it has the same scale factor. Because the triangles are similar, the corresponding angle measurements are the same, so the measure of angle *F* is 94°. Angle *B* and corresponding angle *E* are each 30°. **Note:** Students will need to use the fact that the sum of the interior angles of a triangle is 180°.

The student edition pages for this investigation begin on the next page.

Notes _____

_____

_____

_____

Similar Polygons

In *Shapes and Designs*, you learned that some polygons can fit together to cover, or tile, a flat surface. For example, the surface of a honeycomb is covered with a pattern of regular hexagons. Many bathroom and kitchen floors are covered with a pattern of square tiles.

   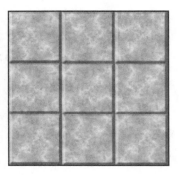

If you look closely at the pattern of squares on the right above, you can see that the large square, which consists of nine small squares, is similar to each of the nine small squares. The nine-tile square has sides made of three small squares, so the scale factor from the small square to the nine-tile square is 3. You can also take four small squares and put them together to make a four-tile square that is similar to the nine-tile square. The scale factor in this case is 2.

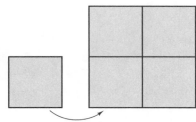

Similar; scale factor is 2.

However, no matter how closely you look at the hexagon pattern, you cannot find a large hexagon made up of similar smaller hexagons.

If congruent copies of a shape can be put together to make a larger, similar shape, the original shape is called a **rep-tile.** A square is a rep-tile, but a regular hexagon is not.

3.1 Rep-Tile Quadrilaterals

In the next problem, you will see if rectangles and non-rectangular quadrilaterals are also rep-tiles.

Problem 3.1 Forming Rep-Tiles With Similar Quadrilaterals

Sketch and make several copies of each of the following shapes:

- a non-square rectangle
- a non-rectangular parallelogram
- a trapezoid

A. Which of these shapes can fit together to make a larger shape that is similar to the original? Make a sketch to show how the copies fit together.

B. Look at your sketches from Question A.

   1. What is the scale factor from the original figure to the larger figure? Explain.

   2. How does the perimeter of the new figure relate to the perimeter of the original?

   3. How does the area of the new figure relate to the area of the original?

C. 1. Extend the rep-tile patterns you made in Question A. Do this by adding copies of the original figure to make larger figures that are similar to the original.

   2. Make sketches showing how the figures fit together.

   3. Find the scale factor from each original figure to each new figure. Explain.

   4. Explain what the scale factor indicates about the corresponding side lengths, perimeters, and areas.

ACE Homework starts on page 44.

Notes _____

_____

_____

_____

3.2 Rep-Tile Triangles

While rep-tiles must tessellate, not every shape that tessellates is a rep-tile.

Are the birds in the tessellation below rep-tiles?

All triangles tessellate. Are all triangles rep-tiles?

Problem 3.2 Forming Rep-Tiles With Similar Triangles

Sketch and make several copies of each of the following shapes:

- a right triangle
- an isosceles triangle
- a scalene triangle

A. Which of these triangles fit together to make a larger triangle that is similar to the original? Make a sketch to show how the copies fit together.

B. Look at your sketches from Question A.

   1. What is the scale factor from each original triangle to each larger triangle? Explain.

   2. How is the perimeter of the new triangle related to the perimeter of the original?

   3. How is the area of the new triangle related to the area of the original?

Notes _____

_____

_____

_____

C. 1. Extend the rep-tile patterns you made in Question A. Do this by adding copies of the original triangle to make larger triangles that are similar to the original.

  2. Make sketches to show how the triangles fit together.

  3. Find the scale factor from each original triangle to each new triangle. Explain.

  4. Explain what the scale factor indicates about the corresponding side lengths, perimeters, and areas.

D. Study the rep-tile patterns. See if you can find a strategy for dividing each of the triangles below into four or more similar triangles. Make sketches to show your ideas.

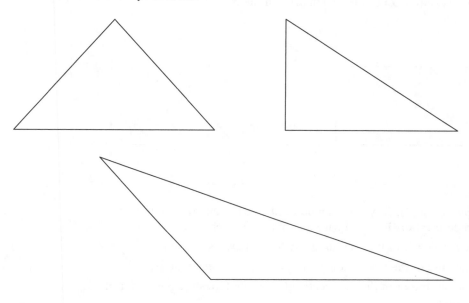

ACE Homework starts on page 44.

Notes _____

_____

_____

_____

3.3 Scale Factors and Similar Shapes

You know that the scale factor from one figure to a similar figure gives you information about how the side lengths, perimeters, and areas of the figures are related. You will use what you learned in the next problem.

Problem 3.3 Scale Factors and Similar Shapes

For Questions A and B, use the two figures on the grid.

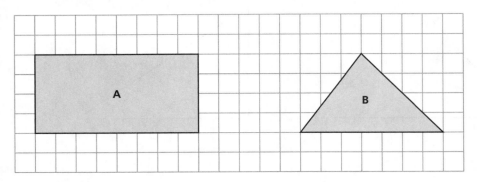

A. For parts (1)–(3), draw a rectangle similar to rectangle A that fits the given description. Find the base and height of each new rectangle.

1. The scale factor from rectangle A to the new rectangle is 2.5.

2. The area of the new rectangle is $\frac{1}{4}$ the area of rectangle A.

3. The perimeter of the new rectangle is three times the perimeter of rectangle A.

B. For parts (1)–(2), draw a triangle similar to triangle B that fits the given description. Find the base and height of each new triangle.

1. The area of the new triangle is nine times the area of triangle B.

2. The scale factor from triangle B to the new triangle is $\frac{1}{2}$.

Notes _____

_____

_____

_____

C. 1. Rectangles *ABCD* and *EFGH* are similar. Find the length of side *AD*. Explain.

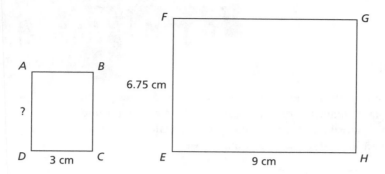
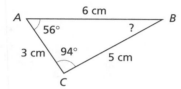

2. Triangles *ABC* and *DEF* are similar.

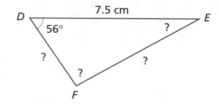

a. By what number do you multiply the length of side *AB* to get the length of side *DE*?

b. Find the missing side lengths and angle measures. Explain.

ACE Homework starts on page 44.

STUDENT PAGE

Notes _____

_____

_____

_____

Applications

1. Look for rep-tile patterns in the designs below. For each design, tell whether the small quadrilaterals are similar to the large quadrilateral. Explain. If the quadrilaterals are similar, give the scale factor from each small quadrilateral to the large quadrilateral.

a.

b.

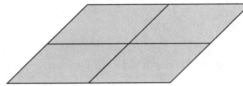

c.

d.

Notes _____

_____

_____

_____

2. Suppose you put together nine copies of a rectangle to make a larger, similar rectangle.

   a. What is the scale factor from the smaller rectangle to the larger rectangle?

   b. How is the area of the larger rectangle related to the area of the smaller rectangle?

3. Suppose you divide a rectangle into 25 smaller rectangles. Each rectangle is similar to the original rectangle.

   a. What is the scale factor from the original rectangle to each of the smaller rectangles?

   b. How is the area of each of the smaller rectangles related to the area of the original rectangle?

4. Look for rep-tile patterns in the designs below. For each design, tell whether the small triangles seem to be similar to the large triangle. Explain. When the triangles are similar, give the scale factor from each small triangle to the large triangle.

   a.

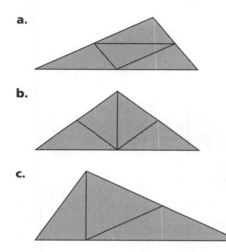

   b.

   c.

   d.

Notes _____

_____

_____

_____

5. Copy polygons A–D onto grid paper. Draw line segments that divide each of the polygons into four congruent polygons that are similar to the original polygon.

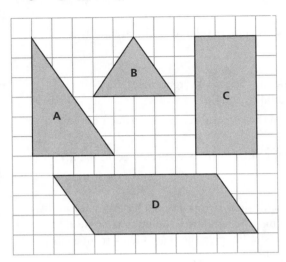

6. a. For rectangles E–G, give the length and width of a different similar rectangle. Explain how you know the new rectangles are similar.

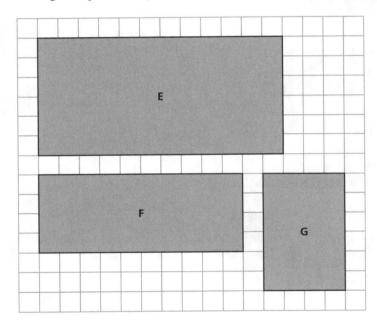

Notes _____

_____

_____

_____

b. Give the scale factor from each original rectangle in part (a) to the similar rectangles you described. Explain what the scale factor tells you about the corresponding lengths, perimeters, and areas.

7. Use the polygons below.

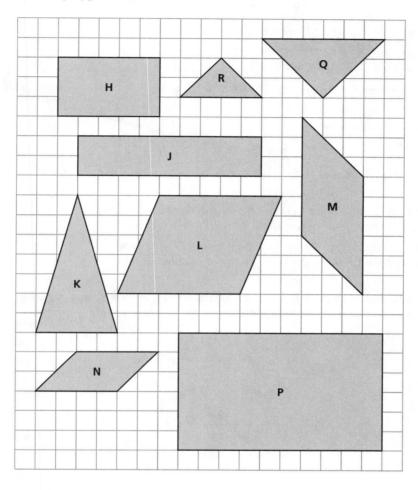

a. List the pairs of similar shapes.

b. For each pair of similar shapes, find the scale factor from the smaller shape to the larger shape.

STUDENT PAGE

Notes _____

_____

_____

_____

8. For parts (a)–(c), use grid paper.

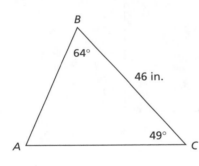

a. Sketch a triangle similar to triangle X with an area that is $\frac{1}{4}$ the area of triangle X.

b. Sketch a rectangle similar to rectangle Y with a perimeter that is 0.5 times the perimeter of rectangle Y.

c. Sketch a parallelogram similar to parallelogram Z with side lengths that are 1.5 times the side lengths of parallelogram Z.

Triangle *ABC* is similar to triangle *PQR*. For Exercises 9–14, use the given side and angle measurements to find the indicated angle measure or side length.

Go Online
PHSchool.com
For: Multiple-Choice
Skills Practice
Web Code: ana-2354

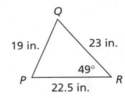

9. angle *A*

10. angle *Q*

11. angle *P*

12. length of side *AB*

13. length of side *AC*

14. perimeter of triangle *ABC*

Notes _____

_____

_____

_____

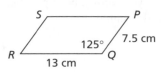
Multiple Choice For Exercises 15–18, use the similar parallelograms below.

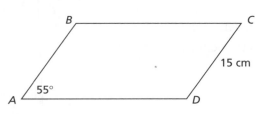

15. What is the measure of angle *D*?

    A. 55°   **B.** 97.5°   **C.** 125°   **D.** 135°

16. What is the measure of angle *R*?

    F. 55°   **G.** 97.5°   **H.** 125°   **J.** 135°

17. What is the measure of angle *S*?

    A. 55°   **B.** 97.5°   **C.** 125°   **D.** 135°

18. What is the length of side *AB* in centimeters?

    F. 3.75   **G.** 13   **H.** 15   **J.** 26

19. Suppose a rectangle B is similar to rectangle A below. If the scale factor from rectangle A to rectangle B is 4, what is the area of rectangle B?

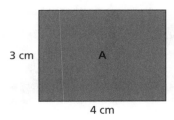

20. Suppose rectangle E has an area of 9 square centimeters and rectangle F has an area of 900 square centimeters. The two rectangles are similar. What is the scale factor from rectangle E to rectangle F?

21. Suppose rectangles X and Y are similar. The dimensions of rectangle X are 5 centimeters by 7 centimeters. The area of rectangle Y is 140 square centimeters. What are the dimensions of rectangle Y?

Investigation 3 Similar Polygons   **49**

Notes _____

_____

_____

_____

Connections

22. In the figure below, lines L_1 and L_2 are parallel.

a. Use what you know about parallel lines to find the measures of angles *a* through *g*.

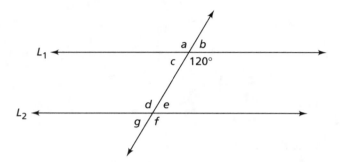

b. When the sum of the measures of two angles is 180°, the angles are **supplementary angles.** For example, angles *a* and *b* above are supplementary angles because they fit together to form a straight line (180°). List all pairs of supplementary angles in the diagram.

23. Suppose you have two supplementary angles (explained above). The measure of one angle is given. Find the measure of the other angle.

a. 160°   **b.** 90°   **c.** $x°$

24. The two right triangles are similar.

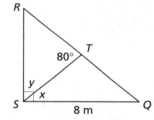

a. Find the length of side *RS*.

b. Find the length of side *RQ*.

c. Suppose the measure of angle *x* is 40°. Find the measure of angle *y*.

Notes _____
_____
_____
_____

d. Find the measure of angle R. Explain how you can find the measure of angle C.

Angle x and angle y are called **complementary angles.** Complementary angles are a pair of angles whose measures add to 90°.

e. Find two more pairs of complementary angles in triangles ABC and QRS besides angles x and y.

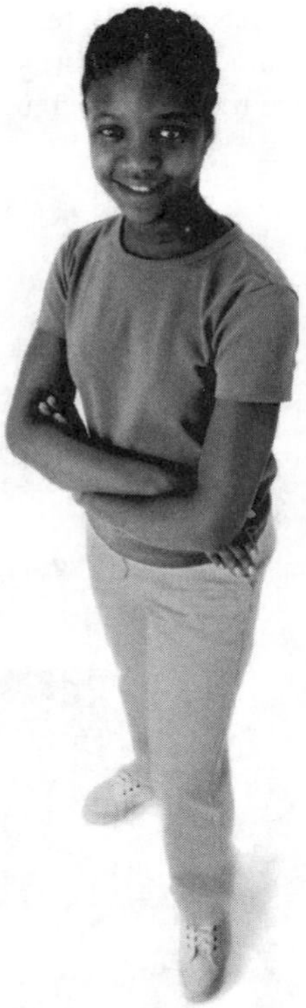

25. For parts (a)–(f), find the number that makes the fractions equivalent.

a. $\frac{1}{2} = \frac{3}{\blacksquare}$

b. $\frac{5}{6} = \frac{\blacksquare}{24}$

c. $\frac{3}{4} = \frac{6}{\blacksquare}$

d. $\frac{8}{12} = \frac{2}{\blacksquare}$

e. $\frac{3}{5} = \frac{\blacksquare}{100}$

f. $\frac{6}{4} = \frac{\blacksquare}{10}$

26. For parts (a)–(f), suppose you copy a figure on a copier using the given size factor. Find the scale factor from the original figure to the copy in decimal form.

a. 200%

b. 50%

c. 150%

d. 125%

e. 75%

f. 25%

27. Write each fraction as a decimal and as a percent.

a. $\frac{2}{5}$

b. $\frac{3}{4}$

c. $\frac{3}{10}$

d. $\frac{1}{4}$

e. $\frac{7}{10}$

f. $\frac{7}{20}$

g. $\frac{4}{5}$

h. $\frac{7}{8}$

i. $\frac{3}{5}$

j. $\frac{15}{20}$

Notes _____

_____

_____

_____

28. For parts (a)–(d), tell whether the figures are mathematically similar. Explain. If the figures are similar, give the scale factor from the left figure to the right figure.

a.

b.

c.

d.

Notes _____

_____

_____

_____

For Exercises 29–31, decide if the statement is true or false. Justify your answer.

29. All squares are similar.

30. All rectangles are similar.

31. If the scale factor between two similar shapes is 1, then the two shapes are the same size. (Note: If two similar figures have a scale factor of 1, they are *congruent*.)

32. a. Suppose the following rectangle is reduced by a scale factor of 50%. What are the dimensions of the reduced rectangle?

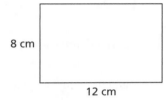

8 cm

12 cm

b. Suppose the reduced rectangle in part (a) is reduced again by a scale factor of 50%. Now, what are the dimensions of the rectangle?

c. How does the reduced rectangle from part (b) compare to the original rectangle from part (a)?

Extensions

33. Trace each shape. Divide each shape into four smaller pieces that are similar to the original shape.

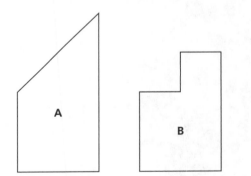

A

B

C

Investigation 3 Similar Polygons   **53**

Notes _____

_____

_____

_____

34. The **midpoint** is a point that divides a line segment into two segments of equal length. Draw a figure on grid paper by following these steps:

Step 1 Draw a square.

Step 2 Mark the midpoint of each side.

Step 3 Connect the midpoints in order with four line segments to form a new figure. (The line segments should not intersect inside the square.)

Step 4 Repeat Steps 2 and 3 three more times. Work with the newest figure each time.

   a. What kind of figure is formed when the midpoints of the sides of a square are connected?

   b. Find the area of the original square.

   c. Find the area of the new figure that is formed at each step.

   d. How do the areas change between successive figures?

   e. Are there any similar figures in your final drawing? Explain.

35. Repeat Exercise 34 using an equilateral triangle.

36. Suppose rectangle A is similar to rectangle B and to rectangle C. Can you conclude that rectangle B is similar to rectangle C? Explain. Use drawings and examples to illustrate your answer.

37. The mathematician Benoit Mandelbrot called attention to the fact that you can subdivide figures to get smaller figures that are mathematically similar to the original. He called these figures *fractals*. A famous example is the Sierpinski triangle.

Notes _____

_____

_____

_____

You can follow these steps to make the Sierpinski triangle.

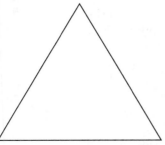

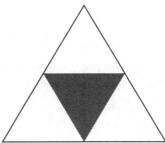

Step 1 Draw a large triangle.

Step 2 Mark the midpoint of each side. Connect the midpoints to form four identical triangles that are similar to the original. Shade the center triangle.

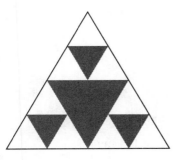

Step 3 For each unshaded triangle, mark the midpoints. Connect them in order to form four identical triangles. Shade the center triangle in each case.

Step 4 Repeat Steps 2 and 3 over and over. To make a real Sierpinski triangle, you need to repeat the process an infinite number of times! This triangle shows five subdivisions.

a. Follow the steps for making the Sierpinski triangle until you subdivide the original triangle three times.

b. Describe any patterns you observe in your figure.

c. Mandelbrot used the term *self-similar* to describe fractals like the Sierpinski triangle. What do you think this term means?

STUDENT PAGE

Notes _____

_____

_____

_____

For Exercises 38–42, read the paragraph below and answer the questions that follow.

When you find the area of a square, you multiply the length of the side by itself. For a square with a side length of 3 units, you multiply 3×3 (or 3^2) to get 9 square units. For this reason, you call 9 the *square* of 3.

Three is called the *square root* of 9. The symbol, "$\sqrt{}$" is used for the square root. This gives the fact family below.

$$3^2 = 9$$
$$\sqrt{9} = 3$$

38. The square has an area of 10 square units. Write the side length of this square using the square root symbol.

39. Multiple Choice What is the square root of 144?

    A. 7   **B.** 12   **C.** 72   **D.** 20,736

40. What is the length of the side of a square with an area of 144 square units?

41. You have learned that if a figure grows by a scale factor of s, the area of the figure grows by a factor of s^2. If the area of a figure grows by a factor of f, what is the scale factor?

42. Find three examples of squares and square roots in the work you have done so far in this unit.

Notes _____

_____

_____

_____

Mathematical Reflections 3

This investigation explored similar polygons and scale factors. These questions will help you summarize what you learned.

Think about your answers to these questions. Discuss your ideas with other students and your teacher. Then write a summary of your findings in your notebook.

1. How can you tell if two polygons are similar?

2. If two polygons are similar, how can you find the scale factor from one polygon to the other? Show specific examples. Describe how you find the scale factor from the smaller figure to the enlarged figure. Then, describe how you find the scale factor from the larger figure to the smaller figure.

3. For parts (a)–(c), what does the scale factor between two similar figures tell you about the given measurements?

   a. side lengths

   b. perimeters

   c. areas

Notes _____

_____

_____

_____

Investigation 3

ACE Assignment Choices

Differentiated Instruction
Solutions for All Learners

Problem 3.1

Core 1, 2
Other *Applications* 3, *Connections* 22–25, *Extensions* 33, 34

Problem 3.2

Core 4–6
Other *Connections* 26–31; *Extensions* 35–37; unassigned choices from previous problems

Problem 3.3

Core 7–18
Other *Applications* 19– 21; *Connections* 32; *Extensions* 38–42; unassigned choices from previous problems

Adapted For suggestions about adapting Exercise 1 and other ACE exercises, see the CMP *Special Needs Handbook*.
Connecting to Prior Units 22–24, 29–31: *Shapes and Designs*; 25: *Bits and Pieces II*; 26–28: *Bits and Pieces III*

Applications

1. **a.** No, they are not similar. One of the small figures is a square, so it does not have the same shape as the original rectangle, which is *not* a square.

   b. Yes, they are similar because their corresponding interior angles are congruent. The side lengths of the larger shape are double that of the smaller shape. The scale factor is 2.

   c. Yes, they are similar because their corresponding interior angles are congruent. The side lengths of the larger shape are triple that of the smaller shape. The scale factor is 3.

   d. Yes, they are similar because their corresponding interior angles are

congruent. The side lengths of the larger shape are double that of the smaller one. The scale factor is 2.

2. **a.** 3

   b. The area of the large rectangle is 9 times the area of the small rectangle. You might suggest that students provide a sketch to verify their answer.

3. **a.** $\frac{1}{5}$

   b. The area of the small rectangle is $\frac{1}{25}$ the area of the large rectangle. You might suggest that students provide a sketch to verify their answer.

4. **a.** The small triangles are similar to the large triangle. The scale factor is 2.

   b. The small triangles on the left and right corners are similar to the large triangle with scale factor $\frac{1}{2}$ but the other two small triangles are not similar.

   c. None of the small triangles are similar to the large one.

   d. The small triangles are similar to the large triangle. The scale factor is 2. (Compare this figure with the figure of part (a). They look different but their constructions are essentially the same.)

5.

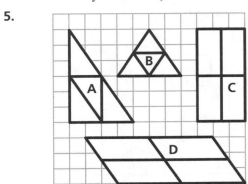

6. Answers will vary.

Rectangle E:

a. Any rectangle with dimensions $6k$ by $12k$, where k is any positive number, is similar to rectangle E, because the ratio of the corresponding sides will be the same.

b. The scale factor from rectangle E to the new rectangle is k.

Rectangle F:

a. Any rectangle with dimensions $4k$ by $10k$, where k is any positive number, is similar to rectangle F, because the ratio of the corresponding sides will be the same.

b. The scale factor from rectangle F to the new rectangle is k.

Rectangle G:

a. Any rectangle with dimensions $6k$ by $4k$, where k is any positive number, is similar to rectangle G, because the ratio of the corresponding sides will be the same.

b. The scale factor from rectangle G to the new rectangle is k.

7. a. Rectangles H and P, triangles R and Q, and parallelograms M and N.

b. The scale factor from H to P is 2, from R to Q is $\frac{3}{2}$, and from N to M is $\frac{3}{2}$.

8. a.

base: 2.5
height: 2.5

b.

base: 1.5
height: 2

c.

base: 9
height: 3

9. angle $A = 67°$ 10. angle $Q = 64°$

11. angle $P = 67°$ 12. side $AB = 38$ in.

13. side $AC = 45$ in.

14. perimeter $ABC = 129$ in.

15. C   16. F   17. C   18. H

19. 192 cm^2 20. 10   21. 10 cm by 14 cm

Connections

22. a. $a = 120°, b = 60°, c = 60°, d = 120°, e = 60°, f = 120°, g = 60°$

b. Student may list any combination of angles as long as the pairs sum to 180°. See answer in Question A. For example: angles a and b, a and c, a and e are all pairs of supplementary angles.

23. a. 20°   b. 90°   c. $180° - x$

24. a. 6 m; since the scale factor from the smaller to the larger is 2, side RS is 6 m.

b. 10 m; 10 m = 5 m × 2.

c. 50°

d. 50°; since the sum of the angles in triangle STR is 180° and two angles are known, 80° and angle $y = 50°$, we know that angle R must be $180° - (80° + 50°) = 50°$. Since the triangles are similar angle C is also 50° since it corresponds to angle R.

e. Angles R and Q, angles C and B, angles R and B, and angles Q and C are all complementary.

25. Students may have a couple of ways of solving these problems. Below is one possible solution for part (d). Similar thinking can apply to all parts.

The scale factor that takes 8 to 2 is $\frac{1}{4}$.

Therefore, I need $\frac{1}{4}$ of 12, which is 3.

a. 6   b. 20   c. 8

d. 3   e. 60   f. 15

26. a. 2   b. 0.5   c. 1.5

d. 1.25   e. 0.75   f. 0.25

27. a. $\frac{2}{5} = \frac{40}{100} = 40\% = 0.4$

b. $\frac{3}{4} = \frac{75}{100} = 75\% = 0.75$

c. $\frac{3}{10} = \frac{30}{100} = 30\% = 0.3$

d. $\frac{1}{4} = \frac{25}{100} = 25\% = 0.25$

e. $\frac{7}{10} = \frac{70}{100} = 70\% = 0.7$

f. $\frac{7}{20} = \frac{35}{100} = 35\% = 0.35$

g. $\frac{4}{5} = \frac{80}{100} = 80\% = 0.8$

h. $\frac{7}{8} = \frac{87.5}{100} = 87.5\% = 0.875$

i. $\frac{3}{5} = \frac{60}{100} = 60\% = 0.6$

j. $\frac{15}{20} = \frac{75}{100} = 75\% = 0.75$

28. a. The birds are not similar since the ratio of base length of the larger figure to the base length of the smaller figure is not the same as the ratio of the height of the larger figure to the height of the smaller figure. Another possible answer is: the width of the first figure is reduced more than half while the height is reduced only about 80%. Because the two reduction scales are different, the figures are not similar.

b. The figures are similar because the ratio of base length of the larger figure to the base length of the smaller figure is the same as the ratio of the height of the larger figure to the height of the smaller figure. Another possible answer is: For both width and height the same reduction scale is applied; so, the figures are similar. The scale factor is about 0.7.

c. The figures are not similar because the height of the first figure is reduced by about 56%, while the width is reduced by a smaller percent.

d. The lighthouses are not similar because the height is reduced but the width is enlarged.

29. True. The corresponding angles will always be equal to each other since they are all 90° and the ratio of any two sides of a square is 1. Alternatively, students might notice that if they choose any side of one square and any side of the other square, the scale factor must be the same, regardless of which sides they chose.

30. False. While the angles of any two rectangles will be the same (90°), it is not the case that the ratios of sides will be equal.

31. True. The fact that there is a consistent scale factor implies that the shapes are similar, and so the corresponding angle measures are equal. The fact that the scale factor is 1 means that the side lengths are unchanged. Equal angle measures and equal side lengths yield congruent figures.

32. a. 4 cm by 6 cm **b.** 2 cm by 3 cm

c. The dimensions are $\frac{1}{4}$ of the lengths of the original dimensions. (**Note:** One thing students often have difficulty with conceptually is that multiplying by a number smaller than 1 reduces the original. Multiplication has been taught as a "makes larger" operation in the elementary grades. This concept makes the new world of rational numbers harder for students to enter.)

Suppose you take a piece of rope that is 12 m long and reduce its length by a factor of 0.5 (or $\frac{1}{2}$). The new length of the rope is 6 m. Suppose you reduced the new length of the rope by a factor of 0.5 again. The length of the rope is 3 m. A physical model of what is happening to the rope is shown.

3 m   3 m   6 m

Extensions

33.

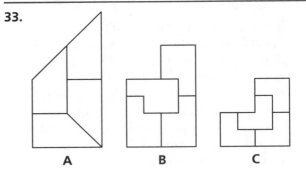

A   B   C

34.

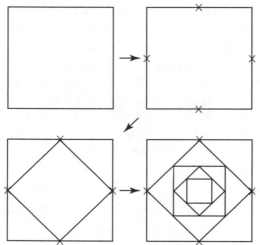

a. Another square.

b. Answers will vary.

c. Answers will vary, but each square should be $\frac{1}{2}$ the area of the square before it.

d. At each step, the area of the new square is $\frac{1}{2}$ the area of the previous square.

e. All the squares are similar to each other. Also, all the triangles are similar to each other.

35. a. Another equilateral triangle is formed.

b. Answers will vary.

c. The answer should be $\frac{1}{4}$ the area of the original triangle.

d. At each step, the area of the new triangle is $\frac{1}{4}$ the area of the previous triangle.

e. All the triangles in the figure are similar to each other.

36. Yes, rectangle B is similar to rectangle C. Possible explanation: Because rectangle A is similar to rectangle B, the ratio of the short side of rectangle A to the long side of rectangle A is the same as the ratio of the short side of rectangle B to the long side of rectangle B. Because rectangle B is similar to rectangle C, the ratio of the short side of rectangle C to the long side of rectangle C must equal this same ratio. This means the ratio between sides in rectangle C equals the ratio between sides in rectangle A, making rectangles C and A similar.

37. a.

b. Some of the patterns in the picture: At each step, the side length of the new triangle is $\frac{1}{2}$ the side length of the triangle of the previous step. The area of the new triangle is $\frac{1}{4}$ the area of the triangle of the previous step. The number of new shaded triangles obtained at each step follows the following pattern: $1, 3, 9, 27, \ldots, 3^n$ (for the $n + 1$st step).

c. "Self-similar" means that the original figure is similar to a smaller part of itself. You can apply a reduction to the original figure and obtain a new figure that is the same as a part of the original figure.

38. $\sqrt{10}$ **39.** B

40. The side length of the square is 12 units.

41. $\sqrt{f}$

42. Answers will vary. Possible answers: For rep-tiles, when we used a scale factor of 2, we needed 4 (the square of 2) tiles to make the larger tile. In Problem 3.3, when we needed a rectangle whose area was $\frac{1}{4}$ of the original, we used a scale factor of $\frac{1}{2} = \sqrt{\frac{1}{4}}$. In Problem 2.3, when we compared the areas of similar rectangles, we found that they grew by the square of the scale factor.

Possible Answers to Mathematical Reflections

1. When two polygons are similar, they must have the same shape, but their sizes might be different. The two polygons are similar if their corresponding angles have equal measures, and the scale factor between their corresponding sides is the same (or the side lengths of one figure are multiplied by the same number to get the corresponding side lengths in a second figure).

2. The ratio of a side of the second polygon to its corresponding side in the first polygon gives the scale factor from the first to the second polygon. Check students' examples.

3. **a.** The scale factor tells us how many times longer (or shorter if less than 1) the sides of the image are than the sides of the original.

   b. The scale factor tells us how many times longer (or shorter if less than 1) the perimeter of the image is than the perimeter of the original.

   c. The scale factor *squared* tells us how many times as large (or as small, if less than 1) the area of the image is compared to the area of the original.

Investigation 4 — Similarity and Ratios

Mathematical and Problem-Solving Goals

- Use ratios of corresponding sides within a figure to determine whether two figures are similar
- Use ratios to identify similar triangles
- Use ratios of corresponding sides or scale factors to find missing lengths in similar figures

Mathematics Background

For background on equivalent ratios and similarity of triangles, see page 6.

Note of Caution About Using Rulers to Find Lengths: In the beginning of the unit students use informal measurements to gain intuitions about similar figures. However, students need to be aware that pictures of an object or shape may not be drawn to scale. Measuring lengths and angles in a picture may not (and often does not) work to show that two figures are or are not similar. One of the main goals of this unit is to help students develop techniques that do not rely on direct measurement, but rather on properties of similar figures. Sometimes figures are marked with "not drawn to scale." For the most part, the art should be representative of the conditions given for the object.

Occasionally students will be asked to measure attributes. For example, in Investigation 5 students will measure the lengths of shadows to find the height of buildings or trees. They then make sketches of the triangles formed by the object and its shadow and label these figures with the measurements. They use properties of similar figures to find the missing height.

As you move through the unit watch for students who are trying to find missing measurements by measuring. Remind them that figures may not be drawn to scale and help them to use properties.

Summary of Problems

Problem 4.1 Ratios Within Similar Parallelograms

Students first determine which parallelograms are similar and then they compare the ratios of corresponding lengths in one parallelogram with the corresponding ratio of corresponding lengths in the other.

Problem 4.2 Ratios Within Similar Triangles

Students repeat the process in Problem 4.1 with triangles. Students also compare the information that is given by a scale factor or by the ratios of corresponding sides.

Problem 4.3 Finding Missing Parts

Students use the information about the ratios of corresponding lengths within a figure to find missing measurements in two similar polygons. Ratios formed this way for similar figures are equal.

	Suggested Pacing	Materials for Students	Materials for Teachers	ACE Assignments
All	$3\frac{1}{2}$ days	Centimeter and inch rulers (1 per student), angle rulers or protractors (1 per group or pair)	Transparent centimeter ruler (optional), angle ruler (optional)	
4.1	1 day		Transparencies 4.1A–C	1, 3–4, 15–26, 37
4.2	1 day	Labsheet 4.2 (1 per student)	Transparency of Labsheet 4.2 (optional)	2, 27–30, 35, 36, 38
4.3	1 day	Labsheet 4.3 (1 per student)	Transparencies 4.3A–C (optional)	5–14, 31–34, 39
MR	$\frac{1}{2}$ day			

Ratios Within Similar Parallelograms

Goal

- Use ratios of corresponding sides within a figure to determine whether two figures are similar

Launch 4.1

Put Transparency 4.1A on the overhead from the Getting Ready. Tell the class the images were formed on a computer.

Suggested Questions

- *How do you think this technique produced these variations of the original shape?* (Answers may vary.)

- *If we think of these images as we did the Wumps, which ones would be in the same family? How do you know?* (The image on the right because she has the same shape of the original. The figure on the left is too tall and thin. The figure in the middle is too short and wide.)

- *Are these the similar figures?* (The image on the right appears to be similar to the original figure.)

- *These figures don't have straight sides to measure as the Wumps did. What can we measure?* (You could measure their heights and widths.)

Put up the following table.

Figure	Height (cm)	Width (cm)	Ratio: Height to Width	Ratio
Original	10	8	10 to 8	
Left	8	3	8 to 3	
Middle	3	6	3 to 6	
Right	5	4	5 to 4	

- *What patterns do you notice about these measures?* (Some students might compare length to length and width to width. This comparison gives the scale factor. Students might notice that each measurement of the original figure is twice the measurement of the corresponding lengths in the figure on the right.)

Fill in the last column of your table with the ratio written in fraction form.

Tell the class that, just as we talk about equivalent fractions, we can talk about equivalent ratios. In this example, the height-to-width ratios for the original and the image on the right's are equivalent. If the ratios are not equivalent, the figures cannot be similar.

Ratio
$\frac{10}{8} = 1.25$
$\frac{8}{3} = 2.\bar{6}$
$\frac{3}{6} = 0.5$
$\frac{5}{4} = 1.25$

Suggested Questions Ask:

- *A new figure is created that is similar to the original girl. The height of the girl in this figure is 15 cm. What is her width?* (Students might suggest various ways to find the width—perhaps finding scale factor first. Some might suggest using ratios.)

If students don't suggest using ratios, ask:

- *How could you use ratios to find the width of the girl in the figure?* (Write equivalent fractions: $\frac{10}{8} = \frac{15}{\blacksquare}$. To make these two fractions equal, students might rewrite the first one as $\frac{5}{4}$ and reason that since the numerator has been multiplied by 3, the denominator must be multiplied by 3. So, the new width is 12. Also note that $\frac{5}{4}, \frac{10}{8}$, and $\frac{15}{12}$ are all equal to 1.25. Students may have other ways to find the missing number.)

- *In this problem, you will find ratios of short side to long side for each rectangle. Then you will compare the information that the ratios and the scale factors give about similar figures.*

Let students work in pairs.

Explore 4.1

As you move around, check to make sure that students are writing correct ratios and provide any necessary help in keeping track of the place of corresponding measures in the ratios.

Be sure that students label their work in some way such as length to width or width to length.

- *Can you form a different ratio?* (Yes, length to width if width to length was written or vice versa.)

- *How do these two ratios compare?* (They are reciprocals of each other.)

Summarize 4.1

Discuss the answers. Be sure that students compare the ratios of corresponding side lengths in similar figures. This is an opportunity to review or assess their understanding of equivalent fractions.

Suggested Questions

- *Why is it necessary to check angle measures in non-rectangular parallelograms, but not in rectangles?*

- *Can you show two non-rectangular parallelograms that have equal corresponding angle measures but are not similar?* (One way to show this is to draw a parallelogram and extend a pair of sides. The angles remain congruent, but the side lengths of two sides have changed and the other two side lengths have not changed.)

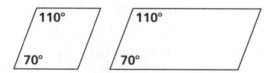

- *Describe the criteria that is necessary for two parallelograms to be similar.* (Corresponding angle measures are equal and ratios of corresponding sides lengths are equal. In place of ratios students might suggest the scale factor between corresponding shapes must be the same. Both criteria for side lengths are correct.)

If your class is ready, you might ask about the ratios of the height of original to the height of the similar figure and the width of the original to the width of the similar figure. These ratios give the scale factor from the smaller figure to the larger figure.

Use this summary to lead into the next problem, which is identical to this problem except it uses triangles. You might want to assign this as homework and discuss it in class the next day.

Check for Understanding

Use ratios of corresponding side lengths and corresponding angle measures to determine if the two parallelograms are similar.

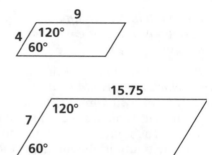

4.1 Ratios Within Similar Parallelograms

Mathematical Goal

- Use ratios of corresponding sides within a figure to determine whether two figures are similar

Launch

Put a transparency of the picture of the girl and its images on the overhead. Tell the class the images were formed on the computer.

- *How do you think this technique produced these variations of the original shape?*
- *If we think of these girls as we did the Wumps, which ones would be in the same family? How do you know?*
- *Are these similar figures?*
- *These figures don't have straight sides to measure as the Wumps did. What can we measure?*

After you have discussed these questions, put up a chart with the measurements for the original figure and the three images.

- *What patterns do you notice about these measures?*

Fill in the last column with the ratio written in fraction form.

Tell the class that, just as we talk about equivalent fractions, we can talk about equivalent ratios. Have students solve a couple of simple ratio problems to get started.

- *A new figure is created that is similar to the original girl. The height of the girl in this figure is 15 cm. What is her width?*
- *How could you use ratios to find the width of the man in the figure?*

Let students work in pairs.

Materials
- Transparencies 4.1 A-C

Vocabulary
- ratio
- equivalent ratio

Explore

As you move around check to make sure that students are writing correct ratios and provide any necessary help in keeping track of the place of corresponding measures in the ratios.

Summarize

Discuss the answers. Discuss the relationship between these internal ratios and the scale factor. Be sure that students compare the ratios of corresponding side lengths in similar figures. Review or assess their understanding of equivalent fractions.

If your class is ready, you might ask about the ratios of the height of the original to the height of the similar figure and the width of the original to the width of the similar figure. These ratios give the scale factor from the smaller figure to the larger figure.

Materials
- Student notebooks

continued on next page

Use this summary to lead into the next problem, which is identical to this problem except it uses triangles. You might want to assign this as homework and discuss it in class the next day.

Use the Check for Understanding.

ACE Assignment Guide for Problem 4.1

Core 1, 3–4, 15–20
Other *Connections* 21–26, *Extensions* 37

Adapted For suggestions about adapting ACE exercises, see the CMP *Special Needs Handbook*.
Connecting to Prior Units 15–25: *Bits and Pieces I*; 26: *Bits and Pieces III*

Answers to Problem 4.1

A. 1. rectangle A : $\frac{12}{20}$ = 0.6;

rectangle B : $\frac{6}{10}$ = 0.6;

rectangle C : $\frac{9}{15}$ = 0.6;

rectangle D : $\frac{6}{20}$ = 0.3

2. The ratio of the length of the short side to the length of the long side is the same for all three similar rectangles. The rectangle that is not similar to the others has a different ratio. (Rectangles A, B, and C are similar to each other.)

3. Possible answers: The scale factor from rectangle B to rectangle A is 2. The scale factor from rectangle B to rectangle C is 1.5. The scale factor from rectangle C to rectangle A is $\frac{4}{3}$. The scale factor identifies how many times as great the side lengths and the perimeter are for the similar figures.

4. If they are similar figures, their scale factor and ratio of corresponding side lengths will be the same.

B. 1. parallelogram E : $\frac{10}{8}$ = 1.25;

parallelogram F : $\frac{7.5}{6}$ = 1.25;

parallelogram G : $\frac{6}{4.8}$ = 1.25

All the ratios are equivalent.

2. Parallelograms F and G are similar, because their angles have the same measure and the ratio of their sides is the same.

C. No! One must also check the corresponding angle measures to see if they are congruent. As seen above, E and F have the same ratio, but they are not similar.

Ratios Within Similar Triangles

Goal

- Use ratios to identify similar triangles

Launch 4.2

Display Transparency 4.2. Tell the class that this problem is similar to the last problem. They are to identify which triangles are similar and then look at the ratios of corresponding lengths in the similar triangles.

Suggested Questions Ask:

- *Is it enough just to check relationships amongst side lengths?* (No. corresponding angle measures must also be equal.)

- *Look at triangle A. Only two angle measures are given. How can you find the missing angle measure?* (The sum of the angle measures in a triangle is 180°. We can use this fact to find the missing angle.)

Students can work in pairs.

Explore 4.2

Look for ways that students are forming the ratios. Continue to ask students questions that force them to be clear about what is being compared in each ratio.

Note: Be sure students align corresponding angles and sides when comparing.

Going Further:

You might challenge students to find the ratios of corresponding lengths across two similar figures.

Suggested Question

- *What information does this ratio give for two similar figures?* (The scale factor.)

Summarize 4.2

Discuss answers. Be sure to record all the ratios. For example, side a to side b and side b to side a.

In triangles A and D some students may form the ratio, $\frac{7.3}{12.5} = \frac{18.3}{31.3}$. Others may write it as $\frac{12.5}{7.3} = \frac{31.3}{18.3}$. Help students to understand that the order they choose to compare (e.g., height : width vs. width : height) doesn't matter, as long as the comparisons are consistent.

Suggested Question Ask:

- *Does it make a difference if we write $\frac{7.3}{12.5} = \frac{18.3}{31.3}$ instead of $\frac{12.5}{7.3} = \frac{31.3}{18.3}$?* (No, as long as we keep corresponding measures in the numerators and corresponding measures in the denominators.)

If you talked about ratios of corresponding side lengths across two shapes in the last problem, you can continue the conversation with triangles. These ratios give the scale factor from the smaller figure to the larger figure. Pick a pair of similar triangles and ask students to sketch two more triangles that are similar to them, including side lengths. Have them check the ratios of the side lengths. ACE Exercise 35 discusses these ratios for triangles and would provide more practice with this idea.

Note: Some students may observe that for triangles to be similar we only need to check corresponding angle measures. A discussion on why this is true is on page 7.

Mathematics Background

For background on corresponding angle measures in similarity, see page 7.

Check for Understanding

Sketch the following three triangles on the overhead. Ask the class to use ratios and angle measures to determine which are similar.

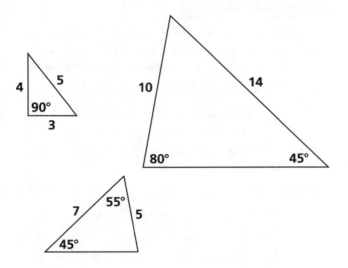

Ask the class to sketch another triangle that is similar to one of the triangles.

4.2 Ratios Within Similar Triangles

Mathematical Goal

• Use ratios to identify similar triangles

Launch

Display Transparency 4.2. Tell the class that this problem is similar to the last problem. They are to identify which triangles are similar and then use the ratios of corresponding lengths to find missing side lengths. Remind students that they also need to check that corresponding angles are congruent.

Students can work in pairs.

Materials
• Transparency 4.2
• Labsheet 4.2

Explore

Look for ways that students are forming the ratios. Continue to ask students questions that force them to be clear about what is being compared in each ratio.

You might challenge students to find the ratios of corresponding lengths across two similar figures and ask,

• *What information does this ratio give for two similar figures?*

Materials

Summarize

Discuss answers.

Help students to understand that the order they choose to compare (e.g. height : width vs. width : height) doesn't matter, as long as the comparisons are consistent.

• *Does it make a difference if we write $\frac{7.3}{12.5} = \frac{18.3}{31.3}$ instead of $\frac{12.5}{7.3} = \frac{31.3}{18.3}$?*

Pick a pair of similar triangles and ask students to sketch two more triangles that are similar to them, including side lengths. Have them check the ratios of the side lengths.

Use the Check for Understanding.

Materials
• Student notebooks

ACE Assignment Guide
for Problem 4.2

Differentiated
Instruction
Solutions for All Learners

Core 2, 27

Other *Connections* 28–30; *Extensions* 35, 36, 38;
unassigned choices from previous problems

Adapted For suggestions about adapting ACE
exercises, see the CMP *Special Needs Handbook*.

Connecting to Prior Units 27, 29–30: *Covering and Surrounding*; 28: *Shapes and Designs*

Answers to Problem 4.2

A. Triangles A, C, and D are similar. The corresponding angle measures and ratios between the corresponding sides are the same. (Note that the students have to use the fact that the sum of the angles in a triangle are 180°.) Students may find various scale factors. The scale factors include:

from A to C is 1.5 and from C to A is $\frac{2}{3}$

from A to D is 2.5 and from D to A is 0.4

from C to D is $\frac{5}{3}$ and from D to C is 0.6

B. 1. In order to keep track of work, students can label the vertices in each of the similar triangles.

Triangle A: $\frac{7.3}{12.5} \approx 0.58, \frac{7.3}{9} \approx 0.81$

Triangle B: $\frac{6}{8.8} \approx 0.68, \frac{6}{7.6} \approx 0.79$

Triangle C: $\frac{11}{18.8} \approx 0.58, \frac{11}{13.5} \approx 0.81$

Triangle D: $\frac{18.3}{31.3} \approx 0.58, \frac{18.3}{22.5} \approx 0.81$

2. The ratios of corresponding side lengths of similar triangles are equal. See answers for corresponding ratios above.

3. In the case of triangles A and B one can think that shortest sides correspond to each other and the longest sides correspond to each other. Then looking at the ratio for shortest side to longest side in

triangle A: $\frac{7.3}{12.5} = 0.58$ versus

triangle B: $\frac{6}{8.8} \approx 0.68$, one can see that they

are not the same. You will usually get non-equivalent ratios for non-similar triangles. However, for some non-similar triangles some of the corresponding ratios, but not all, may be equivalent.

4.3 Finding Missing Parts

Goal

- Use ratios of corresponding sides or scale factors to find missing lengths in similar figures

Caution on Cross-Multiplication

There may be some temptation at this point to introduce a method called "cross multiplication." Past experience shows that students who use this method very often misuse it or make mistakes. But more importantly, cross multiplication can interfere with the development of proportional reasoning. To find the missing lengths using equivalent ratios, students do not need any new information or new algorithms. They will apply their understanding of equivalent fractions—a critical part of developing understanding of ratios and proportions. And cross-multiplication does not save time! Using the concept of equivalent fractions is as quick and is less likely to lead to misconceptions and mistakes and it builds on prior understandings.

By the end of this investigation, students should be comfortable with finding lengths of missing sides using scale factors or ratios within a figure. Additionally, they should be able to correctly use the language of *scale factor* and *ratio*.

Launch 4.3

Show the students the pair of similar triangles in Question B.

Suggested Questions Ask:

- *Which sides are corresponding across the triangles?* (Students might use the strategy of small to small and large to large, with the third side in between. You might also compare the angles. They could label the angles in some way to show which ones correspond. This might help them determine the correct corresponding side lengths.)

- *How can you find the missing side length?* (Students should be able to describe how they can use either scale factors or internal ratios to find the missing side lengths.)

Let the class work in pairs. Question E could be assigned as homework.

Explore 4.3

Establishing which sides correspond may still be problematic for students. Use some of the suggestions in the launch to guide students. Try to do this by asking questions.

Suggested Question Point to a side in one figure and ask:

- *Which side does it correspond to in the other triangle? How do you know?*

You could also have students trace one of the triangles, cut it out, and turn it to match the orientation of the other one.

Summarize 4.3

Discuss the answers. Be sure to let different groups share their strategies, particularly for Question E. Be sure that students are using the concept of equivalent fractions or scale factor to find the missing lengths. They may use language like "find common denominators . . ." or "find the number that I must multiply the numerator and denominator by to get an equivalent fraction whose denominator is . . ." or "find the corresponding side length and multiply (divide) by the scale factor."

- *Find the perimeter of one of the parallelograms in Question D. Use the perimeter and your knowledge of similar figures to determine the perimeter of the second parallelogram. (Students can use ratios or scale factors.)*

- *Find the perimeter of one of the triangles in Question B. Use the perimeter and your knowledge of similar figures to determine the perimeter of the second triangle. (Students can use ratios or scale factors.)*

Check for Understanding

Put up two similar rectangles with two side labels with measures on one and the corresponding sides labeled—one with a measure and the other with a question mark. Ask students to find a missing side length.

Suggested Question Then, ask:

- *What is the area of the two rectangles? What is the perimeter of the two rectangles?*

Repeat for two similar triangles.

4.3 Finding Missing Parts

PACING 1 day

Mathematical Goal

- Use ratios of corresponding sides or scale factors to find missing lengths in similar figures

Launch

Show the students the pair of similar triangles in Question B.

- *Which sides are corresponding?*

Compare the angles. Label the angles in some way to show which ones correspond. This might help them determine the correct corresponding side lengths.

- *How can you find the missing side length?*

Then ask students for another method. Students should be able to describe how they can use either scale factors or internal ratios to find the missing side lengths.

Have students work in pairs.

Materials
- Transparency 4.3A
- Labsheet 4.3

Explore

Establishing which sides correspond may still be problematic for students. Guide students by asking questions.

- *Which side does this side correspond to in the other triangle? How do you know?*

You could also have students trace one of the triangles, cut it out, and turn it to match the orientation of the other one.

Summarize

Discuss the answers. Be sure to let different groups share their strategies, particularly for Question E. Be sure that students are using the concept of equivalent fractions to find the missing lengths.

Use the Check for Understanding.

Materials
- Transparencies 4.3B and 4.3C
- Student notebooks

ACE Assignment Guide
for Problem 4.3

Differentiated
Instruction
Solutions for All Learners

Core 5–12
Other *Applications* 13–14; *Connections* 31–34;
Extensions 39; unassigned choices from previous
problems

Adapted For suggestions about adapting Exercise
13 and other ACE exercises, see the CMP *Special
Needs Handbook*.
Connecting to Prior Units 31: *Data About Us*;
32–33: *How Likely Is It?*

Answers to Problem 4.3

A. $x = 10$ cm. One possible answer: the scale
factor from the small to the large triangle is 2.
Therefore, x will be 2 times its corresponding
side. $x = 2 \times 5 = 10$.

B. 13.75 cm. The ratio of the longest side to the
second longest side in the small triangle is $\frac{6.2}{5.5}$.
The corresponding ratio in the other triangle
is $\frac{15.5}{x}$. Find the value of x that will make these
ratios equivalent. $x = 13.75$. Students can also
find the value for x by using the scale factor of
0.4 from small to large and dividing 5.5 by 0.4.

C. $x = 2.5$ cm. Compare the ratios of the sides:
$\frac{x}{1.5} = \frac{10}{6}$ and find the value of x that will make
these ratios equivalent. Or find the scale
factor (4) from small to large and divide it
into 10 to get 2.5.

D. $x = 41.25$ m. Compare the ratios of the sides:
$\frac{18.75}{12.5} = \frac{x}{27.5}$ and find the value of x that will
make these ratios equivalent. Another way of
solving for x is using the scale factor of the
smaller parallelogram to the larger
parallelogram, which is 2.2. One simply
multiplies 18.75 by 2.2 to get 41.25.

Angle $a = 112°$, angle $b = 68°$,
angle $c = 112°$, angle $d = 112°$,
angle $e = 68°$, angle $f = 112°$

E. 1. $x = 1$ in. Find the value of x that will
make this an equivalent ratio: $\frac{8}{14} = \frac{x}{1.75}$.
Note: The first ratio compares the top side
of the smaller figure to the top side of the
larger figure. However, students can choose
any corresponding sides for the first ratio.
The easiest way to see this with ratios is to
look at the bottom left corner and set up
the equation $\frac{x}{2} = \frac{1.75}{3.5}$. Since $\frac{1.75}{3.5} = \frac{1}{2}$, x is 1.

2. $y = 7$ in. Multiply the scale factor (1.75) by
4 to get y.

3. The area of the small figure is 40 in.^{2}.

4. The area of the large figure is 122.5 in.^{2}.
The scale factor is 1.75. Therefore, the area
of the larger figure will be
$40 \times 1.75 \times 1.75 = 122.5$ in.^{2}.

The student edition pages for this investigation begin on the next page.

Notes _____

_____

_____

_____

Similarity and Ratios

You can enhance a report or story by adding photographs, drawings, or diagrams. Once you place a graphic in an electronic document, you can enlarge, reduce, or move it. In most programs, clicking on a graphic causes it to appear inside a frame with buttons along the sides, like the figure below.

You can change the size and shape of the image by grabbing and dragging the buttons.

STUDENT PAGE

Notes _____

_____

_____

_____

Here are examples of the image after it has been resized.

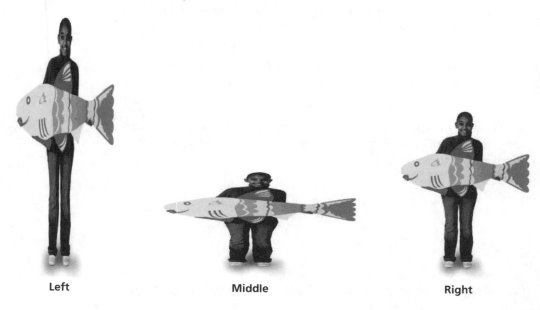

Left   Middle   Right

Getting Ready for Problem 4.1

- How do you think this technique produced these variations of the original shape?
- Which of these images appears to be similar to the original? Why?

One way to describe and compare shapes is by using **ratios.** A ratio is a comparison of two quantities such as two lengths. The original figure is about 10 centimeters tall and 8 centimeters wide. You say, "the *ratio* of height to width is 10 to 8."

This table gives the ratio of height to width for the images.

Image Information

Figure	Height (cm)	Width (cm)	Height to Width Ratio
Original	10	8	10 to 8
Left	8	3	8 to 3
Middle	3	6	3 to 6
Right	5	4	5 to 4

- What do you observe about the ratios of height to width in the similar figures?

STUDENT PAGE

Notes _____

_____

_____

_____

The comparisons "10 to 8" and "5 to 4" are **equivalent ratios.** Equivalent ratios name the same number. In both cases, if you write the ratio of height to width as a decimal, you get the same number.

$$10 \div 8 = 1.25 \qquad\qquad 5 \div 4 = 1.25$$

The same is true if you write the ratio of width to height as a decimal.

"8 to 10"   "4 to 5"

$$8 \div 10 = 0.8 \qquad\qquad 4 \div 5 = 0.8$$

Equivalence of ratios is a lot like equivalence of fractions. In fact, ratios are often written in the form of fractions. You can express equivalent ratios with equations like these:

$$\frac{10}{8} = \frac{5}{4}$$

$$\frac{8}{10} = \frac{4}{5}$$

4.1 Ratios Within Similar Parallelograms

When two figures are similar, you know there is a scale factor that relates each length in one figure to the corresponding length in the other. You can also find a ratio between any two lengths in a figure. This ratio will describe the relationship between the corresponding lengths in a similar figure. You will explore this relationship in the next problem.

When you work with the diagrams in this investigation, assume that all measurements are in centimeters. Many of the drawings are not shown at actual size.

Notes _____

_____

_____

_____

A. The lengths of two sides are given for each rectangle.

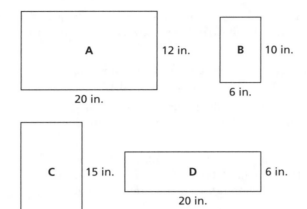

1. For each rectangle, find the ratio of the length of a short side to the length of a long side.

2. What do you notice about the ratios in part (1) for similar rectangles? About the ratios for non-similar rectangles?

3. For two similar rectangles, find the scale factor from the smaller rectangle to the larger rectangle. What information does the scale factor give about two similar figures?

4. Compare the information given by the scale factor to the information given by the ratios of side lengths.

B. 1. For each parallelogram, find the ratio of the length of a longer side to the length of a shorter side. How do the ratios compare?

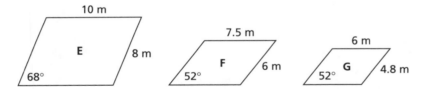

2. Which of the parallelograms are similar? Explain.

C. If the ratio of adjacent side lengths in one parallelogram is equal to the ratio of the corresponding side lengths in another, can you say that the parallelograms are similar? Explain.

ACE Homework starts on page 66.

STUDENT PAGE

Notes _____

_____

_____

_____

4.2 Ratios Within Similar Triangles

Since all rectangles contain four 90° angles, you can show that rectangles are similar just by comparing side lengths. You now know two ways to show that rectangles are similar.

(1) Show that the scale factors between corresponding side lengths are equal. (compare length to length and width to width)

(2) Show that the ratios of corresponding sides within each shape are equal. (compare length to width in one rectangle and length to width in the other)

However, comparing only side lengths of a non-rectangular parallelogram or a triangle is not enough to understand its shape. In this problem, you will use angle measures and side-length ratios to find similar triangles.

Notes _____

_____

_____

_____

For Questions A and B, use the triangles below. Side lengths are approximate.

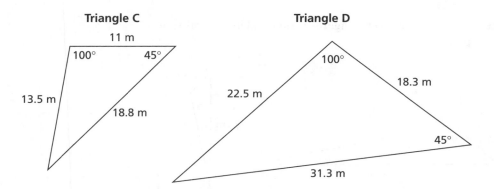

Triangle A

7.3 m   9 m

45°   35°

12.5 m

Triangle B

8.8 m

42°   58°

7.6 m   6 m

Triangle C

11 m

100°   45°

13.5 m

18.8 m

Triangle D

100°

18.3 m

22.5 m

45°

31.3 m

A. Identify the triangles that are similar to each other. Explain how you use the angles and sides to identify the similar triangles.

B. 1. Within each triangle, find the ratio of shortest side to longest side. Find the ratio of shortest side to "middle" side.

   2. How do the ratios of side lengths compare for similar triangles?

   3. How do the ratios of side lengths compare for triangles that are *not* similar?

ACE Homework starts on page 66.

Investigation 4 Similarity and Ratios   **63**

Notes _____

_____

_____

_____

4.3 Finding Missing Parts

When you know that two figures are similar, you can find missing lengths in two ways.

(1) Use the scale factor from one figure to the other.

(2) Use the ratios of the side lengths within each figure.

Problem 4.3 Using Similarity to Find Measurements

For Questions A–C, each pair of figures is similar. Find the missing side lengths. Explain.

A.

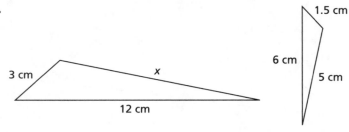

B.

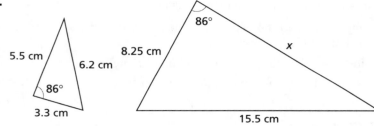

C.

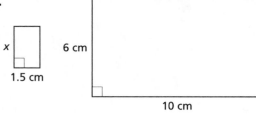

64   Stretching and Shrinking

Notes _____

_____

_____

_____

D. The figures are similar. Find the missing measurements. Explain.

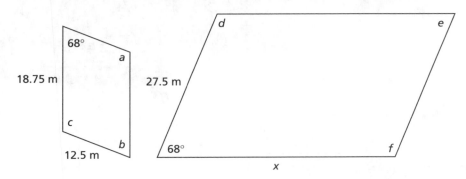

E. The figures below are similar. The measurements shown are in inches.

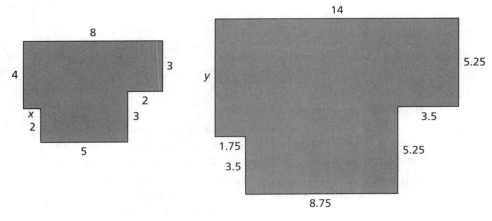

1. Find the value of *x* using ratios.
2. Find the value of *y* using scale factors.
3. Find the area of one of the figures.
4. Use your answer to part (3) and the scale factor. Find the area of the other figure. Explain.

ACE **Homework starts on page 66.**

Notes _____

_____

_____

_____

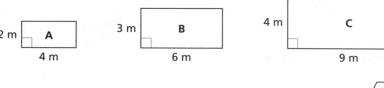

Applications

1. Figures A–F are parallelograms.

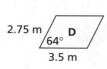

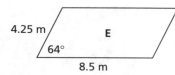

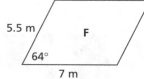

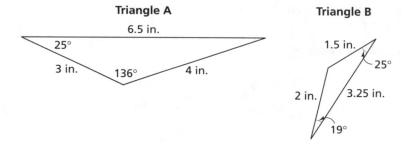

a. List all the pairs of similar parallelograms.

b. For each pair of similar parallelograms, find the ratio of two adjacent side lengths in one parallelogram and compare it to the ratio of the corresponding side lengths in the other parallelogram.

c. For each pair of similar parallelograms, find the scale factor from one shape to the other. Explain how the information given by the scale factors is different from the information given by the ratios of side lengths.

2. For parts (a)–(c), use the triangles below and on the next page.

Triangle A

6.5 in.

25°

3 in.   136°   4 in.

Triangle B

1.5 in.

25°

2 in.   3.25 in.

19°

Notes _____

_____

_____

_____

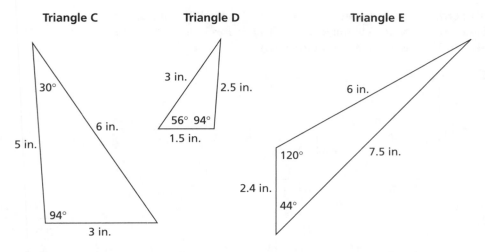

Triangle C   Triangle D   Triangle E

a. List all the pairs of similar triangles.

b. For each pair of similar triangles, find the ratio of two side lengths in one triangle and the ratio of the corresponding pair of side lengths in the other. How do these ratios compare?

c. For each pair of similar triangles, find the scale factor from one shape to the other. Explain how the information given by the scale factors is different than the information given by the ratios of side lengths.

3. a. On grid paper, draw two similar rectangles so that the scale factor from one rectangle to the other is 2.5. Label the length and width of each rectangle.

b. Find the ratio of the length to the width for each rectangle.

4. a. Draw a third rectangle that is similar to one of the rectangles in Exercise 3. Find the scale factor from one rectangle to the other.

b. Find the ratio of the length to the width for the new rectangle.

c. What can you say about the ratios of the length to the width for the three rectangles? Is this true for another rectangle that is similar to one of the three rectangles? Explain.

Investigation 4 Similarity and Ratios   **67**

Notes _____
_____
_____
_____

For Exercises 5–8, each pair of figures is similar. Find the missing measurement. (Note: Although each pair of figures is drawn to scale, the scales for Exercises 5–8 are not the same.)

5.

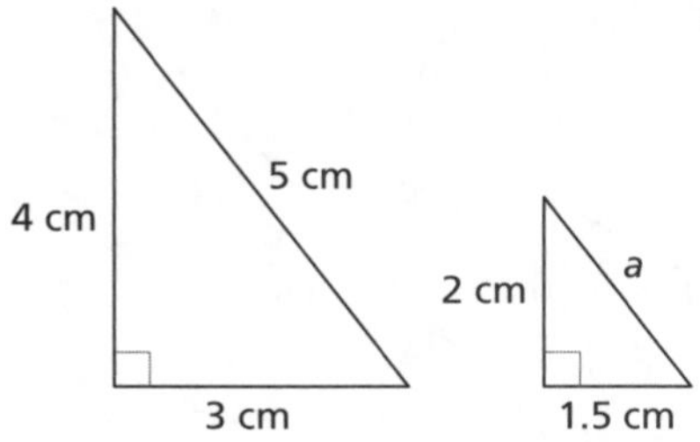

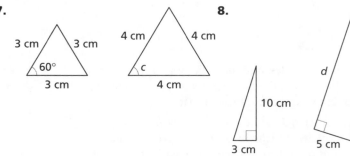

6.

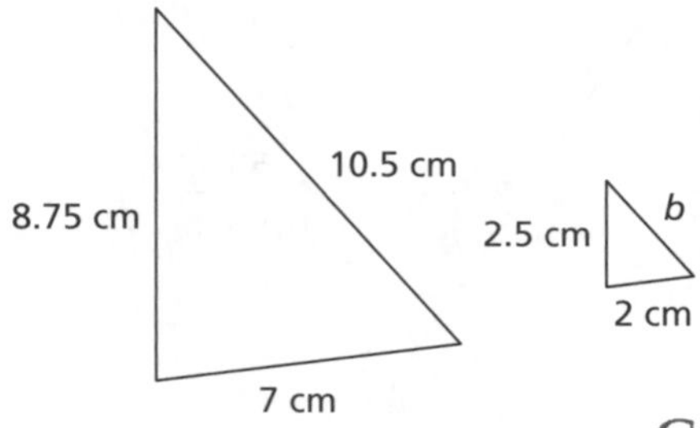

Go Online
PHSchool.com

For: Multiple-Choice Skills
Practice
Web Code: ana-2454

7.

8.

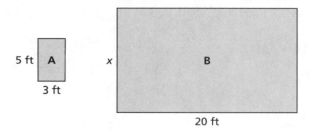

For Exercises 9–11, rectangles A and B are similar.

5 ft | A | x   B

3 ft

20 ft

9. Multiple Choice What is the value of x?

   A. 4   **B.** 12   **C.** 15   **D.** $33\frac{1}{3}$

10. What is the scale factor from rectangle B to rectangle A?

11. Find the area of each rectangle. How are the areas related?

STUDENT PAGE

STUDENT PAGE

Notes _____

_____

_____

_____

12. Rectangles C and D are similar.

Homework
Help **O**nline
PHSchool.com
For: Help with Exercise 12
Web Code: ane-2412

x [C] 8 in.   4 in. [D] 1 in.

a. What is the value of *x*?

b. What is the scale factor from rectangle C to rectangle D?

c. Find the area of each rectangle. How are the areas related?

13. Suppose you want to buy new carpeting for your bedroom. The bedroom floor is a 9-foot-by-12-foot rectangle. Carpeting is sold by the square yard.

a. How much carpeting do you need to buy?

b. The carpeting costs $22 per square yard. How much will the carpet for the bedroom cost?

14. Suppose you want to buy the same carpet described in Exercise 13 for a library. The library floor is similar to the floor of the 9-foot-by-12-foot bedroom. The scale factor from the bedroom to the library is 2.5.

a. What are the dimensions of the library? Explain.

b. How much carpeting do you need for the library?

c. How much will the carpet for the library cost?

STUDENT PAGE

Notes _____

_____

_____

_____

Connections

For Exercises 15–20, tell whether each pair of ratios is equivalent.

15. 3 to 2 *and* 5 to 4

16. 8 to 4 *and* 12 to 8

17. 7 to 5 *and* 21 to 15

18. 1.5 to 0.5 *and* 6 to 2

19. 1 to 2 *and* 3.5 to 6

20. 2 to 3 *and* 4 to 6

21. Choose a pair of equivalent ratios from Exercises 15–20. Write a similarity problem that uses the ratios. Explain how to solve your problem.

For Exercises 22–25, write two other ratios equivalent to the given ratio.

22. 5 to 3

23. 4 to 1

24. 3 to 7

25. 1.5 to 1

26. Here is a picture of Duke, a real dog. The scale factor from Duke to the picture is 12.5%. Use an inch ruler to make any measurements.

a. How long is Duke from his nose to the tip of his tail?

b. To build a doghouse for Duke, you need to know his height so you can make a doorway to accommodate him. How tall is Duke?

c. The local copy center has a machine that prints on poster-size paper. You can enlarge or reduce a document with a setting between 50% and 200%. How can you use the machine to make a life-size picture of Duke?

Notes _____

_____

_____

_____

27. Samantha draws triangle ABC on a grid. She applies a rule to make the triangle on the right.

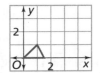

a. What rule did Samantha apply to make the new triangle?

b. Is the new triangle similar to triangle ABC? Explain. If the triangles are similar, give the scale factor from triangle ABC to the new triangle.

28. a. Find the ratio of the circumference to the diameter for each circle.

b. How do the ratios you found in part (a) compare? Explain.

For Exercises 29–30, read the paragraph below.

The Rosavilla School District wants to build a new middle school building. They ask architects to make scale drawings of possible layouts for the building. The district narrows the possibilities to the layouts shown.

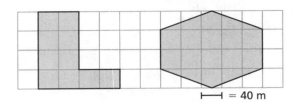

$\longmapsto = 40$ m

29. a. Suppose the layouts above are on centimeter grid paper. What is the area of each scale drawing?

b. What will be the area of each building?

30. Multiple Choice The board likes the L-shaped layout but wants a building with more space. They increase the L-shaped layout by a scale factor of 2. For the new layout, choose the correct statement.

A. The area is two times the original.

B. The area is four times the original.

C. The area is eight times the original.

D. None of the statements above is correct.

Connections

STUDENT PAGE

Notes _____

_____

_____

_____

31. Use the table for parts (a)–(c).

Student Heights and Arm Spans

Height (in.)	60	65	63	50	58	66	60	63	67	65
Arm Span (in.)	55	60	60	48	60	65	60	67	62	70

   a. Find the ratio of arm span to height for each student. Write the ratio as a fraction. Then write the ratio as an equivalent decimal. How do the ratios compare?

   b. Find the mean of the ratios.

   c. Use your answer from part (b). Predict the arm span of a person who is 62 inches tall. Explain.

32. Suppose you enlarge this spinner by a factor of 3. Does this change the probabilities of the pointer landing in any of the areas? Explain.

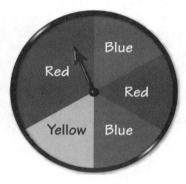

33. Suppose you enlarge the square dartboard below by a scale factor of 3. Will the probabilities that the dart will land in each region change? Explain.

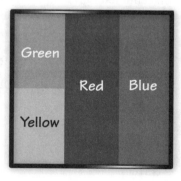

Notes _____

_____

_____

_____

34. For each angle measure, find the measure of its complement and the measure of its supplement.

   Sample 30°
   complement: 60°
   supplement: 150°

   a. 20°   **b.** 70°   **c.** 45°

Extensions

35. For parts (a)−(e), use the similar triangles below.

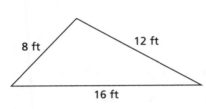
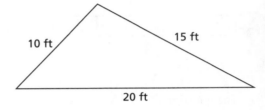

   a. What is the scale factor from the smaller triangle to the larger triangle? Give your answer as a fraction and a decimal.

   b. Choose any side of the larger triangle. What is the ratio of the length of this side to the corresponding side length in the smaller triangle? Write your answer as a fraction and as a decimal. How does the ratio compare to the scale factor in part (a)?

   c. What is the scale factor from the larger triangle to the smaller triangle? Write your answer as a fraction and a decimal.

   d. Choose any side of the smaller triangle. What is the ratio of the length of this side to the corresponding side length in the larger triangle? Write your answer as a fraction and as a decimal. How does the ratio compare to the scale factor in part (c)?

   e. Is the pattern for scale factors and ratios in this exercise the same for any pair of similar figures? Explain.

Notes _____

_____

_____

_____

36. For parts (a) and (b), use a straightedge and an angle ruler or protractor.

a. Draw two different triangles that each have angle measures of 30°, 60°, and 90°. Do the triangles appear to be similar?

b. Draw two different triangles that each have angle measures of 40°, 80°, and 60°. Do the triangles appear to be similar?

c. Based on your findings for parts (a) and (b), make a conjecture about triangles with congruent angle measures.

37. Which rectangle below do you think is "most pleasing to the eye?"

A

B

C

The question of what shapes are attractive has interested builders, artists, and craftspeople for thousands of years. The ancient Greeks were particularly attracted to rectangular shapes similar to rectangle B above. They referred to such shapes as "golden rectangles." They used golden rectangles frequently in buildings and monuments.

The photograph of the Parthenon (a temple in Athens, Greece) below shows several examples of golden rectangles.

Notes _____

_____

_____

_____

The ratio of the length to the width in a golden rectangle is called the "golden ratio."

a. Measure the length and width of rectangles A, B, and C in inches. In each case, estimate the ratio of the length to the width as accurately as possible. The ratio for rectangle B is an approximation of the golden ratio.

b. Measure the dimensions of the three golden rectangles in the photograph in centimeters. Write the ratio of length to width in each case. Write each ratio as a fraction and then as a decimal. Compare the ratios to each other and to the ratio for rectangle B.

c. You can divide a golden rectangle into a square and a smaller rectangle similar to the original rectangle.

Golden Rectangle

The smaller rectangle is similar to the larger rectangle.

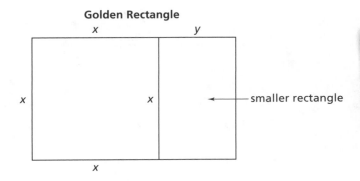

Copy rectangle B from the previous page. Divide this golden rectangle into a square and a rectangle. Is the smaller rectangle a golden rectangle? Explain.

Notes _____

_____

_____

_____

38. For parts (a) and (b), use the triangles below.

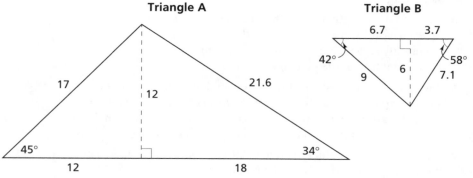

Triangle A

Triangle B

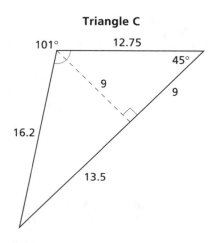

Triangle C

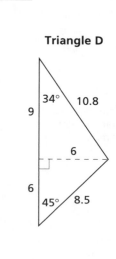

Triangle D

a. Identify the triangles that are similar to each other. Explain.

b. For each triangle, find the ratio of the base to the height. How do these ratios compare for the similar triangles? How do these ratios compare for the non-similar triangles?

39. The following sequence of numbers is called the *Fibonacci sequence*. It is named after an Italian mathematician in the 14th century who contributed to the early development of algebra.

1, 1, 2, 3, 5, 8, 13, 21, 34, 55, 89, 144, 233, 377 . . .

a. Look for patterns in this sequence. Figure out how the numbers are found. Use your idea to find the next four terms.

b. Find the ratio of each term to the term before. For example, 1 to 1, 2 to 1, 3 to 2, and so on. Write each of the ratios as a fraction and then as an equivalent decimal. Compare the results to the golden ratios you found in Exercise 37. Describe similarities and differences.

Mathematical Reflections 4

In this investigation, you used the idea of ratios to describe and compare the size and shape of rectangles, triangles, and other figures. These questions will help you summarize what you learned.

Think about your answers to these questions. Discuss your ideas with other students and your teacher. Then write a summary of your findings in your notebook.

1. If two parallelograms are similar, what do you know about the ratios of the two side lengths within one parallelogram and the ratios of the corresponding side lengths in the other parallelogram?

2. If two triangles are similar, what can you say about the ratios of the two side lengths within one triangle and the ratios of the corresponding side lengths in the other triangle?

3. Describe at least two ways of finding a missing side length in a pair of similar figures.

STUDENT PAGE

STUDENT PAGE

Notes _____

_____

_____

_____

Investigation

ACE Assignment Choices

Differentiated Instruction
Solutions for All Learners

Problem 4.1
Core 1, 3–4, 15–20
Other *Connections* 21–26, *Extensions* 37

Problem 4.2
Core 2, 27
Other *Connections* 28–30; *Extensions* 35, 36, 38; unassigned choices from previous problems

Problem 4.3
Core 5–12
Other *Applications* 13–14; *Connections* 31–34; *Extensions* 39; unassigned choices from previous problems

Adapted For suggestions about adapting Exercise 13 and other ACE exercises, see the CMP *Special Needs Handbook*.
Connecting to Prior Units 15–25: *Bits and Pieces I*; 26: *Bits and Pieces III*; 27, 29–30: *Covering and Surrounding*; 28: *Shapes and Designs*; 31: *Data About Us*; 32–33: *How Likely Is It?*

Applications

1. **a.** Rectangles A and B are similar since the ratio of "2 to 4" is equivalent to the ratio of "3 to 6". Parallelograms D and F are similar since the ratio of "2.75 to 3.5" is equivalent to the ratio of "5.5 to 7" and the corresponding angles are the same measure.

   b. For A: $\frac{2}{4} = 0.5$;

   for B: $\frac{3}{6} = 0.5$;

   for D: $\frac{2.75}{3.5} \approx 0.786$;

   for F: $\frac{5.5}{7} \approx 0.786$.

   The ratios for A and B are equivalent; also the ratios for D and F are equivalent.

   c. The scale factor from A to B is 1.5 which is different from the ratio of "3 to 6" or the

   ratio of "6 to 3". The scale factor from D to F is 2 which is different from the ratio of "5.5 to 7" or the ratio of "7 to 5.5". The scale factor compares the corresponding sides of two shapes while the ratio of the side lengths within a shape is compared to the ratio of the corresponding sides in another shape.

2. **a.** A and B are similar. C and D are similar.

   b. For triangle A we have the ratio "3 to 4" and corresponding ratio in triangle B is "1.5 to 2", then $\frac{3}{4} = 0.75$ and $\frac{1.5}{2} = 0.75$, which are equivalent to each other. For triangle C we have the ratio "3 to 5" and the corresponding ratio in triangle D is "1.5 to 2.5," which are equivalent to each other (0.6).

   c. One possible answer: The scale factor from A to B is $\frac{1}{2}$ which is different from the ratio of "3 to 4" or the ratio of "1.5 to 2". The scale factor from C to D is $\frac{1}{2}$, which is different from the ratio of the sides in one triangle either "3 to 5" or "1.5 to 2.5". The scale factors of these similar triangles implies how many times as great the corresponding side lengths or perimeter are of two similar figures. The ratios of side lengths in the same triangle tells how many times as great one side length of the triangle is to another side length.

3. **a–b.** The answer varies depending on the dimensions of the rectangles drawn.

4. **a–b.** The answer varies depending on the dimensions of the rectangles drawn.

   c. The ratios of length to width are equivalent in all similar rectangles.

5. The scale factor from big triangle to small triangle is 0.5. Therefore, $5 \times 0.5 = 2.5$ cm is the value of *a*.

6. The ratio of "10.5 to 7" is 1.5. Therefore, the ratio of "b to 2" should also be 1.5. Thus, $b = 2 \times 1.5 = 3$ cm.

7. $c = 60°$, because the corresponding angle measures are the same.

8. $\frac{10}{3} = \frac{d}{5}$, hence $d = \frac{50}{3} \approx 16.7$ cm

9. B   10. 0.25

11. Area of A is 15 ft^2. Area of B is 240 ft^2. The area of rectangle B is 16 or 42 (square of the scale factor) times that of rectangle A.

12. a. $x = 2$ in.

    b. 0.5

    c. Area of C is 16 in.^{2}. Area of D is 4 in.^{2}. The area of D is $\frac{1}{4}$ the area of C, where the factor $\frac{1}{4}$ is obtained by taking the square of the scale factor, i.e. $\frac{1}{4} = (\frac{1}{2})^2$.

13. a. 108 ft^2, or 12 yd^2.

    b. $264

14. a. 22.5 ft by 30 ft. The dimensions of the library are 2.5 times the corresponding dimensions of the bedroom.

    b. 675 ft^2, or 75 yd^2.

    c. $1,650

Connections

15. not equivalent   16. not equivalent

17. equivalent   18. equivalent

19. not equivalent   20. equivalent

21. Answers will vary.

22–25. Answers will vary. In each answer, the division of the first number by the second should give the same result as the division of the numbers in the question.

26. a. about 44 in.

    b. about 24.5 in.

    c. Duke is 8 times as large as the picture. Using 200% enlargement one can double the size of the picture. One may use the 200% enlargement three times in a row to get $2 \times 2 \times 2 = 8$ times as large a picture.

27. a. $(0.5x, 0.5y)$

    b. Yes, they are similar. The scale factor is 0.5.

28. a. For each circle, the ratio of circumference to diameter will give the number π.

    b. They are all equivalent since in a circle we have circumference = diameter $\times \pi$, so the ratio $\frac{\text{circumference}}{\text{diameter}} = \pi$, regardless of the size of the circle.

29. a. 10 cm^2; 15 cm^2

    b. 16,000 m^2; 24,000 m^2

30. B.

31. a. $\frac{55}{60} \approx 0.92$; $\frac{60}{65} \approx 0.92$; $\frac{60}{63} \approx 0.95$; $\frac{48}{50} = 0.96$; $\frac{60}{58} \approx 1.03$; $\frac{65}{66} \approx 0.98$; $\frac{60}{60} = 1.0$; $\frac{67}{63} \approx 1.06$; $\frac{62}{67} \approx 0.93$; $\frac{70}{65} \approx 1.08$.

    b. The mean is about 0.98.

    c. About 60.76 in. $\frac{\text{Arm span}}{62}$ will be about 0.98, so, arm span $\approx 62(0.98) \approx 60.76$ in.

32. It will not change the probabilities since the central angles of each section remain the same, hence each section occupies the same fraction of the whole as before.

33. It will not change the probabilities since the area of each region will be enlarged by the same factor, which is 9. (However, a student may argue that a larger dartboard is easier to hit with a given aim.)

34. a. complement: 70°, supplement: 160°

    b. complement: 20°, supplement: 110°

    c. complement: 45°, supplement: 135°

Extensions

35. a. $\frac{10}{8} = 1.25$

    b. The ratio using the longest sides is $\frac{20}{16} = 1.25$. (The same ratio is obtained using other sides as well.) This ratio is the same as the scale factor in part (a).

    c. Scale factor is $\frac{8}{10} = 0.8$

    d. The ratio using the longest sides is $\frac{16}{20} = 0.8$. (the same ratio would be obtained using other sides as well.) This ratio is the same as the scale factor in part (c).

e. Yes, the pattern will be true in general. The scale factor tells by what factor each side is enlarged or reduced. The ratio of the corresponding sides is measuring the same quantity. The ratio of corresponding sides between two similar figures gives the scale factor of the larger figure to the smaller figure or vice versa.

36. a–b. The drawings vary, however all triangles with the given angles will be similar to each other.

   c. Conjecture: "If the interior angle measures of a triangle are the same as those of another triangle, then the triangles are similar."

37. a. Rectangle A: ratio is "2.25 to 0.25"

   Rectangle B: ratio is "2 to 1.25," which gives 1.6 as a decimal number.

   Rectangle C: ratio is "1 to 0.75"

   b. (The measurements are done in centimeters for better accuracy.)

   Large rectangle: ratio is $\frac{7.65}{4.65} \approx 1.65$;

   middle rectangle: $\frac{2.6}{1.6} \approx 1.625$;

   small rectangle: $\frac{1.1}{0.65} \approx 1.69$. These ratios are about the same.

   c. The smaller rectangle is a golden rectangle.

38. a. Triangles A, C, and D are similar. The corresponding angle measures and ratios between the corresponding sides are the same.

   Triangle A : $\frac{17}{30} \approx 0.57$ versus

   Triangle D : $\frac{8.5}{15} \approx 0.57$. They are the same.

   Triangle A : $\frac{17}{21.6} \approx 0.79$ versus

   Triangle C : $\frac{12.75}{16.2} \approx 0.79$. They are again the

   same. (Note that the students have to use the fact that the sum of the angles in a triangle are 180°.)

   b. Triangle A: $\frac{30}{12} = 2.5$, Triangle B: $\frac{10.4}{6} = 1.7\overline{3}$,

   Triangle C: $\frac{22.5}{9} = 2.5$, Triangle D: $\frac{15}{6} = 2.5$;

   Similar triangles have the same base to height ratio.

39. a. You obtain each number in the sequence by adding the previous two numbers. The following four numbers in the sequence will be: 610; 987; 1,597; 2,584.

   b. $\frac{1}{1} = 1, \frac{2}{1} = 2, \frac{3}{2} = 0.5, \frac{5}{3} = 1.6, \frac{8}{5} = 1.6,$

   $\frac{13}{8} = 1.625, \frac{21}{13} \approx 1.615, \frac{34}{21} \approx 1.619,$

   $\frac{55}{34} \approx 1.618, \frac{89}{55} \approx 1.618, \frac{144}{89} \approx 1.618,$

   $\frac{233}{144} \approx 1.618, \frac{377}{233} \approx 1.618 \dots (1.618$ repeats$)$.

   The sequence approaches a number that is very close to the estimation of the golden ratio in Exercise 37. (In fact, the "limit" of this sequence will be equal to the golden ratio.)

Possible Answers to Mathematical Reflections

1. For similar parallelograms, the ratios of the two side lengths within the parallelogram and the ratios of the corresponding side lengths in the other parallelogram will be equivalent.

2. For similar triangles, the ratio of side lengths in one triangle will be equivalent to the corresponding ratio of side lengths in the other triangle. Similar triangles will also have the same base to height ratio.

3. One possible example: Let's call the triangle with the missing length triangle A, and the other triangle B.

   First way: Find the scale factor from triangle B to triangle A. Take the known side length in triangle B that corresponds to the missing length in triangle A and multiply this length by the scale factor.

   Second way: In triangle A, write a ratio using the missing length and one of the known lengths in a triangle. Find the corresponding ratio in triangle B. Find the missing value that will make these two ratios equal to each other.

   Note: Some students may also use ratios of corresponding side lengths between the two triangles. This is similar to applying the scale factor.

Investigation 5
Using Similar Triangles and Rectangles

Mathematical and Problem-Solving Goals

- Apply knowledge of similar triangles and similar quadrilaterals

- Develop a technique for indirect measurement

- Practice measuring lengths to solve problems

Mathematics Background

For background on solving problems using similar figures, see page 7.

Summary of Problems

Problem 5.1 Using Shadows to Find Heights

Students use shadows to estimate the height of a real-world object.

Problem 5.2 Using Mirrors to Find Heights

Students use mirrors to estimate the height of an object.

Problem 5.3 On the Ground. . . but Still Out of Reach

Students use similar triangles to measure distances on the ground that cannot be measured directly.

	Suggested Pacing	Materials for Students	Materials for Teachers	ACE Assignments
All	$3\frac{1}{2}$ days	Centimeter and inch rulers (1 per student), angle rulers or protractors (1 per group or pair), tape measure (optional; 1 per group) meter sticks (1 per group)	Transparent centimeter ruler (optional), angle ruler (optional)	
5.1	1 day		Transparency 5.1	1, 2, 6–21
5.2	1 day	Small mirrors (1 per group)	Transparency 5.2	3, 4, 22–26, 35, 36
5.3	1 day	Labsheet 5.3 (1 per student)	Transparency 5.3, string and stakes for laying out a "pond"	5, 27–34, 37, 38
MR	$\frac{1}{2}$ day			

5.1 Using Shadows to Find Heights

Goals

- Apply knowledge of similar triangles
- Develop a technique for indirect measurement
- Practice measuring lengths to solve problems

Launch 5.1

Many teachers like to begin this problem by having students practice one or two missing parts problems like the one below.

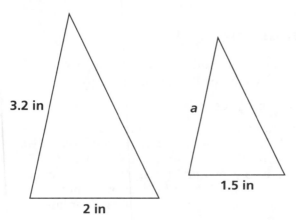

In this example, $a = 2.4$ in. (using a scale factor of 0.75 from the larger triangle to the smaller).

Talk to the students about the situation. Explain that you need to have a pretty good estimate of the height of a tower, a building, a pole, etc. but there does not seem to be any way to measure it directly. The task is to find out how you can use mathematics to make such measurements.

Suggested Questions

- *Today is a sunny day and we are going to use the power of the sun to help us estimate the height we are interested in. When the sun shines on the earth, objects cast a shadow. From your experiences what can you say about the shadows that the sun casts?*

Students may note that the length of the shadow depends on the height of the object. They may note that shadows change their length for an object as the sun moves during the day. Shadows are longer when the sun is near the horizon whether in the morning or evening and very short in the middle of the day when the sun is more nearly overhead.

- *Let's think about the relationship between the length of a shadow and the height of an object. At the same time of day, how will the shadows of two objects that are not the same height compare? (The shadow of the taller object will be longer.)*

- *This means that the length of the shadow depends on the height of the object. Imagine that you are looking at a tall pole when the sun casts a shadow for the pole. In your mind move around until you are standing so that you see the pole and its shadow from the side. Sketch on your paper what you think this would look like. (You just want to have the students see in their mind the two legs of the right triangle made by the pole and the shadow.)*

- *Who would like to share their sketch on the overhead? (Sketch is shown below.)*

- *What do you think? Is your sketch somewhat like this one?*

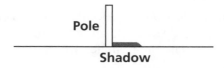

- *Add to your sketch a line to show the triangle formed by the pole, the shadow, and the line from the top of the pole to the tip of the shadow.*

It is not important that students get this completely correct at this stage. This is to increase interest in the setting and to get students thinking about the visual image of the scene.

- *Suppose you took a meter stick outside and held it vertical to the ground. You can picture an imaginary line (the ray of the sun) from the top of the meter stick to the ground.*

- *Do you see a triangle being formed by the meter stick, the ray of the sun, and the shadow? Sketch a picture of the triangle.*

- *If there is another nearby object such as a flagpole or a tree, what do you think will be true about that object, its shadow, and the ray of the sun? Will they form a triangle? Is the triangle similar to the one formed by our meter stick? Explain your reasoning.*

- *How can you use this meter stick and the sun to find out how tall our school is? How can you find similar triangles and what measurements do you need?*

In order to reinforce the importance of checking angles, you might hold the meter stick at an obtuse angle to the ground and ask:

- *Can I hold the meter stick this way and use the resulting shadow length to find the height of the building? Why not?*

Ask the questions in the Getting Ready.

- *Can you explain why each angle of the large triangle is congruent to the corresponding angle of the small triangle?* (The building is at a right angle to the ground and we were careful to hold the stick at a right angle to the ground also. The other angle at the base of each triangle is the angle of the sun. From two nearby points at a common time, the sun appears at the same angle. Finally, the third angle must be the same in each triangle because all three angles must add to 180°.)

- *What does this suggest about similarity of the triangles?* (Because all of the angles are congruent, the triangles are similar.)

After the class gives their ideas, use the picture in the book to talk about how to find the height of the building using the information given. When the students are able to summarize what has to be done to use the sun and a meter stick to estimate the height of an object, give the class directions for going outside to find the height of the school building or tree or lamp post, etc.

Have students work in groups of four. Each group should independently make whatever measurements they need to estimate the height of the object you and the class have chosen.

Explore 5.1

Usually, students have so little opportunity to make actual measurements of distances larger than a desktop that some groups may need help in getting started. One of the important goals of this problem is to give students these measuring experiences, as well as experience using similarity to solve a problem. Be prepared to assist students in their measuring.

Summarize 5.1

Collect the data and form a line plot. Discuss the variations and possible sources of error.

Suggested Questions

- *What is a typical unit of measure to use to tell the height of the building (or other object you choose) based on the class data? Why?* (Possible answer: Meters; they are big enough that we won't have huge answers, but small enough that we will have an answer larger than 1)

- *Who can describe to the class exactly how he or she used similar triangles in the work that he or she did measuring the building?* (Answers will vary.)

- *Can you always use this method to estimate the height of an object? Why or why not?* (Yes, because they used the facts about similar triangles.)

5.1 Using Shadows to Find Heights

Mathematical Goals

- Apply knowledge of similar triangles
- Develop a technique for indirect measurement
- Practice measuring lengths to solve problems

Launch

Have students practice one or two simple missing parts problems.

Talk to the students about the situation. Explain that you need to have a pretty good estimate of the height of a tower, a building, a pole, etc. but there does not seem to be any way to measure it directly. The task is to find out how you can use mathematics to make such measurements.

- *From your experiences, what can you say about the shadows that the sun casts?*

- *At the same time of day, how will the shadows of two objects that are not the same height compare?*

- *This means that the length of the shadow depends on the height of the object. Imagine that you are looking at a tall pole when the sun casts a shadow for the pole. In your mind, move around until you are standing so that you see the pole and its shadow from the side. Sketch on your paper what you think this would look like.*

- *Add to your sketch a line to show the triangle formed by the pole, the shadow, and the line from the top of the pole to the tip of the shadow.*

Continue to guide students through the set-up of the problem, being sure that they understand what is being measured, what is being compared, and how they are to use their knowledge of similar triangles.

Have students work in groups of four. Have each group make their own measurements.

Materials
- Transparency 5.1
- Meter sticks

Explore

Usually, students have so little opportunity to make actual measurements of distances larger than a desktop that some groups may need help in getting started. One of the important goals of this problem is to give students these measuring experiences, as well as experience using similarity, to solve a problem. Be prepared to assist students in their measuring.

Summarize

Collect the data and form a line plot. Discuss the variations and possible sources of error.

- *What is a typical unit of measure to use to tell the height of the building (or other object you choose) based on the class data? Why?*

Materials
- Student notebooks

continued on next page

continued

- *Who can describe to the class exactly how he or she used similar triangles in the work that he or she did measuring the building?*

- *Can you always use this method to estimate the height of an object? Why or why not?*

ACE Assignment Guide for Problem 5.1

Differentiated Instruction
Solutions for All Learners

Core 1, 2
Other *Connections* 6–21

Adapted For suggestions about adapting ACE exercises, see the CMP *Special Needs Handbook*.
Connecting to Prior Units 6–13: *Bits and Pieces I*;
14–21: *Bits and Pieces III*

Answers to Problem 5.1

A. Since the sun's rays are parallel to each other, the angles formed by the shadow and the sun ray in both triangles are going to be congruent to each other. Thus, the interior angles of one of the triangles are congruent to corresponding angles in the other triangle since both also have a 90-degree angle. Hence, the two triangles will be similar.

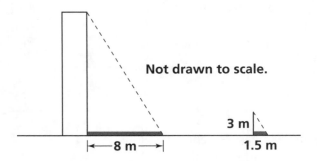

Not drawn to scale.

3 m

8 m

1.5 m

B. The building's height is 16 m. One possible method: The ratio of the height to the shadow of the stick is $\frac{3}{1.5}$ or 2, and the ratio of height to the shadow of the building is $\frac{x}{8} = 2$.

Therefore, $x = 16$.

C. The tree is $33\frac{1}{3}$ ft tall. Use the ratio of height to shadow: $\frac{6}{45} = \frac{x}{25}$ to find the value of x that would make them equivalent.

D. The radio tower is 80 ft high. The same method as part (1) of finding equivalent ratios can be used with the ratios $\frac{x}{120} = \frac{12}{18}$. Students may choose to simplify $\frac{12}{18}$ to $\frac{2}{3}$ to make it easier.

Goals

- Apply knowledge of similar triangles
- Develop a technique for indirect measurement

The method in this problem also involves triangles. Again, the two triangles that are formed are similar. From science classes, students may know why the corresponding angles are congruent.

Suggested Question Ask the questions in the Getting Ready.

- *Can you explain why each angle of the large triangle is congruent to the corresponding angle of the small triangle?* (In each triangle there are corresponding right angles at the foot of the object and at the foot of the person doing the sighting. One fact that we need to use is that the angle of incidence and angle of reflection are the same for the path of the light reflected in the mirror. This means that the two angles at the mirror, the one formed by the line from the mirror to the top of the object and the line of the ground and the one from the mirror to the eyes of the person sighting and the line of the ground, are the same. This will be plausible to most students, but few will know it already. Thus the triangles are similar.)

- *What does this suggest about the triangles?* (If two of the angles are equal, the third angles must be equal since the sum of the angles of a triangle is 180°.)

Since we cannot count on the sun to always shine, we need to find some other ways to estimate the height of a tall object. To get students into this method, use a student to demonstrate the set-up in the classroom. Place the mirror on the floor of the room so that there is an unobstructed space between the mirror and the board. Have a student stand straight and look into the mirror then move either forward or backwards until the top of the board is reflected in the center of the mirror. When the student is satisfied that he or she has the top of the board in the center of the mirror, have the student stand still so that the class can look at the setup.

Suggested Questions

- *Do you see any triangles being formed in what you see here?* (The top of the board to the floor forms a triangle with the ground distance to the mirror and the line drawn from the top of the board to the mirror (line of reflection). Another triangle is formed from the line of sight to the mirror, the height to the eyes of the person, and the distance to the mirror.)

- *Sketch a picture of the set-up with the two triangles shown on your drawing. I will do one at the overhead.*

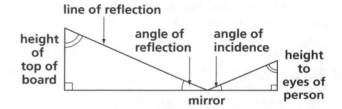

- *Are these two triangles similar? Why or why not?* (They are similar because their corresponding angles are equal.)

See Getting Ready answers for more information. You may need to help students see very explicitly which angles correspond.

- *Now let's move the mirror to a nice, whole-number distance from the bottom of the board. Let's measure a three-meter distance from the base of the wall and use that as the position of the center of the mirror.*

Once the mirror is in place have the student once again sight the top of the board in the center of the mirror. Ask the class to observe how the triangles change. Is the student closer or further from the board and why. The line of sight of the eye always makes the same angle as the line of reflection of the top of the board in the mirror. As the mirror is moved further away, the student must move further from the mirror.

- *What measurements do you need to make to use the similar triangles to estimate the height of the board?* (Distance from *person to mirror* and *mirror to base of wall*, which we already know, as well as the height of the person's eyes. This will give us the scale factor, which

INVESTIGATION 5

we can use to find the missing side—the height we want to estimate.)

- *Let's have two volunteers make the measurements that we need.*

Finish the calculations with the students as an example. Point out that since the group chooses where to place the mirror, it can be placed in a convenient spot. This means a spot that is a "nice" distance from the base of the object whose height the group is estimating (such as 1 meter or 2 meters instead of 79 cm). This makes the number nicer in the calculation.

Then describe the problem to the students and give them directions to complete the example in the problem as practice.

Have students work in groups of four to use the mirror method to measure the same object outdoors that you estimated with the shadow method (if time permits.)

Explore 5.2

Have groups of four estimate the height of the object chosen for the problem. Each group may want to try the method more than once having a different person sight each time. This will give more than one estimate of the height of the object since different people will have different eye heights and different sighting distances. Be prepared to help students with making careful measurements.

Note: When using this method, the mirror must be on a level surface.

Summarize 5.2

Collect the class data and organize it on a line plot. Ask what would be a typical measurement for the class using the mirror method. Discuss possible sources of error.

Then look back to the line plot made for the shadow method. Display both line plots and discuss with the class how the estimates are alike and different. Ask what they think the best estimate of the height of the object is given the data from the two methods. If the data is very different, discuss sources of error in the measurements and ask the students which method they have the most confidence in.

You are just trying to get the students to think about factors that affect the estimates and to see that measurements are approximate and errors can be compounded through calculation with imprecise measurements.

Check for Understanding

Ask students once again to explain what triangles were formed and used by each of the procedures (shadows and mirrors), why the triangles are similar, and how the fact that they are similar allows one to estimate the height of the object.

Note: In Problems 5.1 and 5.2, we are using the fact that if the corresponding angles in two triangles have equal measure, the triangles are similar. At this stage, we only expect students to informally understand this. A proof will occur in later mathematics courses. It is important to show that this fact is not true for other polygons. This can be shown simply with rectangles.

5.2 Using Mirrors to Find Heights

Mathematical Goals

- Apply knowledge of similar triangles
- Develop a technique for indirect measurement

Launch

Explain the mirror method to students. Demonstrate the setup in the classroom. Place the mirror on the floor of the room so that there is an unobstructed space between the mirror and the board. Have a student look into the mirror, then move either forward or backward until the top of the board is reflected in the center of the mirror.

- *Do you see any triangles being formed in what you see here?*
- *Sketch a picture of the set-up with the two triangles shown on your drawing. I will do one at the overhead.*
- *Are these two triangles similar? Why or why not?*

You may need to help students see very explicitly which angles correspond.

Continue to help students understand the set-up of the problem, then describe the problem to the students. Give them directions to complete the example in the problem as practice.

Have students work in groups of four.

Materials

- Transparency 5.2
- small mirrors
- meter sticks

Explore

Have groups of four estimate the height of the object chosen for the problem. Each group may want to try the method more than once having a different person sight each time. This will give more than one estimate of the height of the object since different people will have different eye heights and different sighting distances. Be prepared to help students with making careful measurements.

Summarize

Collect the class data and organize it on a line plot. Ask what would be a typical measurement for the class using the mirror method. Discuss possible sources of error. Then look back to the line plot made for the shadow method. Display both line plots and discuss with the class how the estimates are alike and different. Ask what they think the best estimate of the height of the object is given the data from the two methods. If the data are very different, discuss sources of error in the measurements and ask the students which method they have the most confidence in. You are just trying to get the students to think about factors that affect the estimates and to see that measurements are approximate and errors can be compounded through calculation with imprecise measurements.

Use the Check for Understanding.

Materials

- Student notebooks

ACE Assignment Guide for Problem 5.2

Core 3, 4, 22, 25
Other *Connections* 23, 24, 26; *Extensions* 35, 36; unassigned choices from previous problems

Adapted For suggestions about adapting Exercise 4 and other ACE exercises, see the CMP *Special Needs Handbook*.
Connecting to Prior Units 26: *Shapes and Designs*

Answers to Problem 5.2

A. 1. You will have a picture similar to the one in Problem 5.2 in the Student Edition.

   2. The height of the traffic signal is 675 cm (6.75 m).

B. 1. You will have a picture similar to the one in Problem 5.2 in the student edition, where the traffic light is replaced by the gymnasium wall.

   2. The height of the gymnasium is 12.35 m.

C. Answers will vary from classroom to classroom. The final heights within the same classroom should be the same.

D. Both methods may give accurate results. Possible errors might occur while measuring the distances in each method, in locating the exact location of the middle of the mirror or in holding the stick exactly at a 90-degree angle. The mirror also must be on a level surface.

Goals

- Apply knowledge of similar triangles and similar quadrilaterals

- Develop a technique for indirect measurement

Launch 5.3

Describe the problem to the class. Ask how it is the same and how it is different from the previous two problems. Ask the class to identify the similar triangles and the corresponding angles and sides.

You may want to use the term *nested* in the launch for this problem to describe the two triangles like those pictured in Problem 5.3 of the Student Edition. The term appears in the Mathematical Reflections questions and on assessment items. It is a handy (though non-technical) way to describe the smaller triangle within the larger one in this problem.

Ask the questions in the Getting Ready.

- *In the two previous problems, we used the fact that if two triangles have congruent corresponding angles, then the triangles are similar. This is not true in general for other polygons. What do you know about parallelograms and rectangles that explains this?* (All rectangles have four 90° angles, yet not all rectangles are similar. Likewise, for any parallelogram we can stretch just one pair of sides as in the diagram below, maintaining the same angles, with a result that is not similar to the original. Doing this changes the ratio of sides in the figure.)

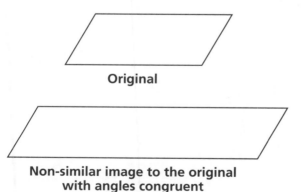

Original

Non-similar image to the original with angles congruent

- *Which triangles in the river diagram are similar? Why?* (The largest triangle with vertices at Stake 3 and Trees 1 and 2 is similar to the smallest one with vertices at the three stakes. The two triangles share the angle at Stake 3. The angle at Stake 1 has the same measure as the angle at Tree 1 because they are corresponding angles created by a transversal crossing two parallel lines. Similarly, the angles at Stake 2 and Tree 2 have the same measure.)

Alternate Approach

If it is impossible for your class to visit a small pond and lay out triangles to measure the distance across, locate an area on the grounds of the school that will be the "pond." Let a group of students mark a boundary for the pretend pond. It does not have to be very large to get the idea. Then, let the class (in groups of four) lay out their triangles and make the measurements needed to estimate the distance across the pond. Be sure that all groups are measuring the pond at the same distance across. Clearly mark the two edges of the distance across the pond that the class is to estimate. Some groups may want to use two different triangles and two sets of measures to check their estimates. Have each group write up a report on how they did the problem, including a sketch with measures given on the sketch of what they found.

Explore 5.3

Be sure the groups have identified the similar triangles and correct parts to measure.

Summarize 5.3

When all groups have made their estimates, give each group a chance to share their work. Make a line plot showing the estimates that were found by each of the groups. Ask the class what they would give as the estimate of the distance across the pond if they can only give one number to represent the work of the class. Most will suggest that the estimates be averaged, which is a good suggestion.

Then, ask what else they would report if they could give more information about what the class found. Here it is reasonable to give the average distance found along with the spread of the estimates.

5.3 On the Ground...but Still Out of Reach

Mathematical Goals

- Apply knowledge of similar triangles and similar quadrilaterals
- Develop a technique for indirect measurement

Launch

Describe the problem to the class. Ask how it is the same and how it is different from the previous two problems. Ask the class to identify the similar triangles and the corresponding angles and sides.

Alternate Approach

If it is impossible for your class to visit a small pond and lay out triangles to measure the distance across, locate an area on the grounds of the school that will be the "pond." Let a group of students mark a boundary for the pretend pond. It does not have to be very large to get the idea. Then, have the class (in groups of four) lay out their triangles and make the measurements needed to estimate the distance across the pond. Be sure that all groups are measuring the pond at the same distance across.

Materials
- Transparency 5.3
- Labsheet 5.3 (optional)
- Meter sticks
- String and stakes
- Large marked area

Vocabulary
- nested triangles

Explore

Be sure the groups have identified the similar triangles and correct parts to measure.

Summarize

When all groups have made their estimates, give each group a chance to share their work. Make a line plot showing the estimates that were found by each of the groups. Ask the class what they would give as the estimate of the distance across the pond if they can only give one number to represent the work of the class. Most will suggest that the estimates be averaged, which is a good suggestion.

Then, ask what else they would report if they could give more information about what the class found. Here it is reasonable to give the average distance found along with the spread of the estimates.

Materials
- Student notebooks

ACE Assignment Guide for Problem 5.3

Core 5, 32–34

Other *Connections* 27–31; *Extensions* 37, 38; unassigned choices from previous problems

Adapted For suggestions about adapting Exercises 6–9 and other ACE exercises, see the CMP *Special Needs Handbook*.

Connecting to Prior Units 27–31: *Bits and Pieces III*

Answers to Problem 5.3

A. The triangle formed by Stakes 1, 2, and 3 is similar to the triangle formed by Stake 3 and Tree 1 and 2. These triangles have angles that are the same. The angle at Tree 1 is 90° and corresponds to the angle at Stake 1 which is also 90°. The triangles both share the angle formed at Stake 3. The angle formed at Tree 2 has the same measure as the angle formed at Stake 2, because the line segment from Tree 1 to Tree 2 is parallel to the line segment from Stake 1 to Stake 2, and the angle at Stake 2 corresponds to the angle at Tree 2.

B. The distance across the river from Stake 1 to Tree 1 is 120 ft. The scale factor from the small triangle to the large one is 2. Thus, the distance from Tree 1 to Stake 3 is 240 ft. 120 + 120 = 240.

C. Standing at Stake 3, look at Tree 1. Have a friend place Stake 1 as close to the river as possible, directly in line between you and Tree 1. Repeat for Tree 2 and Stake 2.

D. Yes, the distance will be the same. This time, the scale factor from the small to the large triangle is 5. This gives the distance between Stake 3 and Tree 1 as 150 ft. From this, we subtract the 30 ft from Stake 3 to Stake 1 to get 120 ft across the river.

The student edition pages for this
investigation begin on the next page.

Notes _____
_____
_____
_____

Using Similar Triangles and Rectangles

You can find the height of a school building by climbing a ladder and using a long tape measure. You can also use easier and less dangerous ways to find the height. In this investigation, you can use similar triangles to estimate heights and distances that are difficult to measure directly.

5.1 Using Shadows to Find Heights

If an object is outdoors, you can use shadows to estimate its height. The diagram below shows how the method works. On a sunny day, any upright object casts a shadow. The diagram below shows two triangles.

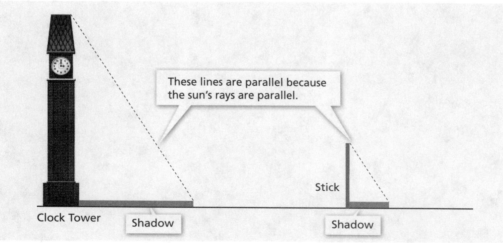

These lines are parallel because the sun's rays are parallel.

Stick

Clock Tower   Shadow   Shadow

A triangle is formed by a clock tower, its shadow, and an imaginary line from the top of the tower to the end of the shadow.

A triangle is formed by a stick, its shadow, and an imaginary line from the top of the stick to the end of its shadow.

78   Stretching and Shrinking

Notes _____

_____

_____

_____

Examine the diagram of the shadow method. Why does each angle of the large triangle have the same measure as the corresponding angle of the small triangle? What does this suggest about the similarity of the triangles?

To find the height of the building, you can measure the lengths of the stick and the two shadows and use similar triangles.

Problem 5.1 Using Shadows to Find Heights

Suppose you want to use the shadow method to estimate the height of a building. You make the following measurements:

- length of the stick: 3 m

- length of the stick's shadow: 1.5 m

- length of the building's shadow: 8 m

A. Make a sketch of the building, the stick, and the shadows. Label each given measurement. What evidence suggests that the two triangles formed are similar?

B. Use similar triangles to find the building's height from the given measurements.

C. A tree casts a 25-foot shadow. At the same time, a 6-foot stick casts a shadow 4.5 feet long. How tall is the tree?

D. A radio tower casts a 120-foot shadow. At the same time, a 12-foot-high basketball backboard (with pole) casts a shadow 18 feet long. How high is the radio tower?

ACE Homework starts on page 84.

Investigation 5 Using Similar Triangles and Rectangles **79**

Notes _____

_____

_____

_____

5.2 Using Mirrors to Find Heights

The shadow method only works outdoors on sunny days. As an alternative, you can also use a mirror to estimate heights. The mirror method works both indoors and outdoors.

The mirror method is shown below. Place a mirror on a level spot at a convenient distance from the object. Back up from the mirror until you can see the top of the object in the center of the mirror.

The two triangles in the diagram are similar. To find the object's height, you need to measure three distances and use similar triangles.

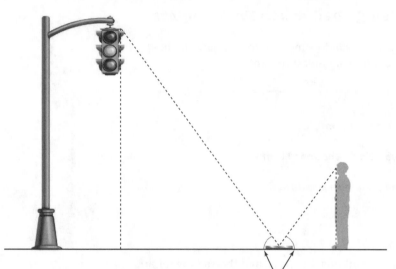

These angles are congruent because light reflects off a mirror at the same angle it arrives.

Getting Ready for Problem 5.2

Examine the diagram above. Explain why each angle of the large triangle has the same measure as the corresponding angle of the small triangle. What does this suggest about the similarity of the triangles?

Notes _____

_____

_____

_____

A. Jim and Su use the mirror method to estimate the height of a traffic signal near their school. They make the following measurements:

> • height from the ground to Jim's eyes: 150 cm
>
> • distance from the middle of the mirror to Jim's feet: 100 cm
>
> • distance from the middle of the mirror to a point directly under the traffic signal: 450 cm

1. Make a sketch. Show the similar triangles formed and label the given measurements.

2. Use similar triangles to find the height of the traffic signal.

B. Jim and Su also use the mirror method to estimate the height of the gymnasium in their school. They make the following measurements:

> • height from the ground to Su's eyes: 130 cm
>
> • distance from the middle of the mirror to Su's feet: 100 cm
>
> • distance from the middle of the mirror to the gym wall: 9.5 m

1. Make a sketch. Show the similar triangles formed and label the given measurements.

2. Use similar triangles to find the height of the gymnasium.

C. Use the mirror method to find the height of your classroom. Make a sketch showing the distances you measured. Explain how you used the measurements to find the height of the room.

D. Compare the two methods (shadow or mirror) for finding missing measurements. What types of problems may arise when using these methods?

ACE **Homework starts on page 84.**

Notes _____

_____

_____

_____

5.3 On the Ground . . . but Still Out of Reach

Darnell, Angie, and Trevor are at a park along the Red Cedar River with their class. They decide to use similar triangles to find the distance across the river. After making several measurements, they sketch the diagram below.

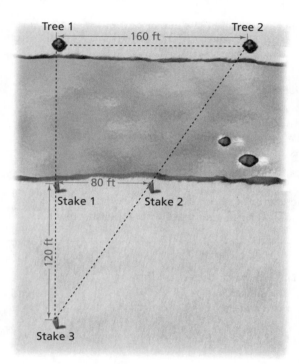

Getting Ready for Problem 5.3

In the two previous problems, you used the fact that if two triangles have corresponding angles with the same measure, then the triangles are similar. This is not true for other polygons in general.

- What do you know about parallelograms and rectangles that explains this?
- Which triangles in the river diagram are similar? Why?

82 Stretching and Shrinking

Notes _____

_____

_____

_____

A. Use the river diagram. Which triangles appear to be similar? Explain.

B. What is the distance across the river from Stake 1 to Tree 1? Explain.

C. The diagram shows three stakes and two trees. In what order do you think Darnell, Angie, and Trevor located the key points and measured the segments?

D. Another group of students repeats the measurement. They put their stakes in different places. The distance from Stake 1 to Stake 2 is 32 feet. The distance from Stake 1 to Stake 3 is 30 feet. Does this second group get the same measurement for the width of the river? Explain.

ACE Homework starts on page 84.

Investigation 5 Using Similar Triangles and Rectangles **83**

Notes _____

_____

_____

_____

Applications

1. The Washington Monument is the tallest structure in Washington, D.C. At the same time the monument casts a shadow that is about 500 feet long, a 40-foot flagpole nearby casts a shadow that is about 36 feet long. Make a sketch. Find the approximate height of the monument.

2. Darius uses the shadow method to estimate the height of a flagpole. He finds that a 5-foot stick casts a 4-foot shadow. At the same time, he finds that the flagpole casts a 20-foot shadow. Make a sketch. Use Darius's measurements to estimate the height of the flagpole.

3. The school principal visits Ashton's class one day. The principal asks Ashton to show her what they are learning. Ashton uses the mirror method to estimate the principal's height. This sketch shows the measurements he records.

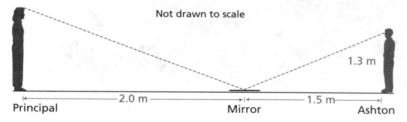

Not drawn to scale

Principal ⊢———2.0 m———⊣⊢———1.5 m———⊣ Ashton
Mirror 1.3 m

a. What estimate should Ashton give for the principal's height?

b. Is your answer to part (a) a reasonable height for an adult?

STUDENT PAGE

Notes

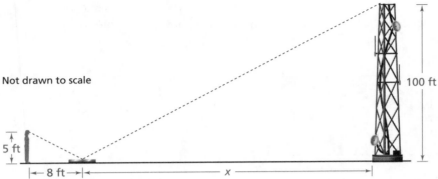
4. Stacia stands 8 feet from a mirror on the ground. She can see the top of a 100-foot radio tower in the center of the mirror. Her eyes are 5 feet from the ground. How far is the mirror from the base of the tower?

Not drawn to scale

5 ft

|← 8 ft →|← ——————— x ——————— →|

100 ft

5. Judy lies on the ground 45 feet from her tent. Both the top of the tent and the top of a tall cliff are in her line of sight. Her tent is 10 feet tall. About how high is the cliff?

Not drawn to scale

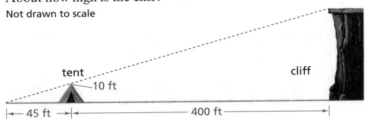

tent

10 ft

cliff

|← 45 ft →|← ——————— 400 ft ——————— →|

Connections

Find the value of x that makes the fractions equivalent.

6. $\frac{5}{2} = \frac{x}{8}$ **7.** $\frac{2}{5} = \frac{7}{x}$ **8.** $\frac{7}{5} = \frac{28}{x}$ **9.** $\frac{7.5}{10} = \frac{3}{x}$

10. $\frac{1}{7} = \frac{x}{35}$ **11.** $\frac{x}{5} = \frac{60}{100}$ **12.** $\frac{4}{10} = \frac{x}{5}$ **13.** $\frac{3}{3.6} = \frac{x}{6}$

Find the given percent or fraction of the number.

14. 30% of 256   **15.** 25% of 2,048

16. $\frac{2}{3}$ of 24   **17.** $\frac{5}{6}$ of 90

Investigation 5 Using Similar Triangles and Rectangles   **85**

Notes _____

_____

_____

_____

Write each comparison as a percent.

18. 55 out of 100

19. 13 out of 39

20. 2.5 out of 10

21. 5 out of 100

22. The rectangles below are similar. The figures are not shown at actual size.

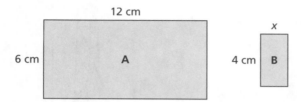

   a. What is the scale factor from rectangle A to rectangle B?

   b. Complete the following sentence in two different ways. Use the side lengths of rectangles A and B.

     The ratio of ▪ *to* ▪ *is equivalent to the ratio of* ▪ *to* ▪.

   c. What is the value of *x*?

   d. What is the ratio of the area of rectangle A to the area of rectangle B?

For Exercises 23 and 24 on page 87, use the rectangles below. The rectangles are not shown at actual size.

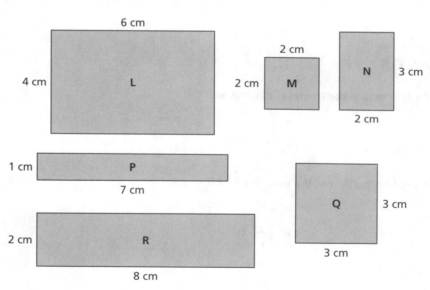

86   Stretching and Shrinking

Notes _____

_____

_____

_____

23. Multiple Choice Which pair of rectangles is similar?

    A. L and M   **B.** L and Q   **C.** L and N   **D.** P and R

24. a. Find at least one more pair of similar rectangles.

    b. For each similar pair, find both the scale factor relating the larger rectangle to the smaller rectangle and the scale factor relating the smaller rectangle to the larger rectangle.

    c. For each similar pair, find the ratio of the area of the larger rectangle to the area of the smaller rectangle.

25. The two triangles are similar.

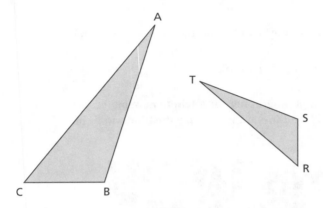

    a. Find the corresponding vertices.

    b. Estimate the scale factor that relates triangle *ABC* to triangle *TSR*.

    c. Estimate the scale factor that relates triangle *TSR* to triangle *ABC*.

    d. Use your result from part (b). Estimate the ratio of the area of triangle *ABC* to the area of triangle *TSR*.

    e. Use the result from part (c). Estimate the ratio of the area of triangle *TSR* to the area of triangle *ABC*.

Notes _____

_____

_____

_____

26. Parallel lines *BD* and *EG* are intersected by line *AH*. Eight angles are formed by the lines, four around point *C* and four around point *F*.

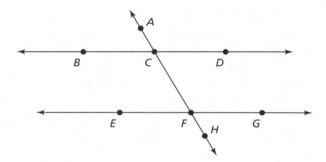

    a. Name every angle that is congruent to (has the same measure as) angle *ACD*.

    b. Name every angle that is congruent to angle *EFC*.

For Exercises 27–31, suppose a photographer for a school newspaper takes this picture for a story. The editors want to resize the photo to fit in a specific space of the paper.

Homework Help Online
PHSchool.com
For: Help with Exercise 27
Web Code: ane-2527

27. The original photo is a rectangle that is 4 inches wide and 6 inches high. Can it be changed to a similar rectangle with the given measurements (in inches)?

    a. 8 by 12   **b.** 9 by 11   **c.** 6 by 9   **d.** 3 by 4.5

28. Suppose that the school copier only has three paper sizes (in inches): $8\frac{1}{2}$ by 11, 11 by 14, and 11 by 17. You can enlarge or reduce documents by specifying a percent from 50% to 200%. Can you make copies of the photo that fit exactly on any of the three paper sizes?

Notes _____

_____

_____

_____

29. How can you use the copy machine to reduce the photo to a copy whose length and width are 25% of the original dimensions? How does the area of the new copy relate to the area of the original photo? (**Hint:** The machine accepts only factors from 50% to 200%.)

30. How can you use the copy machine to reduce the photo to a copy whose length and width are 12.5% of the original dimensions? 36% of the original dimensions? How does the area of the reduced figure compare to the area of the original in each case?

31. What is the greatest enlargement of the photo that will fit on paper that is 11 inches by 17 inches?

32. Multiple Choice What is the correct value for *x*? The figure is not shown at actual size.

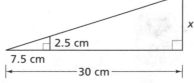

A. 3 cm   **B.** 10 cm

C. 12 cm   **D.** 90 cm

For Exercises 33–34, find each missing measure. The figures are not shown at actual size.

33.

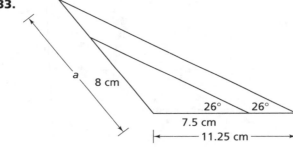

34.

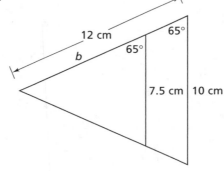

Notes _____

_____

_____

_____

Extensions

35. Use the mirror method, the shadow method, or another method involving similar triangles to find the height of a telephone pole, a light pole, a tall tree, or a tall building in your town. Explain your method.

36. Tang thinks he has found a way to use similar triangles to find the height of the building. He stands 15 meters from a building and holds a 30-centimeter ruler in front of his eyes. The ruler is 45 centimeters from his eyes. He can see the top and bottom of the building as he looks above and below the ruler.

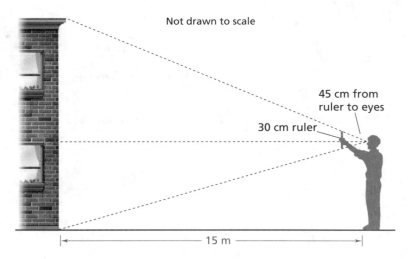

Not drawn to scale

45 cm from ruler to eyes

30 cm ruler

15 m

a. Do you see any similar triangles in the diagram that can help Tang find the height of the building?

b. How tall is the building?

Notes _____

_____

_____

_____

37. In an annular eclipse (a kind of solar eclipse), the moon moves between Earth and the sun, blocking part of the sun's light for a few minutes. Around 240 B.C., a scientist used eclipses to estimate the distances between Earth, the moon, and the sun.

Not drawn to scale

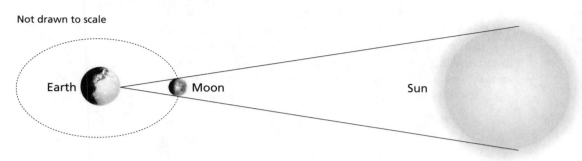

In 1994, there was an annular eclipse. A class constructed a viewing box like the one shown.

Not drawn to scale

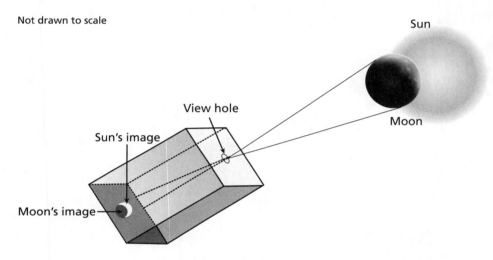

During the eclipse, the image of the moon almost completely covered the sun. The moon's shadow and the ring of light surrounding it appeared on the bottom of the viewing box. The moon's image was 1 meter from the view hole, and its diameter was 0.9 centimeter. The actual diameter of the moon is about 3,500 kilometers. Estimate the distance to the moon at the time of the eclipse.

Investigation 5 Using Similar Triangles and Rectangles **91**

Notes _____

_____

_____

_____

38. Some evening when you see a full moon, go outside with a friend and use a coin to exactly block the image of the moon.

    a. How far from your eyes do you have to hold the coin? Can you hold it yourself or does your friend have to hold it for you?

    b. The diameter of the moon is about 2,160 miles. The distance from the Earth to the moon is about 238,000 miles. Use these numbers, the diameter of your coin, and similar triangles to find the distance you have to hold the coin from your eye to just block the moon. How does the distance you find compare to the distance you measured in part (a)?

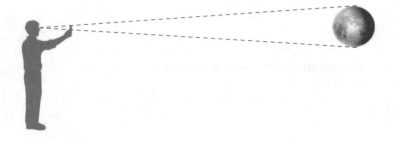

Notes _____

_____

_____

_____

Mathematical Reflections 5

In this investigation, you used what you know about similar triangles to find heights of buildings and to estimate other inaccessible distances. These questions will help you summarize what you learned.

Think about your answers to these questions. Discuss your ideas with other students and your teacher. Then write a summary of your findings in your notebook.

1. How can you estimate heights and distances you can't easily measure with rulers or tape measures by using the following methods?

   a. shadows and similar triangles

   b. mirrors and similar triangles

   c. small triangles nested within larger triangles

2. How can you decide whether a photo or drawing can be enlarged or reduced to fit a space without distorting the shapes?

Notes _____

_____

_____

_____

Investigation

ACE Assignment Choices

Problem 5.1
Core 1, 2
Other *Connections* 6–21

Problem 5.2
Core 3, 4, 22, 25
Other *Connections* 23, 24, 26; *Extensions* 35, 36; unassigned choices from previous problems

Problem 5.3
Core 5, 32–34
Other *Connections* 27–31; *Extensions* 37, 38; unassigned choices from previous problems

Adapted For suggestions about adapting Exercise 4 and other ACE exercises, see the CMP *Special Needs Handbook*.
Connecting to Prior Units 6–13: *Bits and Pieces I*; 14–21, 27–31: *Bits and Pieces III*; 26: *Shapes and Designs*

Applications

1. Sketches should be similar to those in Problem 5.1; 555.5 ft

2. Sketches should be similar to those in Problem 5.1; 25 ft

3. **a.** 1.73 m

   b. Yes; 5 ft 9 in. is a reasonable height.

4. 160 ft

5. About 98.9 ft. Compare the corresponding ratio of the similar triangles: $\frac{x}{10} = \frac{(400 + 45)}{45}$ and solve for x, the height of the cliff.

Connections

6. 20	**7.** 17.5	**8.** 20	**9.** 4
10. 5	**11.** 3	**12.** 2	**13.** 5
14. 76.8	**15.** 512	**16.** 16	**17.** 75
18. 55%	**19.** $33\frac{1}{3}$%	**20.** 25%	**21.** 5%

22. **a.** $\frac{1}{3}$

    b. The ratio of 6 to 12 is equivalent to the ratio of x to 4. The ratio of 6 to x is equivalent to the ratio of 12 to 4.

    c. $x = 2$ cm   **d.** 9 : 1

23. C

24. **a.** M and Q are similar.

    b. Scale factor from Q to M is $\frac{2}{3}$. Scale factor from M to Q is $\frac{3}{2}$. Scale factor from L to N is $\frac{1}{2}$. Scale factor from N to L is 2.

    c. For M and Q, it is $\frac{9}{4}$. For L and N, it is 4.

25. **a.** Angle A corresponds to angle T; angle B corresponds to angle S; angle C corresponds to angle R.

    b. About 0.6 $\left(\frac{6}{10}\right)$ **c.** About 1.6 $\left(\frac{10}{6}\right)$

    d. About 0.36 $\left(\frac{6^2}{10^2}\right)$ **e.** About 2.8 $\left(\frac{10^2}{6^2}\right)$

26. **a.** Angle CFG, angle HFE, and angle FCB are congruent to angle ACD.

    b. Angle BCA, angle FCD, and angle HFG are congruent to angle EFC.

27. **a.** Yes, since $\frac{4}{6} = \frac{8}{12}$.   **b.** No, since $\frac{4}{6} \neq \frac{9}{11}$.

    c. Yes, since $\frac{4}{6} = \frac{6}{9}$.   **d.** Yes, since $\frac{4}{6} = \frac{3}{4.5}$.

28. No. None of the given paper sizes have the same base to height ratio as the drawing does.

29. Use the 50% reduction two times in a row (i.e., copy once and take the image and make its copy again.) Each time the dimensions of the drawing will be reduced to half its size. So, after two reductions the length and width will be $\frac{1}{2} \times \frac{1}{2} = \frac{1}{4}$ of their original size. The area of the smaller image will be $\left(\frac{1}{4}\right)^2$ (or 0.25^2) of the original. For example, a 4 in. × 6 in. photo has an area of 24 in.^{2} and a 1 in. × 1.5 in. photo has an area of 1.5 in.^{2}.

30. (1) Applying a 50% reduction three times in a row using the image each time will reduce the size to 12.5% of its original dimensions.
(2) Possible answer: Apply a 60% reduction two times in a row to get a picture that is 36% of the original size. The area in (1) would be $\frac{1}{64}$ the area of the original. The area in (2) would be $\frac{81}{625}$ $(\frac{9^2}{25^2})$ the area of the original.

31. You can make an enlargement of 200% and then 137%.

32. B

33. $a = 12$ cm

34. $b = 9$ cm

Extensions

35. Answers will vary. It is important that students have an opportunity to try out these methods on real-world objects. They should begin to recognize some of the difficulties in collecting real-world data (for example, finding a flat area to place a mirror, or identifying the top point of a shadow that is cast by an irregularly shaped object such as a tree).

36. a. Yes, the small triangle (ruler to hand to eyes) and the large triangle (building to ground to eyes) are similar to each other.

b. 10 m

37. About 388,889 km

38. a. Answers will vary. Students should find that they need a friend to hold the coin.

b. A dime, with a diameter of $\frac{11}{16}$ in, will need to be held about $\frac{238,000}{2,160} \times \frac{11}{16} = 76$ in. (6 ft 4 in.) away. A penny, with a diameter of $\frac{3}{4}$ in, will need to be held about $\frac{238,000}{2,160} \times \frac{3}{4} = 83$ in (6 ft 11 in.) away. A nickel, with a diameter of $\frac{13}{16}$ in, will need to be held about $\frac{238,000}{2,160} \times \frac{13}{16} = 90$ in. (7 ft 6 in.) away. A quarter, with a diameter of $\frac{15}{16}$ in., will need to be held about $\frac{238,000}{2,160} \times \frac{15}{16} = 103$ in (8 ft 7 in) away. See illustration in the Student Edition. (**Note:** The 238,000 mi from Earth to the Moon is from *surface* to *surface*. These answers assume that the distance is from the Earth's surface to the center of the Moon.)

Possible Answers to Mathematical Reflections

1. a. First measure the shadow of something tall, then compare this to the shadow of something shorter that you have measured, like a meter stick. You must set things up so that all corresponding angles of the triangles formed by each object, its shadow, and the sunbeam have the same measure. Use the scale factor between the shadows to scale the height of the shorter object to find the height of the taller object. For an example, see Problem 5.1.

b. Position yourself so that you can see the top of the object in the center of a mirror placed on level ground between you and the object being measured. This will form two similar right triangles. The triangles are similar because we measure the height of the object and the height of your eyes perpendicular to the ground and the two angles at the mirror will be of equal measure since light reflects off the mirror at the same angle it arrives. The distance along the ground from you to the center of the mirror will correspond to the distance along the ground from the object to the center of the mirror. The relationship between these two sides will give you the scale factor. Use this scale factor to scale the height of your eyes to get the height of the object. For an example, see Problem 5.2.

c. Usually it is the larger triangle you seek to measure. Make sure that the side you wish to measure is parallel to one side of the smaller triangle. This will ensure two pairs of corresponding angles of equal measure. The third angle is shared by the two triangles. Measure one pair of corresponding sides in order to get the scale factor between the triangles. Finally, measure the side of the smaller triangle that corresponds to the side you want to measure on the larger triangle, then apply the scale factor to get the missing side. For an example, see Problem 5.3.

In general, for a, b, and c, use similar triangles to find heights or distances that you can't measure directly. Find a way to make similar triangles with the length you want to measure as one of the sides of one of the triangles and a way to measure the corresponding side in the similar triangle. You must also be able to measure another pair of corresponding sides of the two triangles. These two sets of measures can be used to find the scale factor.

2. A possible answer is that one can compare the ratio of the photo's sides to the corresponding ratio of the space to be fit. If the ratios are equivalent, then it will fit.

Looking Back and Looking Ahead Answers

1. **a.** Triangles A, C, G, and K are similar with the following scale factors:
   A to C: approx. 0.7
   C to A: approx. 1.4 (in fact, it is $\sqrt{2}$)
   A to G: approx. 0.4
   G to A: approx. 2.4
   A to K: approx. 0.3
   K to A: approx. 3.5

C to G: 0.6	G to C: $\frac{5}{3}$
C to K: 0.4	K to C: 2.5
G to K: $\frac{2}{3}$	K to G: 1.5

   Triangles E and F are similar, with a scale factor of 1.

   b. Answers will vary depending on which triangles students choose. In general, the perimeters of the triangles will compare in the same way as the side lengths—their ratios will be the scale factor. The areas compare by the square of the scale factor.

   c. Possible answer: None of the triangles A, C, G, and K are similar to either E or F.

   d. Parallelograms B and H are similar. The scale factor from B to H is 0.4. From H to B the scale factor is 2.5.

   e. There is only one pair of similar parallelograms. The perimeter of B is 2.5 times the perimeter of H (this is the same as the scale factor). The area of B is 6.25 times the area of H (this is the square of the scale factor).

f. Any pair of parallelograms other than B and H will be non-similar.

2. **a.** Rules i, ii, iv, and v will all give similar triangles.

   b. Rule i gives a triangle with a scale factor of 3. Rule ii gives a triangle with a scale factor of 1. Rule iv gives a triangle with a scale factor of 2. Rule v gives a triangle with a scale factor of 1.5.

3. **a.** No. The ratio of sides in the original is 0.6. In the desired image, the ratio of sides is $\frac{2}{3}$.

   b. Yes. The ratio of sides in the original and the image is 0.6. Therefore, the two rectangles are similar. The scale factor from the original to the image is 3.5.

4. Possible answers: "Are the angles congruent in the two figures?, " "Is the scale factor between corresponding sides the same for all pairs?," "Is the ratio of sides within each figure the same?"

5. **a.** The perimeter of shape B will be k times the perimeter of shape A.

   b. The area of shape B will be k^2 times the area of shape A.

6. **a.** Possible answers: The lengths of any two corresponding sides are related by the scale factor. If we form a ratio of the lengths of a pair of sides in the original figure, the ratio of the lengths of the corresponding sides of the image will be the same.

   b. Corresponding angles are congruent.

7. **a.** True; all angles in an equilateral triangle are 60° and the ratio of any two sides is 1.

   b. False; while the angles are all congruent in any two rectangles, the ratio of sides could be anything.

   c. True; squares are rectangles with sides of equal length. This means the ratio of sides must be 1.

   d. False; isosceles triangles can have angles of any measure less than 180°. Therefore, any two isosceles triangles may not have angles with equal measure.

Guide to the Unit Project

Assigning the Unit Project

The first project has two parts. Students are asked to enlarge or shrink a picture using the coordinate graphing system and to identify their scale factor, compare a pair of corresponding angles, and compare two corresponding areas within the drawings. Then, they are asked to write a report that describes techniques they used and compares the original picture to its image. The blackline master for the project appears on page 128.

Grading the Unit Project

Below is a general scoring rubric and specific guidelines for how the rubric can be applied to assessing the activity. A teacher's comments on one student's work follow the suggested rubric.

Suggested Scoring Rubric

This rubric employs a scale from 0 to 4. Use the scoring rubric as presented here, or modify it to fit your needs and your district's requirements for evaluating and reporting students' work and understanding.

4 COMPLETE RESPONSE

- Complete, with clear, coherent work and explanations
- Shows understanding of the mathematical concepts and procedures
- Satisfies all essential conditions of the problem

3 REASONABLY COMPLETE RESPONSE

- Reasonably complete; may lack detail in work or explanations
- Shows understanding of most of the mathematical concepts and procedures
- Satisfies most of the essential conditions of the problem

2 PARTIAL RESPONSE

- Gives response; work or explanation may be unclear or lack detail
- Shows some understanding of some of the mathematical concepts and procedures
- Satisfies some essential conditions of the problem

1 INADEQUATE RESPONSE

- Incomplete; work or explanation is insufficient or not understandable
- Shows little understanding of the mathematical concepts and procedures
- Fails to address essential conditions of problem

0 NO ATTEMPT

- Irrelevant response
- Does not attempt a solution
- Does not address conditions of the problem

Sample Student Project

As her project, one student enlarged a cartoon. Here is her report (her drawings could not be reproduced).

Sample #1

I used ordered pairs to enlarge my cartoon.
(coordinates on other sheet)
The scale factor for my drawing is 12.
The length of the bottom grew up by 12.
The length of Nancy's arm goes up.
The length of the chair goes up by 12.
The corresponding angles stay the same.

on original & enlargement
(chair)   (sleeve)
    on both pictures

The area of the glass is 6 squares on the cartoon and the enlargement, however the squares on the enlargement are 12 times bigger. The glass on the enlargement is 144 times bigger (12²).

(0, 3)
(7, 2)
Stop
(10, 2)
(10½, 2)
Stop
(15, 1½)
(16, 1⅔)
Stop
(5½, 3/4)
(11, 1)
(10½, 1½)
Stop (10½, ½)
(5½, ¾)
(6, 1¼)
(7, 1½)
Stop
(13, 0)
(13, 3)
(15, 3)

(15, 0)
Stop
draw food (It's too hard to plot)
(3½, 1¼)
(3¼, 1½)
make another line of same length
Stop
draw ⌒ on chair
Stop
(3, 3½)
(15, 3½)
(5, 5)
(3, 5)
(3½, 3½)
stop
draw Nancy using grids

A Teacher's Comments on Sample 1

Linda's Drawing Linda shows a good understanding of being able to create an enlarged similar drawing. What she doesn't do is make a drawing (display) that highlights the mathematics involved in the task. Nowhere on the drawing does she identify her scale factor or show how the lengths, angles, or areas of the figures in the two drawings compare. However, she does do this in her report. For that reason, Linda was given a 3 on her drawing. Her report shows that she does understand these ideas but did not demonstrate this understanding in the drawing. Linda needs to revise her drawing but does not need further instruction.

Linda's Report Linda's report is not very neat. However, if I look for the mathematics that she is trying to communicate to me, I can find that she shows considerable understanding of similar figures. She states that her scale factor is 12 (which it is) and that the lengths change by the scale factor ("Nancy's arm goes up by 12," etc.) She also identifies corresponding angles and tells how they are equal and correctly gives the growth relationship between the areas (using the glass in the picture to make her point). Linda states that she used ordered pairs to do the majority of the enlargement. She listed coordinates for many of the important points on the original drawing and then kept the same ordered pairs and used larger grids. This is very interesting yet she doesn't really explain this aspect of her drawing in much detail. It is because of this that Linda was given a 3 for her report. Linda shows clear understanding of the idea of similarity and the majority of the mathematics need for the report is there, but her report is not complete. She lacks details and clarity and did not write a paragraph that discussed what was interesting about her drawing.

Unit Project

1. Shrinking or Enlarging Pictures

Your final project for this unit involves two parts.

(1) the drawing of a similar image of a picture

(2) a written report on making similar figures

Part 1: Drawing

You will enlarge or shrink a picture or cartoon of your choice. You may use the technique of coordinate graphing rules to produce a similar image.

If you enlarge the picture, the image must have a scale factor of at least 4. If you shrink the picture, the image must have a scale factor of at most $\frac{1}{4}$.

94   Stretching and Shrinking

Notes _____

_____

_____

Your final project must be presented in a display for others. Both the original picture and the image need to be in the display, and you must do the following:

- identify the scale factor and show how the lengths compare between the picture and the image
- identify two pairs of corresponding angles and show how the angles compare between the picture and the image
- compare some area of the picture with the corresponding area of the image

Part 2: Write a Report

Write a report describing how you made your similar figure. Your report should include the following:

- a description of the technique or method you used to make the image
- a description of changes in the lengths, angles, and area between the original picture and the image
- A paragraph (or more) on other details you think are interesting or which help readers understand what they see (for example, a description of any problems or challenges you had and decisions you made as a result).

Notes _____

_____

_____

_____

Unit Project

2. All-Similar Shapes

Throughout this unit, you worked with problems that helped you understand the similarity of two shapes. You learned that not all rectangles are similar. For example, an $8\frac{1}{2}$-by-11-inch sheet of paper is rectangular and so is a business-size envelope. However, the envelope is not the same shape as the paper.

A group of students decided to look at rectangles that are square. They find that no matter what size square they drew, every square was similar to shape B in the Shapes Set and to all other squares. They found that *all squares are similar!* They decided to call a square an All-Similar shape.

Notes _____

_____

_____

_____

The students wanted to know whether there were any other All-Similar shapes like the square. That is, are there any other groups of shapes called by the same name that are similar to all other shapes called by that name? Use your Shapes Set to investigate.

Investigate Four Questions

1. Make a list of the names of all the different types of shapes in the Shapes Set (squares, rectangles, triangles, equilateral triangles, circles, and regular hexagons).

2. For each type of shape, list the shapes (using their letter names) that belong in that group.

3. Sort the different types of shapes into two groups: All-Similar shapes (such as squares) and shapes that are not All-Similar (such as rectangles).

4. Describe ways in which All-Similar shapes are alike.

Unit Project Shrinking or Enlarging Pictures   **97**

Notes _____

_____

_____

_____

Looking Back and Looking Ahead

Unit Review

Go Online
PHSchool.com
For: Vocabulary Review Puzzle
Web Code: anj-2051

The problems in this unit helped you understand the concept of similarity as it applies to geometric shapes. You learned how

- to make similar shapes
- to determine whether two shapes are similar
- side lengths, perimeters, angle measures, and areas of similar shapes relate to each other
- to investigate the use of similarity to solve problems

Use Your Understanding: Similarity

Test your understanding of similarity by solving the following problems.

1. The square below is subdivided into six triangles and four parallelograms. Some of the shapes are similar.

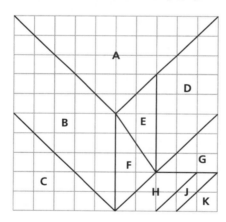

   a. List all the pairs of similar triangles in the figure. For each pair, give the scale factor from one figure to the other.

   b. Pick a pair of similar triangles. Explain how their perimeters are related and how their areas are related.

Notes _____

_____

_____

c. List several pairs of triangles in the figure that are *not* similar.

d. List all pairs of similar parallelograms in the figure. For each pair, give the scale factor from one figure to the other.

e. Pick a pair of similar parallelograms. Explain how their perimeters are related and how their areas are related.

f. List several pairs of parallelograms in the figure that are *not* similar.

2. a. Suppose a triangle is on a coordinate grid. Which of the following rules will change the triangle into a similar triangle?

    i. $(3x, 3y)$ **ii.** $(x + 3, y + 2)$

    iii. $(2x, 4y)$ **iv.** $(2x, 2y + 1)$

    v. $(1.5x, 1.5y)$ **vi.** $(x - 3, 2y - 3)$

b. For each of the rules in part (a) that will produce a similar triangle, give the scale factor from the original triangle to its image.

3. A school photograph measures 12 centimeters by 20 centimeters. The class officers want to enlarge the photo to fit on a large poster.

a. Can the original photo be enlarged to 60 centimeters by 90 centimeters?

b. Can the original photo be enlarged to 42 centimeters by 70 centimeters?

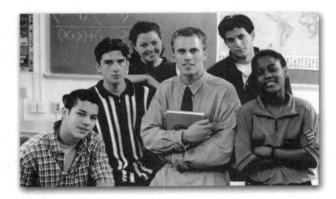

Notes _____

_____

_____

_____

Explain Your Reasoning

Answer the following questions to summarize what you know.

4. What questions do you ask yourself when deciding whether two shapes are similar?

5. Suppose shape A is similar to shape B. The scale factor from shape A to shape B is k.

a. How are the perimeters of the two figures related?

b. How are the areas of the two figures related?

6. If two triangles are similar, what do you know about the following measurements?

a. the side lengths of the two figures

b. the angle measures of the two figures

7. Tell whether each statement is true or false. Explain.

a. Any two equilateral triangles are similar.

b. Any two rectangles are similar.

c. Any two squares are similar.

d. Any two isosceles triangles are similar.

Look Ahead

You will study and use ideas of similarity in several future *Connected Mathematics* units, especially where it is important to compare sizes and shapes of geometric figures. Basic principles of similarity are also used in a variety of practical and scientific problems where figures are enlarged or reduced.

100 Stretching and Shrinking

Notes _____

_____

_____

_____

C

complementary angles Complementary angles are a pair of angles whose measures add to 90°.

ángulos complementarios Los ángulos complementarios son un par de ángulos cuyas medidas suman 90°.

corresponding Corresponding sides or angles have the same relative position in similar figures. In this pair of similar shapes, side *AB* corresponds to side *HJ*, and angle *BCD* corresponds to angle *JKF*.

correspondientes Se dice que los lados o ángulos son correspondientes cuando tienen la misma posición relativa en figuras semejantes. En el siguiente par de figuras semejantes, el lado *AB* es correspondiente con el lado *HJ* y el ángulo *BCD* es correspondiente con el ángulo *JKF*.

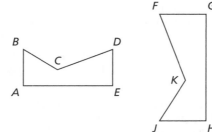

E

equivalent ratios Ratios whose fraction representations are equivalent are called equivalent ratios. For instance, the ratios 3 to 4 and 6 to 8 are equivalent because $\frac{3}{4} = \frac{6}{8}$.

razones equivalentes Las razones, cuyas representaciones de fracciones son equivalentes, se llaman razones equivalentes. Por ejemplo, las razones 3 a 4 y 6 a 8 son equivalentes porque $\frac{3}{4} + \frac{6}{8}$.

I

image The figure that results from some transformation of a figure. It is often of interest to consider what is the same and what is different about a figure and its image.

imagen La figura que resulta de alguna transformación de una figura. A menudo es interesante tener en cuenta en qué se parecen y en qué se diferencian una figura y su imagen.

M

midpoint A point that divides a line segment into two segments of equal length. In the figure below *M* is the midpoint of segment *LN*.

punto medio Punto que divide un segmento de recta en dos segmentos de igual longitud. En la figura de abajo, *M* es el punto medio del segmento de recta *LN*.

Notes _____

_____

_____

_____

nested triangles Triangles that share a common angle are sometimes called nested. In the figure below, triangle *ABC* is nested in triangle *ADE*.

triángulos semejantes Los triángulos que comparten un ángulo común a veces se llaman semejantes. En la siguiente figura, el triángulo *ABC* es semejante al triángulo *ADE*.

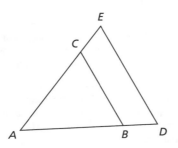

ratio A ratio is a comparison of two quantities. It is sometimes expressed as a fraction. For example, suppose the length of side *AB* is 2 inches and the length of side *CD* is 3 inches. The ratio of the length of side *AB* to the length of side *CD* is 2 to 3, or $\frac{2}{3}$. The ratio of the length of side *CD* to the length of side *AB* is 3 to 2, or $\frac{3}{2}$.

razón La razón es una comparación de dos cantidades. A veces se expresa como una fracción. Por ejemplo, supón que la longitud de *AB* es 2 pulgadas y la longitud de *CD* es 3 pulgadas. La razón de la longitud *AB* a la longitud *CD* es de 2 a 3, es decir, $\frac{2}{3}$. La razón de la longitud *CD* a la longitud *AB* es de 3 a 2, es decir, $\frac{3}{2}$.

rep-tile A figure you can use to make a larger, similar version of the original is called a rep-tile. The smaller figure below is a rep-tile because you can use four copies of it to make a larger similar figure.

baldosa repetida Una figura que puedes usar para hacer una versión más grande y semejante a la original, se llama baldosa repetida. La figura más pequeña de abajo es una baldosa repetida porque se pueden usar cuatro copias de ella para hacer una figura semejante más grande.

Similar Figure

Rep-tile

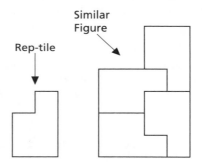

102 Stretching and Shrinking

Notes _____

_____

_____

_____

scale factor The number used to multiply the lengths of a figure to stretch or shrink it to a similar image. If we use a scale factor of 3, all lengths in the image are 3 times as long as the corresponding lengths in the original. When you are given two similar figures, the scale factor is the ratio of the image side length to the corresponding original side length.

factor de escala El número utilizado para multiplicar las longitudes de una figura para ampliarla o reducirla a una imagen semejante. Si el factor de escala es 3, todas las longitudes de la imagen son 3 veces más largas que las longitudes correspondientes de la figura original. Cuando se dan dos figuras semejantes, el factor de escala es la razón de la longitud del lado de la imagen a la longitud del lado original correspondiente.

similar Similar figures have corresponding angles of equal measure and the ratios of each pair of corresponding sides are equivalent.

semejante Las figuras semejantes tienen ángulos correspondientes de igual medida y las razones de cada par de lados correspondientes son equivalentes.

supplementary angles Supplementary angles are two angles that form a straight line. The sum of the angles is 180°.

ángulos suplementarios Los ángulos suplementarios son dos ángulos que forman una recta. La suma de los ángulos es de 180°.

Notes

Academic Vocabulary

Academic vocabulary words are words that you see in textbooks and on tests. These are not math vocabulary terms, but knowing them will help you succeed in mathematics.

Las palabras de vocabulario académico son palabras que ves en los libros de texto y en las pruebas. Éstos no son términos de vocabulario de matemáticas, pero conocerlos te ayudará a tener éxito en matemáticas.

C

compare To tell or show how two things are alike and different.
related terms: analyze, relate, resemble

Sample: Compare the ratios of each of the corresponding side lengths for the similar triangles show below.

The ratios of the corresponding side lengths of two triangles are $\frac{3}{6}$, $\frac{4}{8}$, and $\frac{5}{10}$. Each of these ratios equals $\frac{1}{2}$, so all of the ratios of the corresponding side lengths are equal.

comparar Decir o mostrar en qué se parecen o en qué se diferencian dos cosas.
términos relacionados: analizar, relacionar, asemejar

Ejemplo: Compara las razones de las longitudes de lados correspondientes de los triángulos semejantes que se muestran abajo.

Las razones de las longitudes de lado correspondientes de dos triángulos son $\frac{3}{6}$, $\frac{4}{8}$ y $\frac{5}{10}$. Cada una de estas razones es igual a $\frac{1}{2}$, por lo tanto todas las razones de las longitudes de lado correspondientes son iguales.

E

estimate To find an approximate answer that is relatively close to an exact amount.
related terms: approximate, guess

Sample: Estimate the scale factor for the similar rectangles shown below.

8   6.4

16   12.8

The side length 6.4 in the smaller rectangle corresponds to the side length 8 in the larger rectangle. Since 6.4 is about $\frac{3}{4}$ of 8, the scale factor is about $\frac{3}{4}$.

estimar Hallar una respuesta aproximada, relativamente cercana a una cantidad exacta.
términos relacionados: aproximar, adivinar

Ejemplo: Estima el factor de escala de los rectángulos semejantes a seguir.

8   6.4

16   12.8

La longitud de lado 6.4 del rectángulo más pequeño corresponde a la longitud de lado 8 en el rectángulo más grande. Como 6.4 es aproximadamente $\frac{3}{4}$ de 8. El factor de escala es aproximadamente $\frac{3}{4}$.

104 Stretching and Shrinking

Notes _____

_____

_____

_____

explain To give facts and details that make an idea easier to understand. Explaining can involve a written summary supported by a diagram, chart, table, or a combination of these.

related terms: describe, show, justify, tell, present

Sample: Consider the following similar rectangles. Is it possible to find the missing value *x*? Explain.

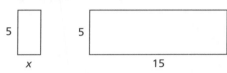

> Since I know the two rectangles are similar, I can find the scale factor. Once I know the scale factor, I can divide the side length of the larger rectangle that corresponds to the missing side length x by the scale factor. This will give me the value of x.
> I can also find the value of x by writing a proportion using the scale factor as one of the ratios, $\frac{x}{5} = \frac{5}{15}$, and then solve for x.

explicar Dar datos y detalles que facilitan el entendimiento de una idea. Explicar puede requerir la preparación de un informe escrito apoyado por un diagrama, una tabla, un esquema o una combinación de éstos.

términos relacionados: describir, mostrar, justificar, decir, presentar

Ejemplo: Considera los siguientes rectángulos semejantes. ¿Es posible hallar el valor que falta *x*? Explica.

> Como sé que los dos rectángulos son semejantes, puedo hallar el factor de escala. Una vez que sepa el factor de escala, puedo dividir la longitud de lado del rectángulo más grande, que corresponde a la longitud de lado x, por el factor de escala. Eso me dará el valor de x.
> También puedo hallar el valor de x al escribir una proporción usando el factor escala como una de las razones, $\frac{x}{5} = \frac{5}{15}$, y después resolver para x.

R

relate To have a connection or impact on something else.

related terms: connect, correlate

Sample: Find the area of the similar triangles below. Relate the area of triangle A to the area of triangle B.

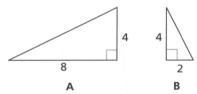

> The area of triangle A is $\frac{1}{2}(4)(8) = 16$. The area of triangle B is $\frac{1}{2}(2)(4) = 4$. The area of triangle A is 4 times the area of triangle B.

relacionar Haber una conexión o impacto entre una cosa y otra.

términos relacionados: unir, correlacionar

Ejemplo: Halla el área de los triángulos semejantes de abajo. Relaciona el área del triángulo A con el área del triángulo B.

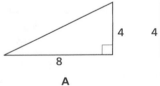

> El área del triángulo A es $\frac{1}{2}(4)(8) = 16$. El área del triángulo B es $\frac{1}{2}(2)(4) = 4$. El área del triángulo A es 4 veces el área del triángulo B.

Academic Vocabulary **105**

Notes _____

_____

_____

_____

Index

Notes _____

_____

_____

_____

STUDENT PAGE

Index

Notes _____

_____

_____

_____

STUDENT PAGE

Notes _____

_____

_____

_____

Acknowledgments

Team Credits

The people who made up the **Connected Mathematics 2** team—representing editorial, editorial services, design services, and production services—are listed below. Bold type denotes core team members.

Leora Adler, Judith Buice, Kerry Cashman, Patrick Culleton, Sheila DeFazio, Katie Hallahan, Richard Heater, **Barbara Hollingdale, Jayne Holman,** Karen Holtzman, **Etta Jacobs,** Christine Lee, Carolyn Lock, Catherine Maglio, **Dotti Marshall,** Rich McMahon, Eve Melnechuk, Kristin Mingrone, Terri Mitchell, **Marsha Novak,** Irene Rubin, Donna Russo, Robin Samper, Siri Schwartzman, **Nancy Smith,** Emily Soltanoff, **Mark Tricca,** Paula Vergith, Roberta Warshaw, Helen Young

Additional Credits

Diana Bonfilio, Mairead Reddin, Michael Torocsik, nSight, Inc.

Illustration

Michelle Barbera: 2, 6, 52

Technical Illustration

WestWords, Inc.

Cover Design

tom white.images

Photos

2, Raoul Minsart/Masterfile; **3,** Lee Snider/The Image Works; **5,** Raoul Minsart/Masterfile; **8 both,** Richard Haynes; **16,** SW Productions/ Getty Images, Inc.; **21,** Ryan McVay/PhotoDisc/ Getty Images, Inc.; **22,** Richard Haynes; **25,** Richard Haynes; **40,** M.C. Escher's "Symmetry Drawing E18" © 2004 The M.C. Escher Company-Baarn-Holland. All rights reserved.; **51,** Richard Haynes; **54,** Geoffrey Clifford/IPN Stock; **58,** Richard Haynes; **59 all,** Richard Haynes; **62,** J. Neubauer/ Robertstock; **69,** F64/Getty Images, Inc.; **74,** Izzet Keribar/Lonely Planet Images; **83,** Raymond Gehman/Corbis; **84,** Alan Schein Photography/Corbis; **88,** Arthur Tilley/ PictureQuest; **94,** Russ Lappa; **96,** Richard Haynes; **99,** Gabe Palmer/Corbis

Note: Every effort has been made to locate the copyright owner of the material reprinted in this book. Omissions brought to our attention will be corrected in subsequent editions.

Acknowledgments **109**

Notes _____

_____

_____

_____

Labsheet 1.2A (right-handed version)

P is the anchor point.

•
P

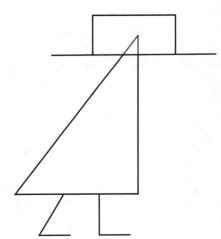

Labsheet 1.2B (left-handed version)

P is the anchor point.

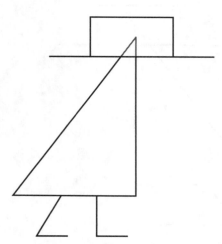

P

Labsheet 1.3

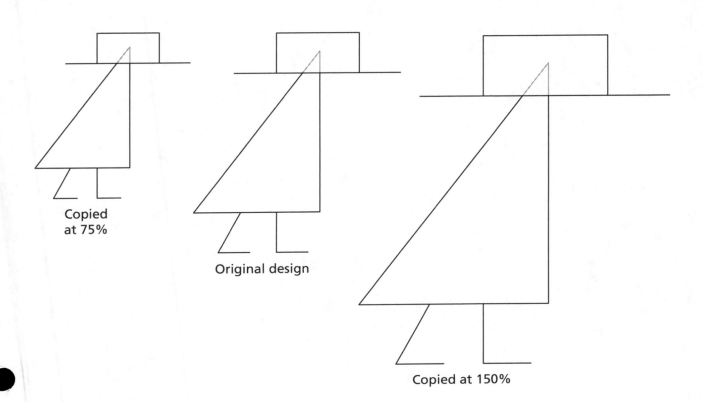

Copied
at 75%

Original design

Copied at 150%

Labsheet 1ACE Exercises 3, 4, and 13 (right-handed version)

3. Square ABCD

•
P

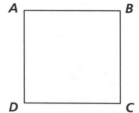

4. Parallelogram ABCD

•
P

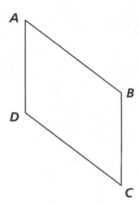

13. Circle C

•
P

Labsheet 1ACE Exercises 3, 4, and 13 (left-handed version)

3. Square ABCD

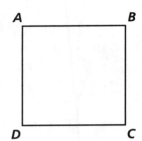

4. Parallelogram ABCD

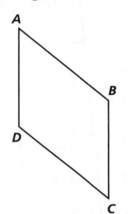

13. Circle C

Labsheet 2.1A

Coordinates of Game Characters

	Mug Wump	Zug	Lug	Bug	Glug
Rule	(x, y)	(2x, 2y)	(3x, y)	(3x, 3y)	(x, 3y)
Point	Part 1				
A	(0, 1)	(0, 2)			
B	(2, 1)	(4, 2)			
C	(2, 0)				
D	(3, 0)				
E	(3, 1)				
F	(5, 1)				
G	(5, 0)				
H	(6, 0)				
I	(6, 1)				
J	(8, 1)				
K	(6, 7)				
L	(2, 7)				
M	(0, 1)				
	Part 2 (start over)				
N	(2, 2)				
O	(6, 2)				
P	(6, 3)				
Q	(2, 3)				
R	(2, 2)				
	Part 3 (start over)				
S	(3, 4)				
T	(4, 5)				
U	(5, 4)				
V	(3, 4)				
	Part 4 (start over)				
W	(2, 5) make a dot				
X	(6, 5) make a dot				

Labsheet 2.1B and 2.2B

Grids

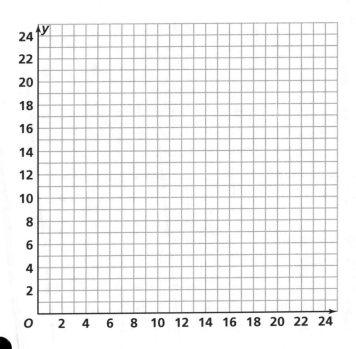

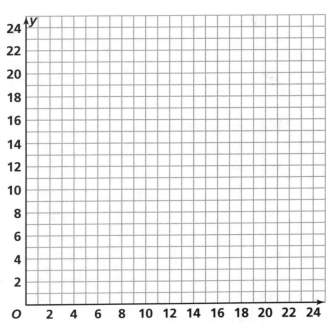

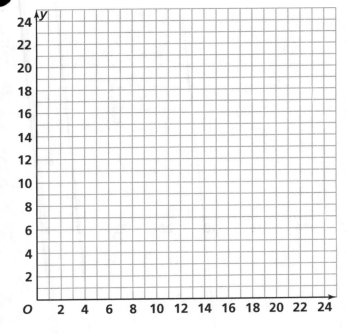

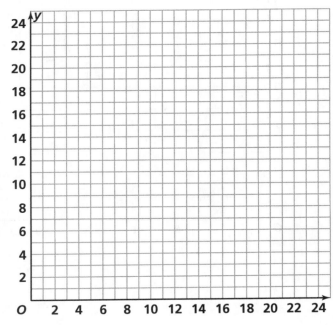

Labsheet 2.1C

Enlarged Grid

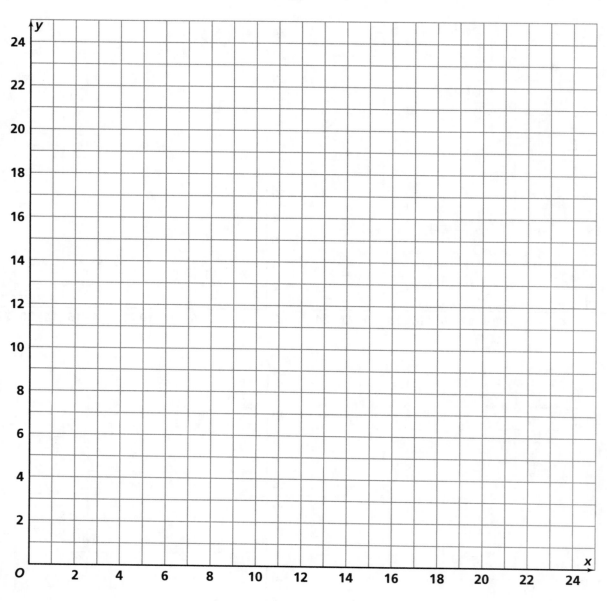

Labsheet 2.2A

Mug's Hat

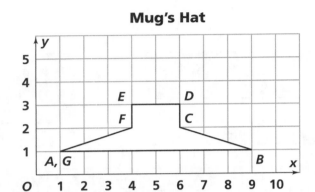

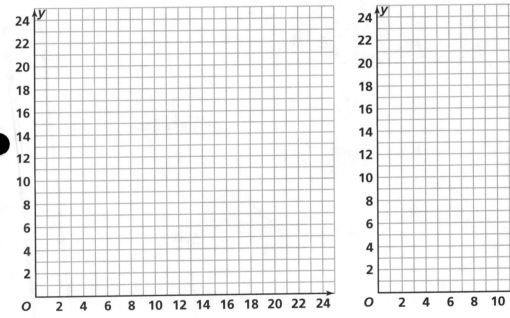 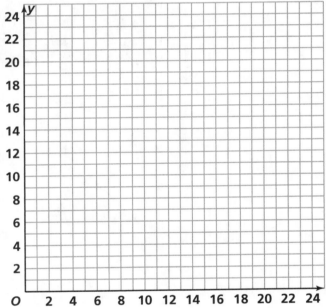

Rules for Mug's Hat

Point	Mug's Hat (x, y)	Hat 1 $(x + 2, y + 3)$	Hat 2 $(x - 1, y + 4)$	Hat 3 $(x + 2, 3y)$	Hat 4 $(0.5x, 0.5y)$	Hat 5 $(2x, 3y)$
A	(1, 1)					
B	(9, 1)					
C						
D						
E						
F						
G						

Labsheet 2.3

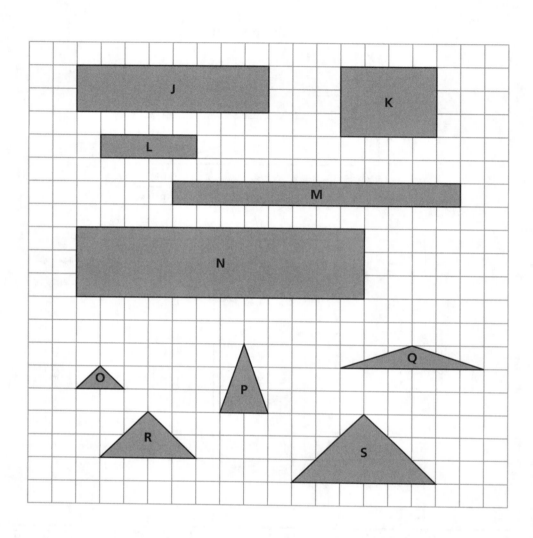

Name _____ Date _____ Class _____

Labsheet 2ACE Exercise 1

Coordinates of Characters

Point	Mug Wump (x, y)	Glum (1.5x, 1.5y)	Sum (3x, 2y)	Tum (4x, 4y)	Crum (2x, y)
Rule	**(x, y)**	**(1.5x, 1.5y)**	**(3x, 2y)**	**(4x, 4y)**	**(2x, y)**
Point	**Mouth**				
M	(2, 2)				
N	(6, 2)				
O	(6, 3)				
P	(2, 3)				
Q	(2, 2) (connect Q to M)				
	Nose (Start Over)				
R	(3, 4)				
S	(4, 5)				
T	(5, 4)				
U	(3, 4) (connect U to R)				

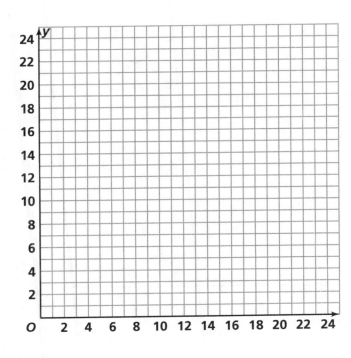

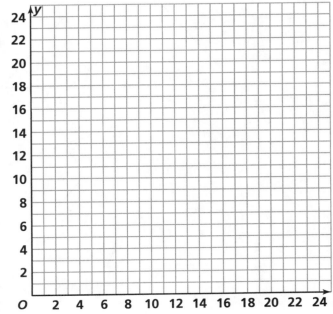

Labsheet 3.2

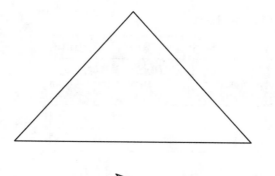
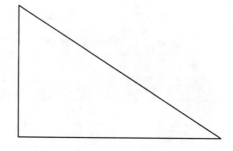
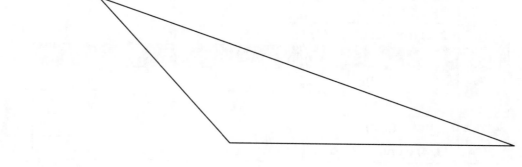
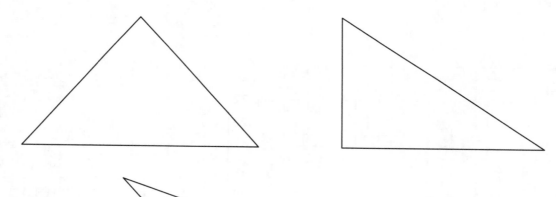

Labsheet 3.3A

Question A

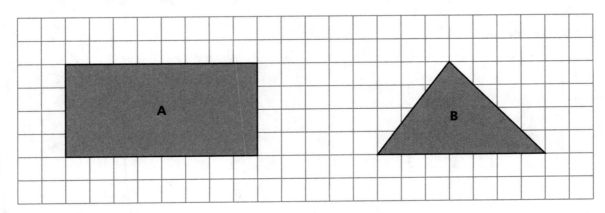

Question C

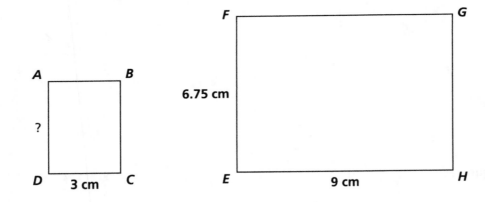

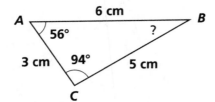

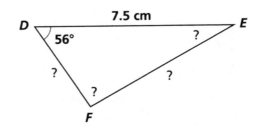

Labsheet 3.3B

Rectangle set

Parallelogram set

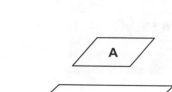
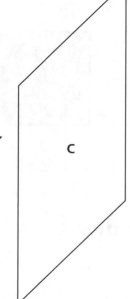

Decagon set

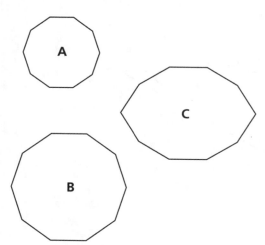

Star set

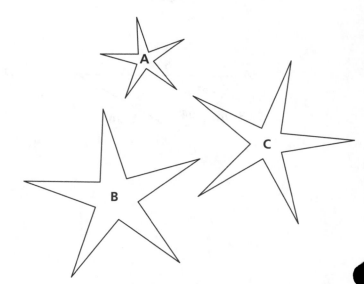

Labsheet 3ACE Exercise 8

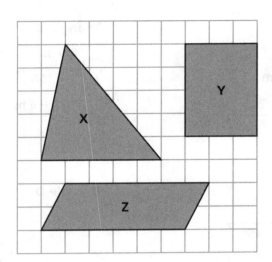

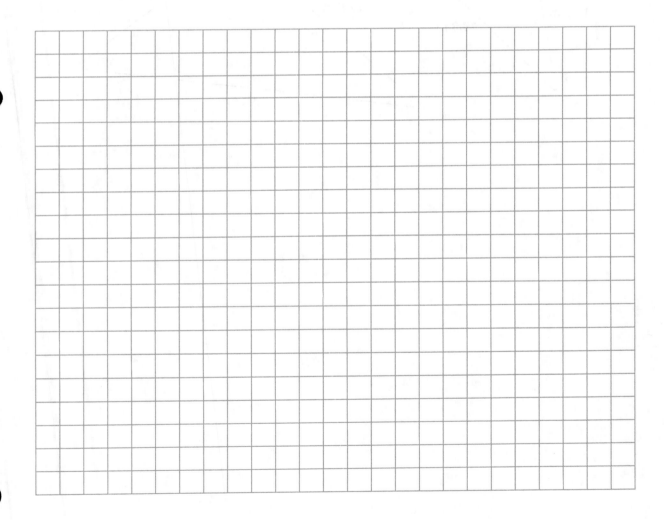

Labsheet 4.2

Triangle A

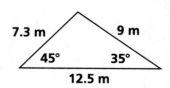

7.3 m   9 m

45°   35°

12.5 m

Triangle B

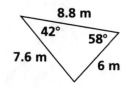

8.8 m

42°   58°

7.6 m   6 m

Triangle C

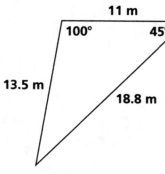

11 m

100°   45°

13.5 m

18.8 m

Triangle D

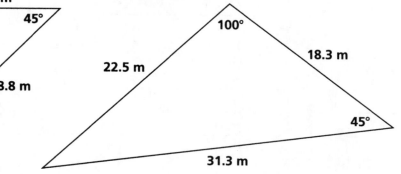

100°

22.5 m   18.3 m

45°

31.3 m

Labsheet 4.3

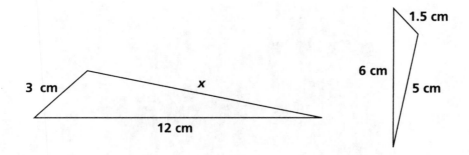

3 cm   *x*   1.5 cm

12 cm   6 cm   5 cm

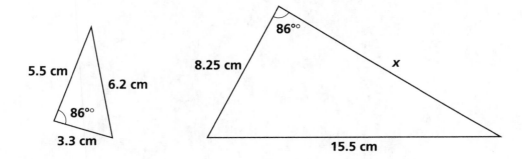

5.5 cm   6.2 cm   86°°   3.3 cm

86°°   8.25 cm   *x*   15.5 cm

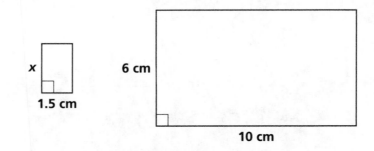

x   1.5 cm   6 cm   10 cm

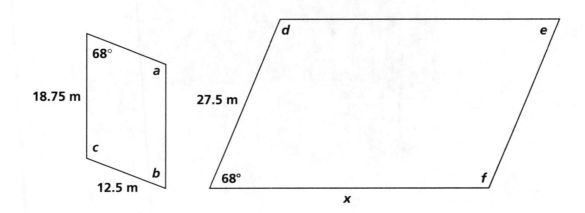

68°   *a*   18.75 m   *c*   *b*   12.5 m

d   *e*   27.5 m   68°   *f*   *x*

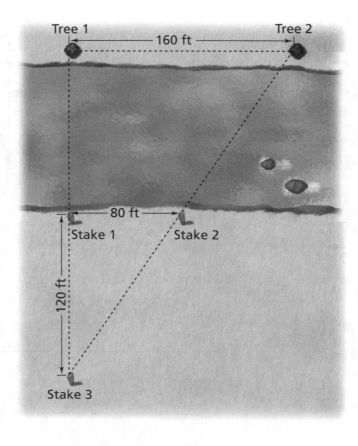

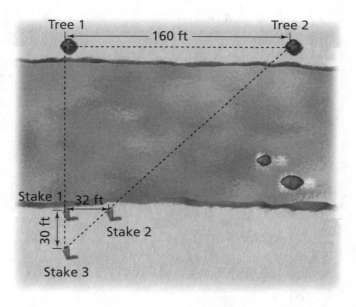

Quarter-inch Grid Paper

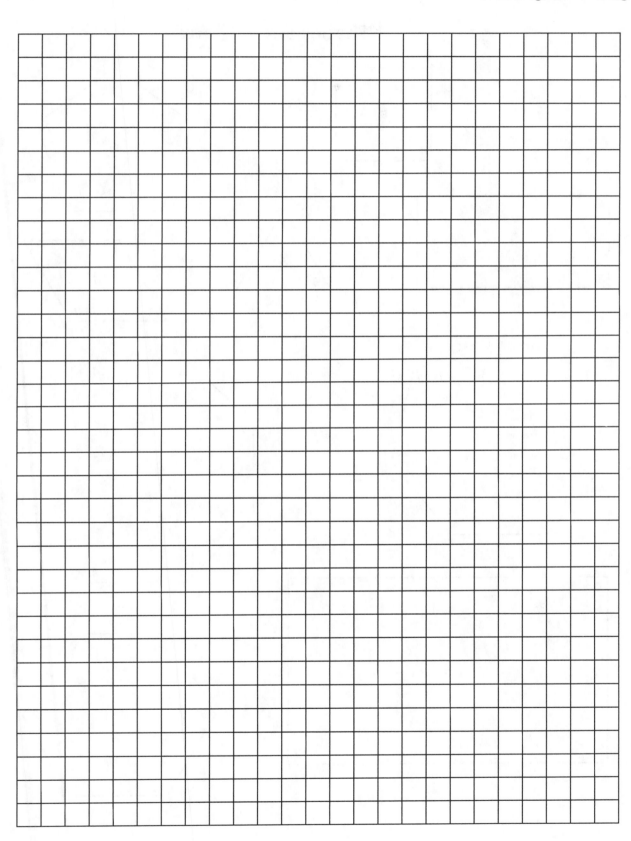

Labsheet

Shapes Set

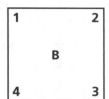

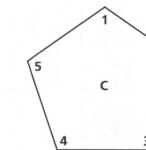

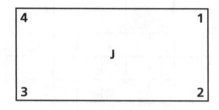

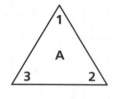

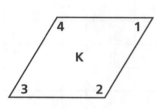

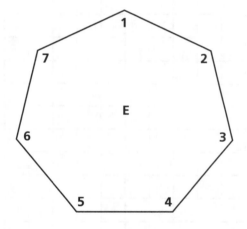

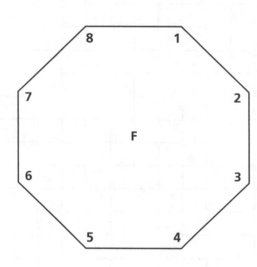

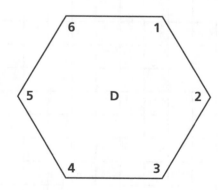

Labsheet

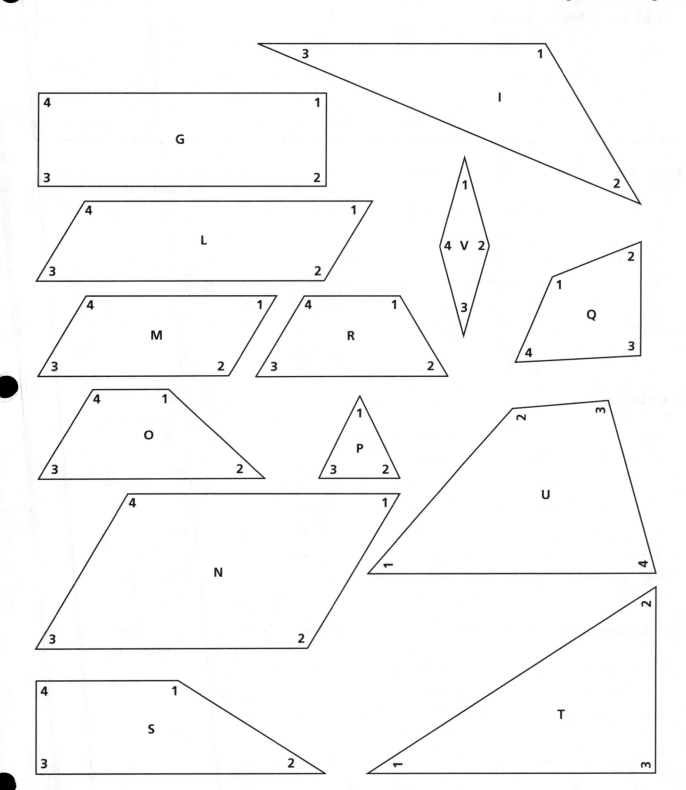

_____

PACING: _____

Mathematical Goals

_____
_____
_____
_____

Launch

_____
_____
_____
_____
_____
_____

Materials

Explore

_____
_____
_____
_____
_____
_____

Materials

Summarize

_____
_____
_____
_____
_____
_____

Materials

Glossary

C

complementary angles Complementary angles are a pair of angles whose measures add to 90°.

corresponding Corresponding sides or angles have the same relative position in similar figures. In this pair of similar shapes, side AB corresponds to side HJ, and angle BCD corresponds to angle JKF.

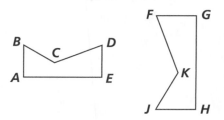

E

equivalent ratios Ratios whose fraction representations are equivalent are called equivalent ratios. For instance, the ratios 3 to 4 and 6 to 8 are equivalent because $\frac{3}{4} = \frac{6}{8}$.

I

image The figure that results from some transformation of a figure. It is often of interest to consider what is the same and what is different about a figure and its image.

M

midpoint A point that divides a line segment into two segments of equal length. In the figure below, M is the midpoint of segment LN.

N

nested triangles Triangles that share a common angle are sometimes called nested. In the figure below, triangle ABC is nested in triangle ADE.

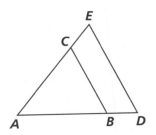

R

ratio A ratio is a comparison of two quantities. It is sometimes expressed as a fraction. For example, suppose length AB is 2 inches and length CD is 3 inches. The ratio of length AB to length CD is 2 to 3, or $\frac{2}{3}$. The ratio of length CD to length AB is 3 to 2, or $\frac{3}{2}$.

rep-tile A figure you can use to make a larger, similar version of the original is called a rep-tile. The smaller figure below is a rep-tile because you can use four copies of it to make a larger, similar figure.

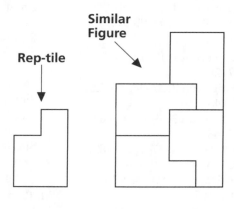

S

scale factor The number used to multiply the lengths of a figure to stretch or shrink it to a similar image. If we use a scale factor of 3, all lengths in the image are 3 times as long as the corresponding lengths in the original. When you are given two similar figures, the scale factor is the ratio of the image side length to the corresponding original side length.

similar Similar figures have corresponding angles of equal measure and the ratios of each pair of corresponding sides are equivalent.

supplementary angles Supplementary angles are two angles that form a straight line. The sum of the angles is 180°.

Index

Acknowledgments

Team Credits

The people who made up the **Connected Mathematics2** team—representing editorial, editorial services, design services, and production services—are listed below. Bold type denotes core team members.

Leora Adler, Judith Buice, Kerry Cashman, Patrick Culleton, Sheila DeFazio, Richard Heater, **Barbara Hollingdale, Jayne Holman,** Karen Holtzman, **Etta Jacobs,** Christine Lee, Carolyn Lock, Catherine Maglio, **Dotti Marshall,** Rich McMahon, Eve Melnechuk, Kristin Mingrone, Terri Mitchell, **Marsha Novak,** Irene Rubin, Donna Russo, Robin Samper, Siri Schwartzman, **Nancy Smith,** Emily Soltanoff, **Mark Tricca,** Paula Vergith, Roberta Warshaw, Helen Young

Additional Credits

Diana Bonfilio, Mairead Reddin, Michael Torocsik, nSight, Inc.

Technical Illustration

Schawk, Inc.

Cover Design

tom white.images